Praise for *Data & AI Imperative*

Consider the landscape of AI projects. More than half will end in failure. And for these doomed projects, they will be lucky if it happens quickly. Others will burn slowly before they run out of cash. Technology will be blamed, but in truth, the writing was already on the wall.

These projects fail because they did not have a proper data strategy. In Data & AI Imperative, *industry veteran Lillian Pierson highlights what companies need to be successful. In many cases, the issues plaguing beleaguered start-ups are not the tech: it's bad market fit, misunderstanding the customer, over promising, and under delivering.*

But by reading this book, companies can get AI right from the get-go, and propel their ideas into exponential growth. In the hyper competitive world of data, Pierson provides the winning strategies.

—Jordan Goldmeier
Author of Bestselling Book, Becoming a Data Head

With Data & AI Imperative *Lillian is addressing an important problem that many companies are now facing, how to derive value from data and AI in practice. Today most companies and organizations realize the transformational power of data and AI, and by reading this book, I believe that companies will have a better chance at deriving this value.*

—Ulrika Jägare
Head of AI, Data, and Architecture at Scania

Data & AI Imperative *is a must-read for data leaders aiming to make real business impact with AI. Lillian breaks down complex strategies into simple, actionable steps, making it easy to align AI projects with business goals. Whether you're just starting out or already deep into data transformations, this book offers practical advice and insights that you can put to work right away.*

—Kate Strachnyi
Founder, DATAcated and
Author of *ColorWise: A Data Storyteller's Guide to the Intentional Use of Color*

We are living in the fastest changing business environment in history. Businesses must adopt tools and processes that drive insight and transformation exponentially faster. Lillian Pierson's Data & AI Imperative *is an essential read for business consultants who are working to navigate the complexities of AI-driven transformation. Her insights into aligning data strategies with business objectives are both practical and forward-thinking. They offer a clear path for consultants to help their clients harness the full potential of AI. This book is a valuable resource for anyone advising organizations on how to turn data and AI into a sustainable competitive advantage.*

—Jim Harris
Leading Keynote Speaker at the WEF and
AI Consultant to Fortune 500 Companies

Data & AI Imperative

Designing Strategies for Exponential Growth

Lillian Pierson, P.E.

WILEY

Published by John Wiley & Sons, Inc., Hoboken, New Jersey.
Published simultaneously in Canada.

ISBNs:
Paperback: 9781394251957   ePDF: 9781394251971   epub: 9781394251964

For general information on our other products and services or for technical support, please contact our Customer Care Department within the United States at (800) 762-2974, outside the United States at (317) 572-3993 or fax (317) 572-4002.

If you believe you've found a mistake in this book, please bring it to our attention by emailing our reader support team at wileysupport@wiley.com with the subject line "Possible Book Errata Submission."

Wiley also publishes its books in a variety of electronic formats. Some content that appears in print may not be available in electronic formats. For more information about Wiley products, visit our website at www.wiley.com.

Library of Congress Cataloging-in-Publication Data
Names: Pierson, Lillian, author. | John Wiley & Sons, publisher.
Title: Data & AI Imperative: designing strategies for exponential growth / Lillian Pierson.
Other titles: Data and AI imperative
Description: Hoboken, New Jersey: John Wiley & Sons, Inc., [2025] | Includes bibliographical references and index. | Summary: "This book covers data landscape analysis, use case identification, planning and strategy development, implementation oversight, and evaluation and scaling of data initiatives. It focuses on applying pre-trained generative AI models rather than developing custom LLMs, which are costly and complex. Using a tested framework, the book guides you in aligning data resources with business objectives, selecting impactful use cases, crafting effective strategies, and ensuring successful execution and scaling of AI initiatives"– Provided by publisher.
Identifiers: LCCN 2024037615 (print) | LCCN 2024037616 (ebook) | ISBN 9781394251957 (paperback) | ISBN 9781394251964 (epub) | ISBN 9781394251971 (ebook)
Subjects: LCSH: Business–Data processing. | Artificial intelligence–Economic aspects. | Artificial intelligence–Financial applications. | Business planning.
Classification: LCC HF5548.2 .P4987 2025 (print) | LCC HF5548.2 (ebook) | DDC 658/.05–dc23/eng/20240924
LC record available at https://lccn.loc.gov/2024037615
LC ebook record available at https://lccn.loc.gov/2024037616

Cover image(s): Graph Paper: © xxmmxx/Getty Images,
                Terrazzo Tiles: © Yuri Parmenov/Getty Images
Cover design: Wiley

SKY10091405_112324

To the decades of pioneers and innovators of data and AI technologies, whose hard work, persistence, and courage have paved the way for the growth of all modern companies. May your contributions inspire a new era of good in the world.

To Vitaly, Ariana, Stanislav, Irina, and Hadas: I'm forever grateful. Your unwavering support has been the foundation upon which I could write this book—the most powerful publication of my career.

Contents

Acknowledgments

I've had the great good fortune of working with some truly talented individuals from the Wiley team to produce this book.

Jim Minatel, Associate Publisher at John Wiley & Sons, led the effort and encouraged me in the writing of this book. It was a pleasure to work with John Sleeva, Project Editor, who helped bring the book from raw manuscript to final production. Thanks to Ashirvad Moses, Managing Editor, for bringing such ease to the final stages of the publishing process.

I appreciate the input of my dear friend Jay, who encouraged me and served as a sounding board as I approached this massive undertaking.

Huge thanks to Damian Wolfgram, who reviewed and contributed from his vast expertise in product leadership and management within the Fortune 500.

Finally, thank you to Satwik Mishra, who reviewed and contributed his AI engineering subject-matter expertise to this book.

—Lillian Pierson

About the Author

Lillian Pierson, P.E. is the founder and fractional CMO at Data-Mania, as well as a globally recognized growth leader in technology.

Through best-in-class marketing strategy, leadership, and advisory support, Lillian helps B2B tech start-ups, scale-ups, and consultancies achieve consistent and predictable revenue growth, all without the full-time CMO price tag.

As a fractional CMO for B2B tech ventures, Lillian specializes in go-to-market and product-led growth strategies, particularly for high-growth data and AI start-ups. Her expertise has supported the expansion of 10% of Fortune 100 companies.

Lillian has a formidable reputation as a data science and AI educator and consultant. She's educated approximately 2 million learners through the dozens of books and courses she's authored as part of deep partnerships with notable publishers such as John Wiley & Sons and LinkedIn Learning, to name two.

She's been a licensed Professional Engineer in good standing since 2014, with approximately 20 years of experience developing in-house strategies for multinational corporations and organizations as large as the US Navy.

Furthermore, Lillian has been a strategic marketing and growth advisor for tech start-ups since 2018. Prior to this, she spent 12 years spearheading marketing campaigns for a diverse range of B2B technology companies, from VC-backed SaaS start-ups like Domino Data Lab to leading enterprise software companies like BMC software, as well as major corporations including IBM, Intel, and Dell.

Introduction

Late-breaking advancements in data science and artificial intelligence have fundamentally and irrevocably changed the face of business. These innovations open many new, untapped avenues for business growth at exponential scale, while simultaneously creating legions of hidden pitfalls for unknowing business leaders.

A methodically prepared, evidence-backed strategy lays a rock solid foundation for driving measurable and predictable business growth from your company's investment into data and AI technologies—investments that are certainly necessary to remain commercially viable now and for the foreseeable future. Well-formed, meticulously executed data and AI strategies deliver an extensive array of benefits, including:

- **A dramatic increase in organizational productivity through automation,** so you can keep your focus on strategic decision-making and innovation.

- **Consistent bottom-line revenue growth** that ensures financial stability and supports long-term investments.

- **Improved customer retention and loyalty** that drives long-term business relationships and decreases customer acquisition costs.

- **Establishment of a clear and unquestionable competitive advantage across the market,** so you can lead in your industry with confidence and foresight.

What Does This Book Cover?

This book guides you through the following topics:

- **Data landscape analysis**—You'll start by identifying the data resources, technologies, and skill sets that your organization currently has, what it needs, and how you can align these with your business objectives.

- **Use case identification and evaluation**—From a plethora of possibilities, you'll learn how to identify the most impactful "Potential Use Cases" and eventually zero in on the "Winning Use Case" to implement. You'll do this through a carefully designed and well-tested framework that I'll be providing in this book.

- **Planning and strategy**—You'll develop a data or AI strategy, complete with a technology assessment, skill gap analysis, and stakeholder engagement strategies.

- **Support for overseeing the implementation**—You'll go beyond theories and simulations and gain the knowledge you need to oversee a responsible execution of your data or AI strategy, in the process transforming it into an operational product or program.

- **Launching and validating in the market**—You'll learn how to bring commercial data and AI solutions to market, validate product-market fit, and scale through powerful AI-driven approaches to growth marketing and product-led growth.

- **Evaluation and scaling**—You'll learn how to measure the impact of your data initiatives, optimize them for better return on investment (ROI), and identify means by which to scale them effectively.

With respect to AI strategy development, this book specifically focuses on the application of pre-trained generative AI models, not on building bespoke LLMs from scratch.

Developing custom LLMs is complicated, novel, and very expensive. It's also risky.

Take, for example, BloombergGPT; a custom LLM that Bloomberg developed. It was trained on its own in-house proprietary financial data. The project required significant investment, to the tune of tens of millions of dollars, and yet recent studies at the Department of Electrical and Computer Engineering & Ingenuity Labs Research Institute Queen's University indicate that both ChatGPT and GPT-4 performed better than BloombergGPT on financial natural language processing tasks.

The AI strategy-building guidance I provide within the pages of this book supports you in leveraging more accessible and versatile pre-trained generative AI models. It provides you with practical insight into the current landscape of generative AI, without digging into the complexities involved in the custom development of generative AI models themselves.

Who Should Read This Book

As implied in its title, this book is written for people who want to drive massive business growth by strategically harnessing data and AI technologies. Naturally, this group of people includes technical founders and leaders, non-technical founders who have sufficient grasp of broad concepts in data and AI, or even data professionals and developers who seek to level up their strategic thinking and approach.

If you're reading this book, I assume you have:

- Some form of expertise in data science methodologies, tools, and techniques.
- A fundamental understanding of the mechanics involved in AI and machine learning.
- Strong analytical skills and some hands-on experience working with data.

After reading this book, you can expect to come away with:

- A holistic understanding of how to align data and AI initiatives with your organization's broader goals and objectives.
- A solid approach for identifying "Potential Use Cases" and rigorously selecting the "Winning Use Case" for optimal ROI.
- Confidence in developing and presenting a data strategy that commands stakeholder buy-in and allocates resources efficiently.
- Preparedness for overseeing the execution of data and AI strategies that deliver measurable bottom-line revenue gains.

By the end of this book, you'll be equipped to think like a strategic driver of data and AI initiatives, you'll have seen how to transform data into immediate business value, and you'll know how to do this in a way that aligns with your organizational objectives while maximizing ROI.

Key Terms

The following key terms are used consistently throughout this book as I work to steer you through each and every nuance involved in data and AI strategy development. Please take note now, as your understanding of these terms is critical to your success with this book.

Current-state—This refers to the existing conditions and operations of a business at a specific point in time. It serves as a baseline for analysis and future planning.

Future-state—This refers to the envisioned or targeted conditions and operations of a business, representing desired improvements and goals from the current state.

Use case—This is an example of how data could be used to achieve a particular business objective. It serves as a blueprint for a data project, outlining what needs to be done, what resources are required, and what outcomes to expect.

Potential use case—This refers to a use case that has been preliminarily assessed as highly relevant and feasible for your organization but hasn't yet undergone an in-depth analysis. It aligns well with the organization's current capabilities, business objectives, and data resources. These are considered "low-hanging fruit" use cases that offer a high likelihood of quick success and clear business value. By designating a use case as a "potential use case," you signal that it meets certain initial criteria and is worthy of further investigation. This serves as a filtering step in the process of choosing the best data initiatives to pursue.

Winning use case—This refers to the single use case that has been thoroughly evaluated and ultimately selected for implementation. It's the use case that, upon rigorous analysis, has been deemed to have the highest likelihood of delivering the most value in terms of meeting business objectives, utilizing available resources efficiently, and being aligned with the technical and skill capabilities of your team.

"Implement a use case"—This refers to the set of actions and processes undertaken to deliver a specific use case—in this book, that use case will be your "winning use case." This includes detailed planning, execution, monitoring, and eventually scaling the solution. The implementation phase is where the rubber meets the road: transforming ideas and analyses into tangible, operational data initiatives.

Growth—For purposes of this book, the word *growth* refers to general bottom-line revenue growth and, more specifically, product-led growth and growth marketing strategies. These are the types of growth driven by the data and AI strategies discussed in this book.

Reader Support for This Book

Companion Download Files

This book comes complete with an exclusive digital resource vault that includes checklists, templates, and spreadsheets to support you every step of the way in your data or AI strategy-building journey. These items are available for free from www.data-mania.com/book.

How to Contact the Author

I appreciate your input and questions about this book! Email me at lillian@data-mania.com, or send me a direct message through my website contact form. (https://www.data-mania.com/contact-our-fractional-cmo-for-hire/).

The Data & AI Advantage in Modern Business

PART I

The Data & AI Advantage in Modern Business

CHAPTER

1

Leveling the Playing Field with Data and AI

Data is the language of the powerholders.

– Jodi Petersen

It was a Tuesday morning, mid-March of 2023. With a warm cup of joe in one hand and my cell phone in the other, I saw an Instagram post from a content repurposer I like to work with. I can't recall the exact contents of the post, but the gist was that something big had happened in the artificial intelligence (AI) space and that it would change our lives forever.

Driven by rabid curiosity, I immediately dug deeper and discovered that OpenAI had just "unleashed" its large language model, GPT-4, onto the world. (The word "unleashed" is a dead ringer for GPT-4 generated content, so pardon the pun.)

You know, we who operate in the AI industry have seen it coming for a long time, but the fact that they actually pulled it off was still the wake-up call of a lifetime. Even for those of us who've been working in the data science industry from its inception, the implications were shocking. This was the day that changed everything.

Evolving Business at Breakneck Speed

We're in the midst of a never-before-seen acceleration of business change, the majority of which has been fueled by advancements in data science, data engineering, and AI. While generative AI technologies, like GPT-4, have radically extended the boundaries of what's possible, they've also served as a warning shot in the dark for all businesses to either get on board or get left behind in the dust.

The transformative potential of data and AI cannot be overstated. Data and AI must take center stage when it comes to how your company drives improvements in growth, operational efficiency, customer engagement, product innovation, and strategic decision-making. Traditional strategies will no longer suffice. You need a dedicated, up-to-date data or AI strategy that's laser-targeted to meet your business's growth objectives in furtherance of the company's mission and vision.

That said, it's no easy feat to make effective use of data and AI technologies. You need a strategy, but building successful data strategies requires one to have a combination of strong technical expertise, business acumen, and astute leadership capabilities. These people are few and far between. My goal for this book is to equip you, the reader, with the strategy development know-how that you need in order to leverage your existing data expertise to drive reliable business growth.

With the extent of digital disruption we're facing, one data strategy seldom suffices. It's highly likely that your company will need a broad overarching strategy to guide the development of high return on investment (ROI) data initiatives across the organization, as well as composite data strategies for each of the use cases that are included within that overarching strategy.

Tip

The methods I'm covering in this book show you how to go about developing a data or AI strategy for a single use case. You can repeat the process for multiple use cases, but if you do, it's highly advisable to map back and optimize the projects against one another in a top-level plan that governs your company-wide data and AI strategy.

A well-built data and AI strategy acts as a road map. It acts as a lighthouse to guide your company through the vast and often overwhelming complexities involved in digital transformation. It's designed to directly transform technological investments into tangible business outcomes, such as improved customer experiences, streamlined operations, or even new revenue streams.

How to Use This Book

Let's look a bit at what this book is meant to be and how to go about getting maximum value from your time within its pages.

My assumption is that, if you're reading this book, you have a solid background in and understanding of data science, analytics, data engineering, and AI. Having a background in strategy development is icing on the cake, but if you don't, that's okay, too.

This book is written in narrative format, yes—but it's more than just a narrative that describes data and AI strategy. Parts I and II are written as an educational primer to supplement and bolster your existing knowledge of applied data, AI, and growth that's required to perform effectively in the data strategist role. Parts III and IV are meant to be used as a step-by-step instruction manual on how to go about building high ROI data strategies.

While Parts I and II detail the foundational knowledge that you should have prior to initiating a data strategy-building effort, these chapters will not be of equal importance to all readers. If you find some areas are less relevant to your current role, you're pretty safe skipping around to other parts of the section. That said, for Parts III and IV, I advise you to follow the instructions as they are presented, in a step-by-step methodical manner.

Caution

Data strategy is a big money game; if your project fails, it could cost the company millions of dollars. Following the meticulous steps. I've laid out for you in great detail throughout Parts III and IV is the most sure-fire way I know to safeguard the success of your data initiatives.

The focus of this book is on business growth and the data and AI strategies that drive it. For this reason, it's essential that we examine two of the biggest growth drivers in modern data-intensive businesses: product-led and growth marketing, introduced in Chapters 4 and 5, respectively. The recent explosive growth of generative AI start-ups also necessitates that we address the basics of ideation and validation around commercial AI products and services. That's covered in Chapter 6.

If you're a product, marketing, or start-up leader, then Chapters 4 through 6 will likely resonate with you. But if your background is mostly in data implementation, then you may prefer Chapters 7 and 8 on ethical and implementation-relevant concerns that are related to data strategy. If you're looking to develop a strategy around the use of generative AI technologies, I've also laid out the implications of working with foundation models for you within Chapters 7 and 13.

How This Book Benefits You

Whether you're a business leader, a product or program manager, or an individual contributor in the tech space, this book is designed to equip you with the insights and strategies you need to harness data and AI innovation to drive growth for your company.

If You're a Business Leader or Executive

Whether you're a Chief Technology Officer, a Chief Financial Officer, a Chief Marketing Officer, or any other type of CXO, you're responsible for the growth and operational health of a core business function. And if you're a Chief Executive Officer, then you know exactly how much of your organization's success is riding on your shoulders.

In all the preceding scenarios, it's imperative that you know the ins and outs of data and AI strategy so that you can oversee such strategies in driving the growth your company needs to stay competitive in today's AI-imbued business environment. In this book, I've included all the insights and strategies you need to do just that.

If You're a Product or Program Manager

Data and AI technology are the basis of growth for a modern organization. Customers and users expect that products and services are delivered with the efficiency advantages that only data and AI can deliver. Not every Product or Program Manager needs to become a technology expert, but you do need to know enough to steer your product and program road maps in the right direction. By reading this book, you'll learn what you need to know to do that.

If You're a Data or Technology Professional

Data scientists, data analysts, data engineers, machine learning (ML) engineers, AI engineers, and software developers–I'm looking at you. Without brilliant individual contributors like yourselves, the data and AI industry would never be where it is today. Though, one challenge most executional team members face is that they aren't in the position to see how the work they do on a daily basis actually drives business growth.

As you read this book, you'll get a clear picture of how what you do each day–all the technical bits and pieces–plays such an important role in the success of the final product that's sent out to the market.

At first glance, the audience that I'm speaking to within the pages of this book may seem excessively broad, but here's the thing: recent developments in AI have radically changed the game for all types of knowledge workers. Every role is impacted. Moreover, business executives, product leaders, and executional team members all have seats at the strategic table here. With its strong focus on data and AI strategies to drive exponential business growth, my goal for this book is to bridge the strategic gap that formerly lay between these diverse roles. By the end of this book, you'll have the solid foundation in data and AI strategy that you need to start leading solutions that drive growth for your company and industry.

To the Business Leaders and Executives

From a strategic perspective, there's never been a time when it's more important for business leaders to truly understand how to harness data and AI to drive growth. The elephant in the room, of course, is generative AI. Entire industries are being upended by the radical change that generative AI has spawned. Chances are, your business and industry are affected, too.

Why Leaders Need a Data or AI Strategy

If your company is not leveraging generative AI to at least streamline its marketing and growth operations, then you're already operating at a major disadvantage. But to make the most of any investment into generative AI projects, you must first have a strategy in place to support that project.

The need for data and AI strategy goes beyond novel generative AI projects in the marketing and growth domains. Competitors are capitalizing on new-found efficiencies across every business function—from software development to customer service, and from financial analysis to product design and innovation. This book helps you lead and champion a data or AI strategy that results in greater efficiencies within your business, regardless of the domain for which the strategy is built.

Caution

The need for astute data leadership is nothing new. Your organization's data initiatives should be designed from the ground up to support one overarching goal. That goal is to fulfill your company's mission. If you've got data operations that are disconnected from that mission, there's a pretty big chance that you're spinning wheels and achieving subpar returns on your investment into data technologies, skill sets, and resources. This book shows you how to align your data initiatives with core business objectives.

To drive business value from data and AI, you need to do so responsibly to safeguard the reputation of your company and the bottom line of its investments. To do that, your company's approach to data and AI must be both ethical and compliant with laws and regulations. Chapter 7 of this book provides you with the foundational knowledge you need about ethical considerations as they relate to data and AI projects. Chapter 13 describes how to go about assessing the current state of your company's AI ethics and compliance.

Lastly, your talent needs your leadership support in helping them upskill and successfully transition to a new data-driven landscape. Chapter 11 will show you the most efficient ways to assess data skill gaps across your organization. Chapter 15 educates you on how to develop effective training programs and make optimal selections for any new hires that might be required for the execution of your data strategy.

Steering the Data and AI Revolution

Not too long ago, generative AI capabilities were mere mental constructs in the minds of only the most creative of innovators. Today, these technologies are facilitating the type of vast data processing and pattern recognition that was only formerly available to big tech companies with the resources and know-how to build these capabilities from scratch in-house.

Like it or not, modern business leaders need to employ AI across the enterprise to achieve both productivity gains and competitive advantages. Naturally, this process involves addressing extremely complex challenges like the technology's potential for making costly errors or its reliance on large volumes of data. To squarely meet these responsibilities, business leaders must be data literate to their core, but that isn't enough. You also need strategies to steer your company's data and AI developments to protect investment while also growing its bottom-line revenue. My goal with this book is to provide you with an approach and methodology on how to do it.

I also emphasize this a lot: modern business leaders must have a fundamental understanding of what's involved in implementing data and AI technologies. Within this book, I'm covering these fundamentals to the extent I am able, but I'm assuming that you're coming to it with at least a basic understanding of data engineering, analytics, data science, and AI.

As you know, integrating AI in business operations requires far more than just technical implementation capabilities. Business leaders need the durable soft skills to lead large-scale technical initiatives in the face of internal resistance to change. Throughout this book, I share leadership tips on how to finesse the finer nuances involved in delivering data and AI strategies that drive growth.

Lastly, leaders need to know how to identify winning use cases for their projects. Winning use cases are the low-risk, high-reward cases around which successful data and AI strategies are built. To drive true competitive advantage, your strategies must be based on an exhaustive assessment of the current state and a thorough analysis of use case alternatives before deciding which one is optimal for your growth goals at this time. Chapters 9 through 14 guide you through the process of selecting a winning use case for strategy development and implementation.

By following the comprehensive approach I've laid out for you in meticulous detail throughout Chapters 9 through 17, I'm confident that you'll quickly be on your way up the path toward leveraging data and AI to drive growth, innovation, and competitive differentiation in your industry.

Two Case Studies to Inspire Your Vision

To inspire your vision, I'm sharing two recent and powerful case studies that were massively effective in driving growth in the telecom and financial services industries. The following Vodafone case study illustrates a data-intensive strategic win that was achieved by Vodafone Italy.

Growth Marketing Case Study

Title: Vodafone Italy's Conversion Boost of 42% with AI-Driven Creativity[1]

Company Name: Vodafone Italy

Industry: Telecom Services

Situation Summary

Vodafone Italy faced the challenge of enhancing customer experiences and loyalty through digital communication channels like mobile push notifications and SMS. The marketing team knew they needed to increase the impact of their marketing messaging to increase customer lifetime value, prevent churn, win back former customers, and boost customer satisfaction through loyalty campaigns.

Challenges

The company struggled with delivering the right message to the right people at the right time. It, also struggled to publish content that resonated with diverse customer types, and this led to missed opportunities in upselling, cross-selling, and customer retention.

Solution

With the goal being to boost their marketing efficiency and results, Vodafone Italy turned to Persado's AI platform. Persado specializes in deploying machine learning and AI to generate optimized marketing creative. The platform analyzes and predicts the effect that specific words and emotions would have on customer decisions. In this way, Persado enabled Vodafone to craft more precise messages to significantly increase the quality and effectiveness of its marketing campaigns across its primary digital channels.

Results

Compared to conventional methods, Vodafone Italy saw a 42% lift in conversion rates for CRM campaigns and a 9% increase for win-back campaigns. The loyalty campaigns saw a 60% average increment in redemption rates at a relatively much lower cost. This strategic partnership improved Vodafone Italy's marketing efficiency and contributed to significant business growth and customer engagement improvements.

Bonus resource

For help in pinpointing the areas where your company's marketing effectiveness could be improved through the strategic use of data and AI like that described previously, I invite you to use my KPI Scorecard and Pipeline Tracker that I've made freely available to all readers here: www.data-mania.com/book.

Another powerful case study that I'm certain business leaders will appreciate is the decision-support win that was recently achieved by DHFL.

Decision-Support / Operations Case Study

Title: DHFL Streamlines Customer Onboarding from 40 Days to just 7 Days[2]

Company Name: DHFL (Dewan Housing Finance Corporation Ltd.)

Industry: Financial Services

Situation Summary

DHFL is committed to providing affordable housing finance in India's semi-urban and rural areas, but it faced challenges in managing its customer onboarding process. Due to the rapid growth of its customer base, the company experienced delays in loan application processing. This decreased customer satisfaction rates across the board. To improve customer satisfaction, DHFL knew it needed more efficient operations.

(continued)

(continued)

Challenges

The primary challenge was in analyzing vast operational data to identify causes for delays in customer onboarding. The process was cumbersome and spanned 35–40 days. At these rates, DHFL was unable to deliver timely financial services. Operational bottlenecks across multiple geographies further complicated the problem. The company needed a solution to streamline the entire onboarding process, despite its complex geographical dependencies.

Solution

DHFL partnered with Gramener to develop visual analytics dashboards using Gramex, Gramener's proprietary development platform. DHFL gained an all-around visibility of its operational KPIs and metrics through the solution. With Gramex, it was able to get a clear picture across different geographies and regions (with different levels of geographical granularity) with regard to cases that were either in processing, pending, or awaiting resolution. Gramex dashboards also enabled DHFL executives to make data-driven decisions and identify and address operational bottlenecks on time.

Results

DHFL saw a dramatic improvement in operational efficiency. Customer onboarding time was reduced by 65%, from 35–40 days to just 7–8 days. Loan application pendency decreased by 52%. Significantly reduced processing times directly improved customer satisfaction. It also reinforced DHFL's commitment to its mission of providing accessible housing finance.

To the Product and Program Managers

The strategic use of data and AI has immense potential for product and program management. In direct correlation with the effective usage of data and AI, product and program outcomes are increasingly data-driven, customer-centric, and efficient. Let's explore just a few of the ways that the data and AI strategy know-how that's imparted in this book is already helping product and program managers score massive wins for their organizations.

Data- and AI-Enabled Product and Program Wins

An effective data or AI strategy has the power to positively transform how your company develops, manages, and evolves its products and services. Decision support, operations, and product growth are often full of quick wins that can be achieved by product and program managers with the help of this book.

Decision-Support Systems That Drive Product and Program Wins

One of the primary ways that you can use data and AI to achieve quick wins in product and program management is by using data to predict future trends and behaviors to improve decision-making processes. AI algorithms help analyze vast amounts of data to predict future trends, customer behavior, and potential market shifts. By leveraging these predictive capabilities, product and program managers can:

- Make better-informed, more timely decisions
- More accurately anticipate market and customer needs
- Proactively adjust strategies based on large bodies of evidence, rather than making strategic decisions on a reactive, ill-informed basis
- Develop tailored product and service recommendations that increase customer satisfaction, build loyalty, and improve customer retention

You can look forward to Parts III and IV, where I share a foolproof, strategic approach to building an effective data strategy around a decision-support use case.

Caution

If you're not leveraging insights from predictive analytics to drive more effective resource allocation, product development prioritization, and risk management strategies, then you're already operating at a disadvantage. This is a pretty standard use case that's already in play at most data-mature organizations. More on data maturity is coming up in Chapter 12.

Automations That Increase Operational Efficiency Generative AI applications are already being used to automate a wide range of routine tasks, including data entry, customer service, and even complex operational decision-making. These types of automations free up product and program managers to focus on their more strategic and creative requirements. They also reduce the likelihood of human error and improve the overall quality of your product and program management processes. This often results in a faster time-to-market for the new products and features you're building. Not to mention that this will also improve the agility of your organization to respond to market changes much more swiftly.

AI-Enabled Product Growth Integrating AI in product and program management has transformed growth strategies, particularly product-led growth. Product-led growth strategies often use AI to enhance customer engagement by providing personalized experiences, predictive future needs, and automated customer support. AI-driven analytics offer deeper insights into how users interact with the product, which in turn enables continuous improvement and innovation based on actual user behavior and feedback in near real-time.

For more insights on AI-enabled product-led growth gains, be sure to study up on Chapter 4.

To the Data and Technology Professionals

Let's be real. If you're reading this book, then the chances are pretty high that you're a data or tech professional working on executional requirements that, hopefully, are part of a coordinated data or AI strategy designed to support your business in reaching its objectives in a timely manner.

Simply put, the work you do on a daily basis is the foundation of all data- and AI-enabled growth. Let's take a look at how your work drives the greatest period of technological advancement ever known to humanity.

Developing Ground-Breaking Innovation at the Speed of Light

Data professionals are tasked with massive responsibilities associated with the development of AI applications, machine learning models, and the data infrastructure that supports these. Your expertise in data science, analytics, data engineering, computer vision, and natural language processing can help you turn manual data strategies into practical applications that dramatically increase efficiency, decision-making, and innovation across your industry.

This book is a data and AI strategy development resource manual. While it does not cover implementation-level details related to building data and AI solutions, Chapter 8 provides useful and practical insights into real-world tactics for a successful AI deployment.

Programming Ethics and Compliance Into Massively Scalable Technologies

As AI systems become an integral part of our daily lives, data and tech professionals must address and implement ethical design principles for responsible use. This demands that you build AI systems that are transparent, fair, and accountable.

While ethicists, legal experts, and policymakers establish guidelines and standards that govern data and AI usage, you're tasked with actually embedding these ethical principles into the design and deployment of data and AI technologies in order to mitigate any privacy, bias, and security issues. The outcome of this collaboration, of course, being data and AI technologies that grow your business bottom line, while also benefiting society as a whole and minimizing potential harms.

Warning

Considering the scale at which many commercial data and AI tools are being adopted, the ethical considerations of your work cannot be understated. As builders, you have the power to transform lives, rewrite history, and shape the future of your company. Build wisely!

Cross-reference

Be sure to read Chapters 13 and 15 to learn the finer points involved in building strategies for ethical, responsible, and compliant data products and services.

How This Book Benefits Individual Contributors

As mentioned at the beginning of this chapter, this book provides individual contributors with the vital perspective that you need to see how what you're building on a daily basis actually drives growth for your company. Gone are the days when you're building with the blinders on, unsure about how a data project you're working on exactly amounts to massive gains for the organization at large.

If you aspire to move into a product or program management role, the data and AI strategy knowledge that's imparted in this book provides a strong foundation for doing so. But, there's more … the knowledge of data and AI strategy you'll get within the pages of this book empowers you to:

- Start asking better-informed questions of leaders and stakeholders, so that you have a clearer picture of outcomes your work should enable.
- Have a much clearer idea of the tools, methods, and approaches you take toward building products.
- Understand your requirements much better by considering the views of multiple stakeholders that are involved in the strategy development process.
- Look at the road map and the tasks you're allotted both from a technical standpoint and a strategic lens—helping you align better with the overall goals of an organization.
- Truly appreciate how your contribution in each step of the development process results in an end product or service that dramatically improves the lives of other people!

Now that I've provided clarifications and communicated expectations as to who this book is written for and how it will help you, let's move into Chapter 2, where you'll learn about the fundamental and introductory prerequisite concepts you need to know in order to make your grand entrance to the data strategy arena.

Notes

1. Persado + Vodafone (2024). *Persado.* https://www.persado.com/resource-library/articles/
2. Gramener (2024). *Gramener.* https://gramener.com/case-studies/data-driven-operational-excellence/

Introduction to Data Strategy

Data is great, but strategy is better.

— Steven Sinofsky

*D*ata & *AI Imperative* is a strategic playbook written to equip you with the tools, frameworks, and strategic expertise you need to build and implement a robust data strategy for your organization.

As you know, data is the linchpin of your business operations, its decision-making, and ultimately, your success. Throughout the pages of this book, I'll be guiding you through the A to Z of transforming raw data into actionable insights that drive immediate business value.

Introduction to the STAR Framework™

Throughout this book, I'm going to use my STAR Framework to walk you through each and every step of the data strategy-building process.

The STAR Framework is a data strategy consulting process I've developed out of my own experience over the last 18 years working as a strategic consultant in the data and technology industry. The purpose of the STAR Framework is to de-risk future data projects and products by following a methodical process. This process helps you select the optimal use case for substantial and reliable ROI given current state conditions within a company. To do this, I teach learners how to select three potential use cases and then produce evidence-based alternatives analysis to support their selection of a single winning use case around which to build their data strategy.

In the context of the book, the STAR Framework acts as a north star to keep learners oriented with respect to how the detailed stages of technical consulting fit together in support of producing a data strategy plan for a low-risk, high-ROI data project or product. Throughout the book, I'll point you back to where we are in the STAR Framework—so in that sense, this framework functions like a high-level road map for the data strategy-building process and the book.

Over the years I've spent supporting Fortune 500 companies, I developed the STAR Framework as my own personal consulting framework to guide me in my strategy development work. I've led many online trainings and face-to-face workshops where I cover the process and teach learners how to make the best use of it. Some organizations with whom I've shared this framework include insightsoftware (formerly LogiAnalytics), Saudi Aramco, Cloudera, GigaOm, Oracle, the Government of Kazakhstan, Central Bank of Malaysia, Pride Microfinance, Women In Data, and others.

Let me explain what this framework is and how it works in the context of this book. The STAR Framework represents a four-phase approach to data strategy building. First, I'll describe each of the four phases, and then I'll show you how we'll apply this process throughout the book.

The Four Phases of the STAR Framework

As illustrated in Figure 2.1, the STAR Framework uses the following four-phase approach:

1. Survey the industry.
2. Take stock and inventory of your organization.
3. Assess your organization's current state conditions.
4. Recommend a strategy for reaching future state goals.

Let's look at each phase a little closer:

Phase 1: Survey the Industry.   This is where you conduct extensive research, looking at all the different use cases and case studies, in order to get yourself up to

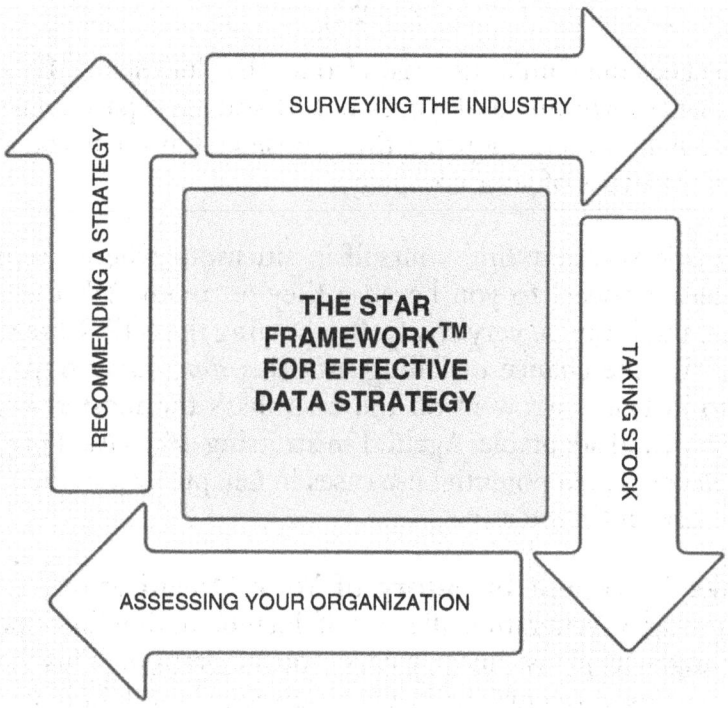

FIGURE 2.1 The STAR Framework's four-phase approach.

speed with all the use cases across the industry. You'll want to pay special attention to the ones that you think, in your best judgment, might be most effective in getting your company a *substantial* ROI.

Note

ROI benchmarks vary significantly based on industry, company maturity, project duration, market conditions, investment scale, business model, and other factors. While there are no hard and fast rules for what qualifies as "substantial" ROI, the following standards may be helpful:

Generally acceptable—≥ 20% ROI
Strong performance—≥ 50% ROI
Exceptional performance—≥ 100% ROI

> ### Tip
>
> Be sure to check out similar use cases from other industries. This will give you an idea of what's working and what's not. If you see a particularly compelling use case from a different industry, then consider ways that you can adapt that use case to the needs of your company.

In some cases, you may find yourself in situations where the use cases that you're considering appeal to you because they're trendy. We call this the *shiny object syndrome*, and it can be very costly. By applying the STAR Framework, you'll be able to de-risk the chance of falling into this *shiny object* trap, and you'll be empowered to instead narrow in on the case that's the most resource-efficient, low-risk, focused, and adaptable. Again, I'm stressing *adaptable*. I'm going to show you how to select optimal potential use cases in Chapter 9 and then how to select a winning use case in Chapter 14.

Phase 2: Take Stock and Inventory of Your Organization.   In this phase, you'll be collecting or generating all sorts of documentation, like operational procedures, contingency plans, and project documentation. This documentation describes all aspects of operations in your business. You definitely don't want to limit yourself to only data operations. You'll need to take a more holistic view of your company and its most urgent needs. I'll be walking you through each and every step.

Phase 3: Assess Your Organization's Current State Conditions.   This is essentially where you take the entire body of documentation you've collected in the previous phase and start evaluating and identifying gaps or areas of opportunity. You also need to consider imminent risks that you can mitigate by implementing the right data use case. After doing an expansive evaluation of your business and its operations, you'd go ahead and hone in on a winning use case—in other words, the one that offers your company the largest ROI given its current state.

Phase 4: Recommend a Strategy for Reaching Future State Goals.   This is the phase where you'll create a robust, well-supported strategic plan for implementing the winning use case you've proposed in prior phases.

Applying the STAR Framework

Now let's look at how we'll apply this framework in the context of this book. Figure 2.2 shows the somewhat iterative process that I'll be guiding you through.

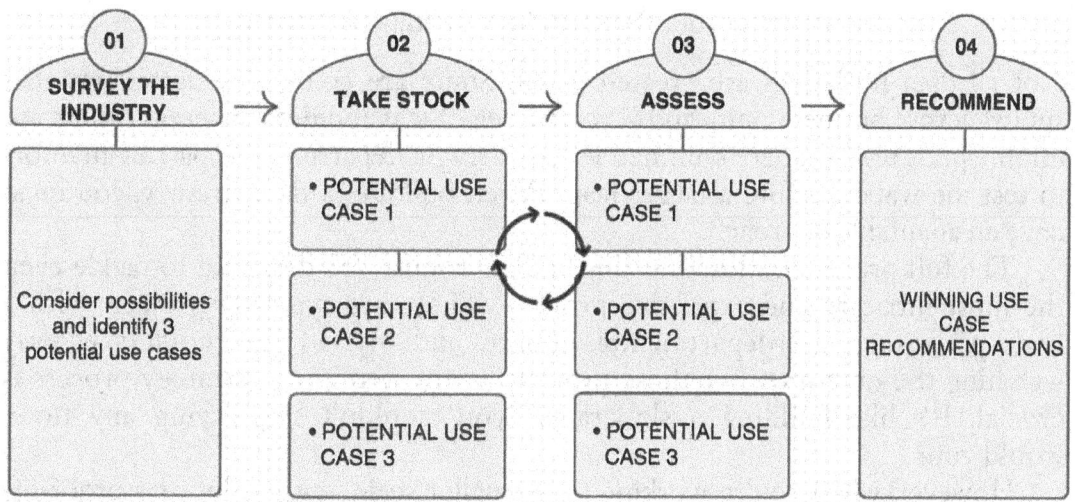

FIGURE 2.2 How to apply the STAR Framework.

In Chapter 9, you'll learn all about surveying the industry via extensive research of use cases and case studies. You'll emerge from Chapter 9 with three potential use cases that you'll use as your basis of investigation as you work through Chapters 10–14. Throughout these chapters, you'll form hypotheses around use cases, including the one that is most appropriate for your organization at this time. Chapters 10–14 cover both the "taking stock" and "assessment" phases of the STAR Framework. You'll be toggling between taking stock and assessing in an iterative process as you work to deeply clarify your organization's most pressing needs and identify which of your three most promising potential use cases is the winning use case upon which you'll build your data strategy.

In Chapter 14, you'll select a "winning" use case around which you'll build your data strategy. Thanks to the work you do throughout the earlier phases of this process, you'll also have an exhaustive body of evidence to support your selection of that use case.

In the remainder of the book, Chapters 15–17, you'll walk through the final phase of the STAR Framework, where you'll recommend a strategy for reaching your organization's future state goals. If you work along with the instructions provided within these pages, you'll emerge from this final portion of the book with a comprehensive data strategy plan that's supported by robust evidence to tie it back to all of your recommendations, as well as a high-level schedule to use in overseeing the execution of the project.

Tailoring Your Data Strategy Building Approach

Not all data initiatives are created equal. Some are colossal undertakings that sprawl across business units and involve a sea of stakeholders, whereas others are nimble pilot tests that are confined within a single department as part of an effort to test the waters before a larger leap. When building a data strategy, you must have an adaptable approach.

The full process outlined in this book is robust. It's designed to tackle even the most intricate and expansive projects. These are typically projects with a high price tag, interdepartmental impact, and myriad stakeholders eagerly watching the outcome. For these projects, every step in our strategy process is crucial. It's like building a skyscraper; you wouldn't skip laying any floor, would you?

However, when you're working on a smaller scale, say, a pilot or a proof-of-concept within your own business unit, flexibility becomes key. Think of this as setting up a camp tent; you might forgo some pegs if the weather's calm, but always know where they are if the winds pick up.

Now, how do you decide which approach is best?

- As a guideline, if you're delivering projects for US companies, you can consider projects with budgets exceeding $250,000 and/or spanning more than three business units as your threshold for the *full process* approach. These projects often carry higher risks due to their scale, complexity, and visibility.
- Projects below this benchmark, particularly those contained within a single department and with fewer stakeholders, might afford you the opportunity to streamline the process.

However, and this is crucial, efficiency shouldn't be an enemy of effectiveness. Your primary goal remains to select and implement a high-ROI use case with minimal risks and maximum efficiency.

So, can you skip some steps? Yes, but proceed with caution. Leaving steps out is like removing safety nets. It can make the process quicker, but if things go wrong, the damage could be much worse.

Quick Win Use Cases vs. Strategic Win Use Cases

Much like in the world of athletics, where there are sprinters and marathon runners, in the world of business strategy, there are *quick win* use cases and *strategic* use cases.

Defining a Quick Win Use Case

A quick win use case is akin to a sprint—its key value propositions are speed and immediate results. Maybe your organization is at a stage where it needs to prove the value of a data strategy promptly, or perhaps you're facing a pressing issue that requires an immediate solution. Or, it might be that you have a use case that you can quickly adopt in your current state without expending a lot of resources. In these cases, you'll want to choose a quick win use case with high ROI and low risk.

The successful implementation of a quick win use case will demonstrate the value of your data initiatives to stakeholders, thereby building momentum and securing further support for more complex, longer-term projects. In the context of data strategy, a quick win use case is a use case that, once implemented, can achieve ROI for the company within its first 90 days.

For example, say your organization already has data resources but has always used them for simple reporting and analysis. Your current state is robust, and you don't have to spend a lot of time or resources on *fixing* your data. So, your quick win use case could be something that's easy to implement and gives results quickly, such as a forecasting or predicting feature on top of your analysis.

Defining a Strategic Win Use Case

A strategic win use case is more of a marathon. With this type of use case, you're thinking from a long-term perspective about building a sustainable advantage and ensuring your organization's data capabilities are robust and future-proof. Companies often look to achieve these long-term strategic wins as part of the next steps once they've achieved a few quick win use cases.

Note

Strategic win use cases generally support more complex, longer-term projects than quick win uses cases.

Identifying the Type of Win You Need

Throughout this book, you'll learn how to select a winning use case. That use case could be a quick win use case, or it could be a strategic win use case, depending on the current needs of your organization.

While this book outlines a unified process that's suitable for achieving success in both scenarios, you need to bring the correct approach with you as you move into your data strategy plan-building work. Here's how you can identify which type of win is most appropriate for your organization at this time.

Start by asking yourself: Are you looking to demonstrate immediate ROI and resolve a current challenge? Or, are you aiming to build a strong data foundation that'll serve your organization for years to come, offering sustainable competitive advantages?

Neither path is better or worse; they simply serve different needs. By understanding your unique context, you'll be better equipped to tailor the insights and methods from this book to your specific situation.

A Brief Introduction to Generative AI and Foundation Models

In the opening paragraph of this book, I described mid-March 2023, the day that OpenAI launched GPT-4, as a watershed moment in the data science and AI world. Truth be told, however, GPT-4 was just another release of the latest and greatest in generative AI technology that's been in research and development since 2017. That was the year that AI researchers from Google and The University of Toronto published a research paper named Attention Is All You Need,[1] in which researchers introduced the transformer model, the model upon which most generative AI systems are built.

But if this is all Greek to you, let me break it down into simpler pieces. First, what *is* generative AI? The term *generative AI* refers to AI systems that generate new data. Whether that data comes in the format of text, audio, or visual, the underlying generative processes are usually built on top of a transformer model.

Generative AI systems are also built on things called *foundation models*. Foundation models are large-scale models that have been pretrained on massive datasets. Large language models (LLMs) are special machine learning models trained on massive datasets and have the ability to both understand and generate human-like text. They can understand the context of a query you provide them and then give you a detailed answer to your question. These are a subset of generative AI.

The GTP-4 LLM is one of the most popular foundation models on the market, but there are many others, such as Llama 2 or Claude 2. Foundation models like these provide the foundational architecture and learned patterns that generative AI systems utilize when generating new datasets.

As innovative leaders, your understanding of generative AI and foundation models is paramount. This understanding determines the effectiveness with which you lead your organization in its growth and monetization of innovative AI products and services moving forward. As you'll learn later in this chapter, not every data strategy is an AI strategy. That said, you still need to have a functional understanding of generative AI and how this technology can radically transform the growth trajectory of your organization.

Introducing Fine-tuning of LLMs, RAG, and AI Agents

Generative AI has taken the world by storm. Everyone's talking about LLMs and what they should be. Several of my contacts are excited about the value they can deliver by embedding generative AI within business processes.

Focusing on Fine-tuning

During my conversations, the word *fine-tuning* comes up often, and there's a lot of confusion around it. Fine-tuning is the process of tuning an already trained model—known as a *pretrained model*—so that the model performs well for the specific task that it's designated to support.

I'll clarify what I mean with an analogy. You're prepping for an exam, and you have a really large textbook as your reference. An LLM is essentially that: a large textbook. You also have a stack of previous years' test questions you can use to prepare. When you study specific chapters and sections that are closely related to those test questions, that's analogous to *fine-tuning* an LLM. When you're *customizing* your studies based on this very narrow guidance, you're not very concerned with the entire body of text within the book, are you? This is similar to fine-tuning in LLMs.

There are two ways in which you can fine-tune models:

- **Feature extraction method**—In this technique, you'd train specific layers of the model on the domain-specific data while keeping the other layers frozen. You should follow this method if your data is similar to the data on which the original model was trained.

- **Full-scale fine-tuning**—Without freezing any model layers, here you'd train all the layers of the model on the domain-specific data. You should go ahead with this method if your data is significantly different from the data on which the original model was trained. Doing so will adjust the weights across multiple layers and may improve model accuracy, but it'll be computationally more expensive and time-consuming if you choose this training technique.

Retrieval-Augmented Generation

The word *RAG* comes up a lot, too. RAG stands for retrieval-augmented generation. RAG works by combining the generative capabilities of an LLM with an information retrieval system. It uses the LLM primarily as a reasoning engine to synthesize and generate responses based on both the pretrained knowledge of the LLM and a custom knowledge base that you provide it as an ancillary, external information source.

While RAG often ends up pulling information from the pretrained LLM model, you can also provide it your own sources of information—or *knowledge bases*—to pull from. A knowledge base could include structured databases (like SQL databases), unstructured data (such as PDF files or text documents), or even data that's made accessible through APIs.

Let me illustrate using the exam analogy. RAG would be like being able to bring with you to the test a whole library that's full of reference books and articles. So, when answering test questions, you'd have access to your textbook plus a plethora of additional material you can refer to. Your answers will be more precise and well-informed. That's similar to how RAG works!

LLMs combined with RAG perform phenomenally well when compared to LLMs that aren't supported with RAG. The answers that you get from the LLMs (combined with RAG) are consistently more creative and better supported by the facts that the LLM has retrieved from the corpus of text it refers to. If you interact with an LLM-powered chatbot, and it provides you up-to-date information on a somewhat conversational basis, then most likely you're interacting with an LLM + RAG.

Let me illustrate LLM + RAG with an example. If you were to ask this type of system *"Who's the best footballer?"* assuming that a list of the most recent names of the best football players has been made available to retrieve from, then this system will return a list of those most recent names. If you were using a traditional LLM (in other words, one that isn't supported by RAG), then you'd only be provided a list that's recent up to the date on which the model was last trained—also known as the *knowledge cut-off date*.

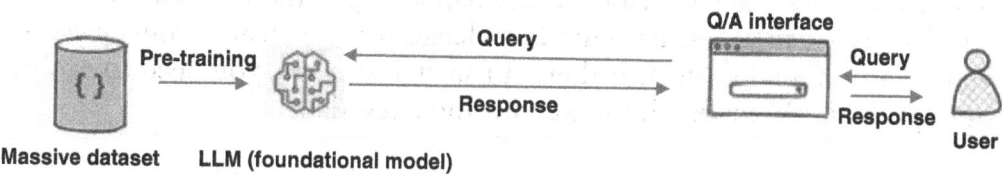

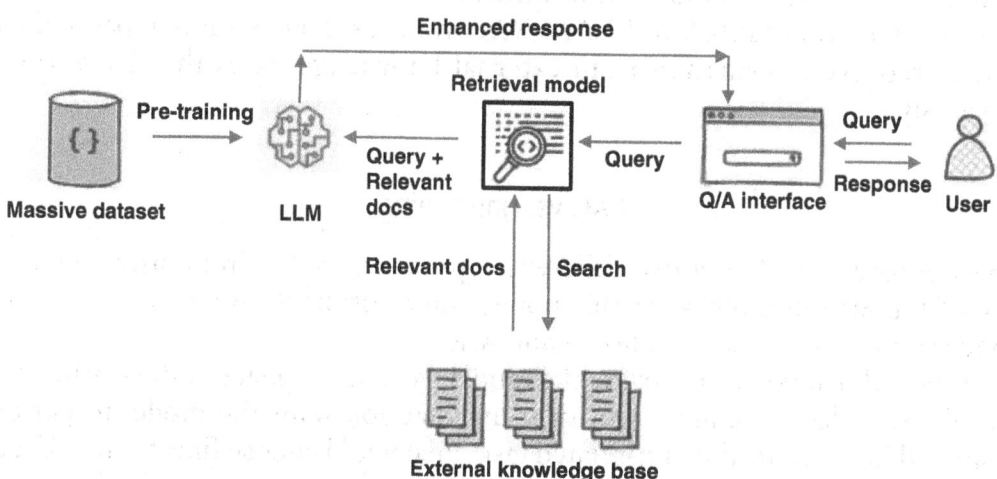

FIGURE 2.3 Traditional LLM vs. RAG-powered LLM.

So, you can relax, an LLM only has access to the information that it has been provided within the training dataset. It doesn't actually *know* who won the recent World Cup or the match you missed yesterday—and it certainly isn't *aware* of any private, personal experiences you may have recently had! Figure 2.3 shows the basic difference between a traditional LLM and an LLM powered by RAG. While the traditional LLM provides a direct answer to the user, the one powered by RAG searches for additional information in an external database to accentuate its response before sending it back to the user.

Warning

GPT 4.0 and later versions have access to the internet and are able to update responses with the latest internet data to answer questions about recent events and happenings. Despite this, you'll often receive back a notice that states

"My training only includes knowledge up until January 2022, and I don't have access to real-time data." In such cases what's happening is the foundation model or LLM is trying to access its static knowledge base to answer your question—and it hasn't found an answer there. In such a scenario, you need to explicitly prompt the LLM to search the web for the latest data.

Speaking of live internet access for information retrieval by LLMs, this use case is a prime example of RAG + LLM working together to produce timely, sometimes accurate results. While information retrieval from the internet is considered a form of RAG, an LLM + RAG system can also—and in parallel—be used to retrieve information from external knowledge bases that I mentioned previously.

RAG vs. Fine-tuning

Fine-tuning and RAG are two different approaches that help improve the accuracy of foundation models. At this point, you're probably scratching your head wondering which method to choose and when.

Provided that you can provide the model with new, updated information periodically to update its knowledge base, and that you want the model to perform really well in a specific domain-related task, then you'd choose fine-tuning. On the other hand, if you just want the model to produce more accurate results by augmenting its output with real-time information or information from an external base, then go ahead with RAG. This will enable you to trace back the model output to its source.

Table 2.1 is an at-a-glance reference to help you choose between fine-tuning and RAG when working with LLMs.

Table 2.1   Fine-tuning vs. RAG

Characteristic	Fine-tuning	Rag
Can utilize external knowledge sources	✕	✓
Adaptable to changing model behavior	✓	✕
Minimizes erroneous fabrications – aka hallucinations	✕	✓
Requires domain-specific training data	✓	✕
Suitable for dynamic data	✕	✓
Offers clear interpretability of outputs	✕	✓

Tip

Do not rule out the possibility of combining the powers of both fine-tuning and RAG. For example, you can fine-tune an existing model with a large domain-specific knowledge base after which you can use RAG to retrieve new information if necessary to supplement your model's output. This can be really useful in the medical domain where you fine-tune an existing model on the medical database and use RAG to access up-to-date medical information from open sources. How this would work is, first the model would process your prompt in order to gather its context, and then if the context is such that it requires the model to look up up-to-date information, then the RAG component would retrieve that information before providing the final output.

Now that you're clear on the basic differences between fine-tuning and RAG, you're equipped to think for yourself. When deciding between RAG and fine-tuning, consider basing your decision on your answers to the following three questions:

1. Do you need the model to excel in a specific task? For example, in historical interpretation or literature analysis. Or, is your requirement more geared toward retrieving recent information, say info about markets or recent developments in a field?

2. Will it suffice if your model is trained once and only fine-tuned periodically with new, unseen data to improve its performance? Or, do you want to supplement the output of your model with up-to-date information retrieved from the internet or another external dataset or source?

3. Are you concerned with why and how the model gave you the output it did? Do you want to trace back the output to its original source?

And since we're talking about LLMs and RAG, I also want to introduce AI agents.

AI Agents

AI agents are like lightweight applications that can behave in a very similar fashion to how humans do. We use them in chatbots, automated customer support, and as virtual assistants. So, when you consider the possibilities that are brought about by AI agents powered by LLMs and RAG, imagine this: A machine that can understand what you're saying, quickly scan through any text corpus, and come up with answers supported by facts. A perfect study companion? Absolutely.

Crafting an Effective Plan: Data Strategy vs. AI Strategy

The cutting-edge data technology development right now is happening within the areas of AI innovation, so naturally there's a lot of talk about and push toward AI product development. That's a great thing, and this book will help you build strategies to support the successful implementation of an AI use case.

Here's the thing though: what I'm sharing with you in this book is an evergreen blueprint for building a strategy to support any type of data-intensive use case. When I say it's "evergreen," I mean that it'll work despite rapid changes and advancements in technology. It also works no matter what type of data project you're building—AI or otherwise.

What we're covering here is an approach you can use to assess your business and its needs in order to custom tailor a data strategy plan that'll support your business in realizing substantial ROI for the data product you're planning.

Figure 2.4 depicts an approach to building an evergreen data strategy. This approach starts with a robust future-proof framework that'll accommodate different use cases that you choose to build your data strategy around. That framework is the STAR Framework introduced earlier in this chapter.

In layer 2 of the pyramid, we're starting from the business: its current state, its needs, and its opportunities. Then, in layer 3, we're using those insights to identify a winning use case that's positioned to deliver substantial ROI to your company. While that use case could be an AI use case, it definitely doesn't need to be. Any sort of data-intensive use case could be relevant.

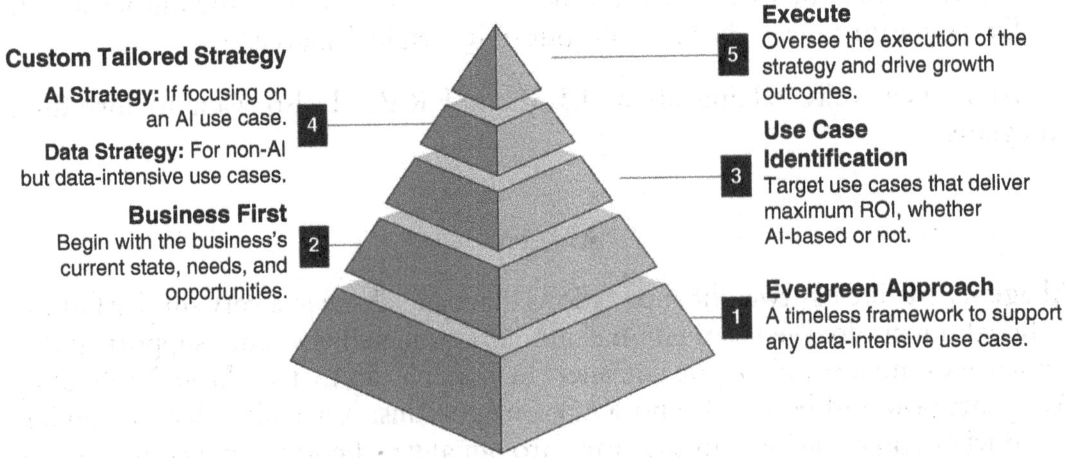

Custom Tailored Strategy

AI Strategy: If focusing on an AI use case.

Data Strategy: For non-AI but data-intensive use cases.

Business First

Begin with the business's current state, needs, and opportunities.

Execute

5 Oversee the execution of the strategy and drive growth outcomes.

Use Case Identification

3 Target use cases that deliver maximum ROI, whether AI-based or not.

Evergreen Approach

1 A timeless framework to support any data-intensive use case.

FIGURE 2.4 Delivering an evergreen data strategy.

Then, in layer 4, we're building a data or AI strategy, and in layer 5 we're overseeing the execution of that strategy to drive growth outcomes.

If you decide to build a data strategy around an AI use case, then indeed the plan you build in this book would be called an *AI strategy*. But in many instances, the use case you identify as the winning use case will not involve AI despite its data-intensive nature. In these situations, the plan you'd build as part of your work in this book would be called a *data strategy*.

Data Product vs. Data Project vs. Data Initiative

This data strategy book teaches you how to plan for and execute data-related efforts that are integral aspects of data product, data project, and data initiative planning. Let's start by clarifying the differences between a data product, a data project, and a data initiative.

A high-level overview of the differences between the three goes like this:

1. The data strategy planning process is about selecting the right use cases to form the backbone of a *data project*.

2. The end goal of each project is generally to build a sustainable *data product or program*.

3. These projects and products should align with and contribute to a larger *data initiative*.

Now that you understand the key differences between these similar terms, you have the basics of what you need to get started, so let's move into Chapter 3, where you'll see the types of use cases that are available to support your business objectives.

Note

1. Vaswani, A., Shazeer, N., Parmar, N. et al. (June 12, 2017). *Attention Is All You Need*. arXiv. https://arxiv.org/abs/1706.03762

Recommended Reading

Li, X., Chan, S., Zhu, X. et al. (December 10, 2023). *Are ChatGPT and GPT-4 General-Purpose Solvers for Financial Text Analytics? A Study on Several Typical Tasks*. arXiv. https://arxiv.org/abs/2305.05862

Vaswani, A., Shazeer, N., Parmar, N. et al. (June 12, 2017). *Attention Is All You Need*. arXiv. https://arxiv.org/pdf/1706.03762.pdf

3

Types of Data-Intensive Use Cases Based on Business Objectives

Data really powers everything that we do.

— Jeff Weiner

As with all types of business-facing strategies, you can categorize data strategies based on the unique business objectives that they support within your organization. You can represent them by the underlying use case around which you build a data strategy. For purposes of data strategy development, I categorize data-intensive use cases as follows:

- **Operational improvements**—Strategies in this category are based on use cases that aim to increase the efficiency and effectiveness of business operations. They generally involve leveraging data resources, technologies, and skill sets to streamline processes and reduce costs

- **Product-led growth improvements**—These strategies concentrate on expanding a product's market presence and user base by using data to inform product development

- **Growth marketing improvements**—Here, the focus is on using data to improve the outcomes of marketing campaigns that drive growth by bolstering market positioning, cultivating deeper relationships, and increasing leads

- **Decision-support improvements**—These data strategies help build and improve the culture of data-driven decision-making within an organization
- **Financial improvements**—This type of data strategy involves leveraging data to optimize financial operations, from budgeting to forecasting and beyond. The goal here is to ensure fiscal health, efficiency, and sustainability
- **Data monetization**—This is a more innovative type of data strategy that focuses on directly converting data resources and skill sets into new or improved revenue streams

Let's take a look at each of these use case types in greater detail.

Operational Improvements Use Cases

Operational improvements use cases focus on improving the efficiency of business processes to reduce operational costs. You may already have something similar in place within your organization. Maybe you're using an advanced tool to streamline project management or to automate repetitive processes in your workflow. Efficient operations reduce waste, lower costs, improve productivity, and ultimately contribute to profit growth over time. It's important for leaders to prioritize these use cases as they directly impact the company's bottom line.

Investing in your company's operations function can yield substantial benefits. Greater operational efficiency often leads to faster turnaround times, improved customer satisfaction, and a better competitive standing in the market. You're also building a culture of continuous improvement by encouraging your employees to switch to efficiency-boosting measures. When you get rid of repetitive, time-consuming procedures by automating them, you're essentially freeing up your employees' time to work on challenging problems that actually need them to use their critical thinking skills. What's more, effective operations management reduces risks associated with supply chain disruptions, quality control, and compliance. At its core, operational improvement is about building a more resilient, agile, and customer-focused business.

Table 3.1 provides a few examples of data-intensive use cases of this type.

A notable example of a company that's using data science to optimize its retail inventory is illustrated in the following Walmart case study.

Table 3.1   Examples of Operational Improvements Use Cases

Use Case	Description
Retail inventory optimization	Using predictive analytics for demand forecasting. This helps optimize and maintain stock levels to reduce overstock and out-of-stock situations.
Patient scheduling in healthcare	Utilizing AI applications to schedule patient appointments more efficiently. This helps reduce wait times, streamline patient flow, and improve customer satisfaction.
Energy consumption analysis	Utilizing automated data analysis at scale to monitor and optimize energy usage in manufacturing for better cost savings and sustainability.
Traffic flow management	Deploying an automated algorithmic approach to analyze vast amounts of traffic data to optimize road usage, reduce congestion, and increase safety.
Predictive maintenance in manufacturing	Using sensors and AI to minimize downtime by predicting equipment failures and scheduling maintenance before breakdowns occur. This reduces the need for manual inspections, abrupt maintenance schedules, and disruptions due to unplanned downtime.
Customer service chatbots	Deploying LLM-based chatbots in customer service to handle routine inquiries. This frees up team members for more complex issues and lets them focus on the customer interactions that require personalized care.

Data Science in Operational Improvements Case Study

Company Name: Walmart[1]

Industry: Retail

Situation Summary

Walmart recognized the need to increase the efficiency and effectiveness of its complex supply chain management processes. The company wanted to ensure better timeliness of deliveries by optimizing their packing process.

Challenges

Optimizing order sourcing and ensuring the fulfillment of on-time delivery promises in e-commerce operations.

Addressing the "Bin Packing Problem" to optimize the packing process for efficient use of packaging materials and space.

Solution

Walmart Labs, the innovation and technology hub of Walmart, utilized data science and ML to build solutions to overcome these challenges. They developed a sophisticated algorithmic approach for estimating delivery dates and for determining the optimal fulfillment center for each order. They also implemented a recommender system to select the most suitable box size for packing. This would minimize space wastage within a predefined time period.

Results

These solutions led to better inventory management and more efficient order fulfillment. Walmart's approach to using data science for inventory optimization illustrates the significant impact of data-driven strategies in retail in order to drive improved operational efficiency, fewer errors, and greater customer satisfaction.

Product-Led Growth Improvements Use Cases

Product-led growth (PLG) strategies are based on the idea that a company's product is the cornerstone of the company's growth trajectory. Within the PLG paradigm, the product serves as the main driver of customer acquisition, activation, retention, and expansion. So, the goal here is to make the product itself exceptional so that it will attract and retain customers on its own, independent of any sales or marketing initiatives that the company has in place.

A great example of this is OpenAI's ChatGPT. The PLG strategies in place demonstrate a continuous effort toward improving the product by adding new features and functionalities that customers want and need.

In practice, PLG shifts the growth focus from traditional sales and marketing efforts to that of the product's "inherent value."

Note

Self-service options are a key marker that indicates whether a company is leveraging PLG strategies.

Tip

You can see for yourself if a SaaS company is leveraging PLG by visiting their website and looking at the primary call to action. If the website copy is pushing you to "book a call" or "sign up for a demonstration," then the product is not self-service and the company is not using PLG as its primary growth driver. If, on the other hand, the website is offering you a free trial or allowing you to "buy now," then it is more than likely deploying PLG.

PLG originally evolved as a response to changing customer expectations, where modern consumers seek powerful functionality that's delivered to them via intuitive and visually appealing products. There's also a lot of effort that goes into using AI to make the products as personalized as possible. For instance, do you know the streaming services that provide movie or TV show recommendations that are very specific to your personality and interests? That's what I call "contact-level" precision. PLG companies like Slack, Zoom, and Atlassian have utilized this model to capitulate untold growth success and customer loyalty.

Table 3.2 provides a few key examples of data-intensive use cases that are being deployed across the industry to accelerate the results of PLG strategies.

While the use cases in Table 3.2 clearly demonstrate the ways in which data is utilized to enhance product-led growth, I'll also be covering PLG in greater detail

Table 3.2 Examples of Data-Intensive Product-Led Growth Use Cases

Use Case	Description
User experience optimization	Utilizing user flow and interaction data to refine the product interface. This increases user-friendliness and overall customer satisfaction.
Feature adoption analytics	Analyzing how users interact with different features to identify popular or underused features and guide future development efforts.
Customer journey personalization	Employing customer data to tailor the product experience so that your users derive value from your product with maximum speed and effectiveness.
Product improvement feedback loop	Deploying built-in feedback systems that automatically collect and analyze user feedback for continuous product improvements. This helps keep the product both relevant and competitive.
Conversion rate optimization (trial-to-paid)	Analyzing trial-to-paid conversion data to refine onboarding processes and promotional strategies to improve conversion rates.
Market trend analysis	Using market research data to align product development with emerging trends and customer needs. An example of this is provided in the following case study.

in Chapter 4. For now, though, I recommend that you read through the following case study. It illustrates how Spotify adopted AI-powered market trend analysis to drive growth and customer satisfaction by better aligning their product with market demands and the customer's preferences.

Product-Led Growth Case Study

Company Name: Spotify[2]

Industry: Entertainment, Technology

Situation Summary

Spotify uses advanced ML algorithms to drive AI systems that improve user experience by offering personalized music recommendations. One of their core features is fully personalized playlists, also known as "Discover Weekly," that are unique to each user's musical taste.

Challenges

- Analyzing user behavior, including play history and playlist creation
- Managing scenarios where new songs or new users have little historical data
- Recommending songs that align with user's known preferences and also introducing new musical styles

Solution

Spotify uses three primary recommendation engines to recommend songs:

- Collaborative filtering involves extensively analyzing user behavior
- Content-based filtering considers descriptions of artists, albums, and songs
- Audio-feature extraction uses deep learning to extract musical features from raw audio files to create a "sonic profile"

(continued)

(continued)

These three models work in tandem to recommend songs that are to people's liking. The engine also learns from user feedback on a continuous basis to provide better recommendations.

Results

Spotify's "Discover Weekly" feature has been very popular and has led to an increase in user satisfaction and engagement. Through this feature, people have discovered new songs, genres, and artists. They then recommend Spotify to their friends and family, which leads to word-of-mouth marketing and a positive brand image. This increases Spotify's subscriptions and revenue.

While PLG is an indispensable growth strategy, it's not without its limitations. One such limitation is that this type of strategic approach omits a clear focus on market positioning and lead acquisition processes. While powerful, PLG can only take your product so far. Left unabated, product-led growth will plateau, and that's exactly where growth marketing comes in.

Growth Marketing Improvements Use Cases

Growth marketing is a growth paradigm wherein a company's marketing activities are optimized through data-driven strategies to drive customer acquisition, retention, and activation. This approach differs significantly from the PLG model that we just examined.

Growth marketing employs methods like content marketing, search engine optimization, community building, event marketing, personalized email marketing, and referral programs. Unlike traditional marketing methods, however, growth marketing relies upon deep data analytics and continuous experimentation to increase brand awareness, generate demand, and drive revenue gains.

To be successful with growth marketing, it's beneficial for a company to have a clear map of their customer journey, all the way from initial consideration to purchase. Many companies are using analytics solutions to identify exactly when those considerations are made, so that they can optimize their positioning in anticipation of the purchasing event. This clarity leads to greatly increased conversion rates and more revenue for businesses that deploy growth marketing as a primary growth approach.

Companies are also using analytics and churn prediction models to identify exactly which phase of the customer journey is causing them to lose customers. Once you have data that shows the precise point in the process where you're losing customers, then you can divert resources to strategically decrease churn at these key junctures.

Tip

Beyond sophisticated analytics and ML approaches, surveys and feedback forms make for simple, readily-accessible diagnostic data tools. Use them to develop an understanding of the reasons that excite, disappoint, or "meh!" your customers, so you can proactively address those issues. Techniques like these are important for customer retention and a core part of growth marketing strategies.

Growth marketing strategies focus on broadening the target consumer segments beyond loyal customers, to include people who may have limited or no prior experience with the brand. By expanding the window for growth potential, growth marketing aims to attract and acquire new leads and customers from a diverse range of consumer segments, including those people who may have previously interacted with the brand but have failed to make a purchase.

Note

In growth marketing, the goal is to drive growth via a data-intensive marketing approach that focuses on the entire customer journey. Growth marketing demands both experimentation and analytics to inform the optimization decisions that drive improvements in customer acquisition, retention, and revenue.

Table 3.3 Examples of Growth Marketing Use Cases

Use Case	Description
Consumer behavior analysis	Utilizing data analytics to understand consumer shopping patterns and preferences. This helps in creating targeted marketing strategies to increase brand loyalty and attract new customers.
Dynamic pricing strategy	Implementing AI to analyze market trends and customer demand. This enables dynamic pricing adjustments for products or services to maximize profits.

(continued)

Table 3.3 Examples of Growth Marketing Use Cases (*continued*)

Use Case	Description
Customer segmentation	Using ML to segment customers and tailor your marketing efforts to hyper-targeted groups based on their buying behavior/history and preferences.
Churn prediction and prevention	Using predictive analytics to identify customers at risk of churning and developing tailored marketing campaigns or incentives to retain them.
Personalized product recommendations	Employing ML algorithms to analyze customer data and provide personalized product recommendations to boost customer engagement and sales.
Marketing campaign optimization	Deploying ML and AI to automatically analyze ad campaign performance data to refine and optimize advertising strategies for effective resource allocation to the most effective channels and tactics. An example of this use case is provided in the DoorDash case study.

For more detailed coverage of growth marketing use cases, see Chapter 5. For now, though, Table 3.3 provides examples of six data-intensive growth marketing use cases.

Growth marketing use cases like those described in Table 3.3 clearly demonstrate how the strategic application of data and AI in marketing can lead to more informed decisions, better customer engagement, and revenue growth. The following DoorDash case study provides a real-life example of how one company leveraged ML to optimize its advertising campaigns for maximum impact and efficiency.

Marketing-Led Growth Case Study (Data Science)

Company Name: DoorDash[3]

Industry: Food Delivery

Situation Summary

DoorDash, a leading food delivery service, faced the challenge of optimizing its marketing and advertising spend to acquire new customers in a more cost-effective manner. With millions of dollars invested in advertising across multiple channels, DoorDash needed to find the perfect balance between spending too little (which would stifle revenue) and overspending on ads (which would hurt profitability).

Challenges

- Managing vast advertising expenditures across multiple channels
- Ensuring optimal allocation of advertising budgets for maximum efficiency
- Overcoming the limitations of manual management in handling tens of thousands of campaigns

Solution

To address these challenges, DoorDash developed an ML-powered marketing automation platform. This platform automatically allocated budgets and published bids to channel partners. It also developed cost curves for each campaign. These curves charted the relationship between advertising spend and the number of new customers acquired. These charts were helpful to DoorDash in quantifying the diminishing returns on increased ad spend. The platform utilized ML to augment historical data with synthetically generated data, which resulted in more reliable and stable cost curve estimations. This led to improved budget allocation across advertising channels and campaigns.

Results

The marketing automation platform significantly increased DoorDash's marketing efficiency. It led to a reduction in advertising costs by 10–30% while maintaining the same customer reach. With this solution in place, the marketing team was freed up to focus more attention on developing and executing strategies, rather than the manual tasks related to monitoring and optimizing ad campaign performance.

Now that you've seen how powerful machine learning and AI can be for driving growth, let's take a look at how these approaches are changing the game for the decision-support function of the modern enterprise.

Decision-Support Improvements Use Cases

Decision-support use cases deploy data technologies, skill sets, and resources to enhance and improve decision-making processes across an organization. Decision-support products usually come in the form of easy-to-understand dashboards that help organizational leaders quickly identify potential risks and opportunities.

Why should leaders care about improved decision support? The answer is simple: better decision-making leads to better outcomes. Effective decision-support products provide a robust interface that's useful for quickly gaining insights from complex data, even if one has only a limited degree of data literacy. This in turn leads to more accurate and timely decisions. This is particularly crucial in today's fast-paced business environment, where the margin for error is increasingly narrow.

Another interesting development in this space is the use of LLMs to "converse" with the data. With an intuitive, easy-to-use chat interface and provision for plots or other visual aids, decision-makers no longer have to rely on complex queries or scripts to get insights from the data. There's also a shorter turnaround time as they're able to get answers to their queries instantly without having to rely on analysts or data scientists. This in turn frees up the analytics team to work on more complex problems; say, for example, model building or building a data pipeline. Though there's ongoing research in the area, it can prove to be a win-win scenario for both parties.

Investing in your company's decision-support function can yield significant benefits. Firstly, it increases efficiency by speeding up the decision-making process. Secondly, it improves the quality of decisions, as data-driven insights are typically more reliable than intuition alone. Lastly, it can give a competitive edge in the market, as companies that leverage advanced decision-support often outperform those that don't. Investing in decision-support leads to the development of more intelligent and responsive business decision-making across the board. The following case study is a powerful example of data-intensive decision-support in action.

Decision-Support Case Study (Business Intelligence)

Company Name: Flinder[4]

Industry: Accounting and Financial Services

Situation Summary

Flinder, an accounting firm, experienced challenges with managing its growing team and client base, particularly during its Monday morning All Hands meetings. These meetings were intended to cover client updates and activities, but they were becoming increasingly lengthy and overwhelming due to information overload.

Challenges

- The firm's team size had quadrupled in 12 months, complicating meeting management
- The excessive level of details that were shared in meetings led to a lack of focus and efficiency
- Their existing project management tool, Asana, didn't provide a strategic, business-wide view

Solution

Flinder adopted a 5D transformation methodology to implement a custom dashboard. They developed Python scripts to manipulate data from Asana, stored and stitched this data in their cloud server, and connected Klipfolio to their bespoke API. This approach circumvented the limitations of Asana's API and enabled Flinder to build a comprehensive view of the business.

Results

The new Asana reporting dashboard on Klipfolio radically improved the effectiveness of Flinder's meetings. It allowed segmentation of management information by team, owner, and status (RAG—red, amber, green). Its focus on critical points saved Flinder significant amounts of time. This strategic approach to data-driven decision-making facilitated more efficient and focused meetings while saving untold employee hours across the company.

Financial Improvements Use Cases

With financial improvement use cases, you're applying data-intensive resources for the purpose of improving a company's financial health and performance. Deploying this type of use case requires you to start by first identifying areas within the finance function that can be optimized, such as cash flow management, cost reduction, or investment strategies. Generally speaking, financial improvement use cases enable strategic investments, foster financial stability, and support overall growth.

When investing in your company's finance function, you can expect several key benefits. Firstly, this type of investment leads to better financial management

Table 3.4   Examples of Data-Intensive Financial Improvements Use Cases

Use Case	Description
Risk assessment automation	Implementing AI to assess and categorize financial risk to improve the speed and accuracy of financial decision-making.
Client portfolio optimization	Using data analytics to optimize investment portfolios by balancing returns and risk exposure.
Fraud detection enhancement	Applying predictive analytics for early detection and prevention of fraudulent activities.
Cost reduction analysis	Utilizing data mining to identify potential cost-saving opportunities without compromising on quality.
Revenue forecasting	Employing statistical models to forecast future revenues in support of strategic planning initiatives.
Compliance monitoring system	Developing an AI-based system for real-time monitoring of financial compliance.

and oversight, along with a substantial reduction in the risk of errors and ineffi-ciencies. Improved accuracy is instrumental in supporting leaders to make better-informed strategic decisions. Secondly, a strong finance function can identify cost-saving opportunities that directly impact the company's bottom line. Lastly, a finance department that's equipped with the latest tools and technologies can pro-vide much deeper insights into market trends and business performance to drive a competitive advantage in decision-making.

Table 3.4 provides six examples of where data technologies, skill sets, and resources can be deployed to drive significant financial improvements.

Financial Improvements Case Study (Machine Learning)

Company Name: Western Union

Industry: Finance/Credit Companies

Situation Summary

Western Union is a global leader in financial and communication services. The company faced challenges in managing fraud and account takeovers, particularly with respect to their digital transactions. With the company han-dling more than $300 billion annually across various countries and curren-cies, the risk of financial loss due to fraud was significant.

Challenges

- High risk of fraud and account takeovers
- Inadequacy of traditional authentication techniques for digital transactions
- The need for safety and security in money transfers

Solution

Western Union implemented a comprehensive digital solution to combat fraud. This involved transitioning from a rules-based system to a suite of advanced analytical tools like SAS, Jupyter, Python, R tools, and H2O.ai. They also integrated Cloudera Data Science Workbench (CDSW), which increased their ability to analyze money transfer orders through ML models. This helped Western Union better validate the reliability of senders and the potential risks of transactions.

Results

The adoption of CDSW and other data science tools significantly reduced Western Union's fraud rates, bringing them well below the industry standard.

Bonus resource

The full Western Union case study and use case are available for you to download for free at www.data-mania.com/book.

Data Monetization Use Cases

Data monetization use cases involve leveraging data resources and skill sets as a strategic asset to build new revenue streams. This is generally achieved through the following three routes:

- **Data resources as a product**—Selling access to your company's data resources
- **Insights as a product**—Selling insights that your company has derived from its existing data resources
- **Data skill sets as a service**—Selling access to your company's in-house data skill sets

Table 3.5 Examples of Data Monetization Use Cases

Use Case	Description
Real estate market prediction SaaS	Offering a subscription service that uses AI and ML to analyze real estate market trends, predict property value fluctuations, and suggest optimal buying and selling times.
AI consultancy services	Monetizing AI expertise by providing consultancy services to businesses looking to implement AI solutions.
Data insights as a service	Selling analytical insights derived from proprietary data to other businesses or sectors needing such information. The SafeGraph case study is a good example of this use case type.
Agricultural data services	Building a platform that collects and analyzes data on weather patterns, soil conditions, and crop growth to provide farmers with actionable insights. Subscribers can use this information to optimize planting schedules, irrigation, and crop rotation to enhance their yield.

Data monetization use cases represent a significant opportunity to grow your company's revenue base by deriving new or improved revenues from your company's existing resources. Table 3.5 offers several examples of data monetization use cases that are being deployed across the industry today.

The following case study demonstrates the power of data monetization in action.

Data Monetization Case Study (Machine Learning)

Company Name: SafeGraph

Industry: Data Analytics and Market Research

Situation Summary

SafeGraph, a Colorado-based data company, recognized the untapped revenue potential in location-based data collected from mobile applications. This data detailed user movements around commercial spaces and presented a significant opportunity for retail companies that sought insights into consumer behavior. SafeGraph's approach involved forming data partnerships with mobile app developers to access and leverage this data.

Challenges

- Ensuring the data collected was accurate, up-to-date, and relevant for clients
- Integrating diverse datasets from various mobile apps into a cohesive, usable format
- Convincing retail companies of the value of this data in improving their decision-making processes

Solution

SafeGraph developed a sophisticated Data-as-a-Service (DaaS) platform that aggregated, cleaned, and processed location-based data from various app developers. This data was analyzed and then made available in a user-friendly web-based mapping application. With a focus on consumer movements and behaviors in commercial areas, the platform was effective in transforming raw data into valuable market research products.

Results

Retail companies purchase SafeGraph's data to make informed decisions about store locations, marketing strategies, and customer engagement. SafeGraph's innovative use of data partnerships led to a substantial increase in revenue and significant capital investments to the tune of $61 million USD.

Bonus resource

The full SafeGraph case study and use case are available for you to download for free at www.data-mania.com/book.

Notes

1. Kaur, M. (October 30, 2023). How Big Data and Data Science Are Reshaping Walmart's Retail Philosophy? *Accredian*. https://blog.accredian.com/how-big-data-and-data-science-are-reshaping-walmarts-retail-philosophy/

2. Velardo, V. (February 11, 2019). Spotify's Discover Weekly explained—Breaking from your music bubble or, maybe not? *Medium*. https://medium.com/the-sound-of-ai/spotifys-discover-weekly-explained-breaking-from-your-music-bubble-or-maybe-not-b506da144123

3. Dhesi, A. (July 31, 2020). Optimizing DoorDash's Marketing Spend with Machine Learning. *DoorDash*. https://doordash.engineering/2020/07/31/optimizing-marketing-spend-with-ml/

4. Barlow, A. (February 1, 2023). How our Asana dashboard changed the rhythm of our meetings. *Klipfolio*. https://www.klipfolio.com/blog/how-asana-dashboards-change-internal-meetings

Recommended Reading

Demyttenaere, M., Roos, A., and Sheth, H. (2023). *Generative AI in the Finance Function of the Future*, Boston Consulting Group. https://www.bcg.com/publications/2023/generative-ai-in-finance-and-accounting

4

Data- and AI-Driven Product-Led Growth

Product-led growth is the only distribution model worth undertaking once the market is mature.

— Pankaj Prasad

It's very easy for specialists of any kind to get so focused on the nuances of their trade that they miss out on the big picture of how their work impacts the business bottom line. Data specialists are no exception. This book is all about growth and the data and AI strategies that drive it, and in this chapter, we'll take a deeper look at how data technologies, skill sets, and resources drive product-led growth. For readers who are new to the term, product-led growth (PLG) is a go-to-market approach that prioritizes the product itself as the primary driver of growth—from user acquisition, activation, and conversion, to referrals and expansion. With the PLG approach, every interaction a user has with a product is meticulously optimized for maximum user satisfaction, conversions, and referrals. Iconic companies like Slack and Dropbox are known to have been massively successful in scaling via the PLG approach.

As a fractional CMO and growth partner, I've had the privilege of working closely with many PLG SaaS companies. It's an absolute honor to help these clients harness cutting-edge PLG strategies to drive substantial user and revenue growth, and I'm equally excited to share some of my learnings with you in this chapter. In Chapter 3, you saw a brief and gentle introduction to PLG, but this chapter provides a deeper exploration of how analytics, ML, and generative AI are driving it. To facilitate this, I'll lay a strong foundation by first detailing what PLG is, how it's measured, and how it works to drive revenue growth. After that, we'll turn our attention to the usefulness of ML and AI in driving PLG.

Harnessing Data for PLG

To optimize a system, you have to first understand the mechanics of how that system works. PLG systems are no different. Figure 4.1 shows the underlying dynamics of how PLG works within a business to drive revenue growth.

As you can see, PLG starts with initial, free user engagement with a product. When the user derives value from the product, this generally leads to a purchase. The product's outstanding features then drive customer satisfaction, turning buyers into loyal customers.

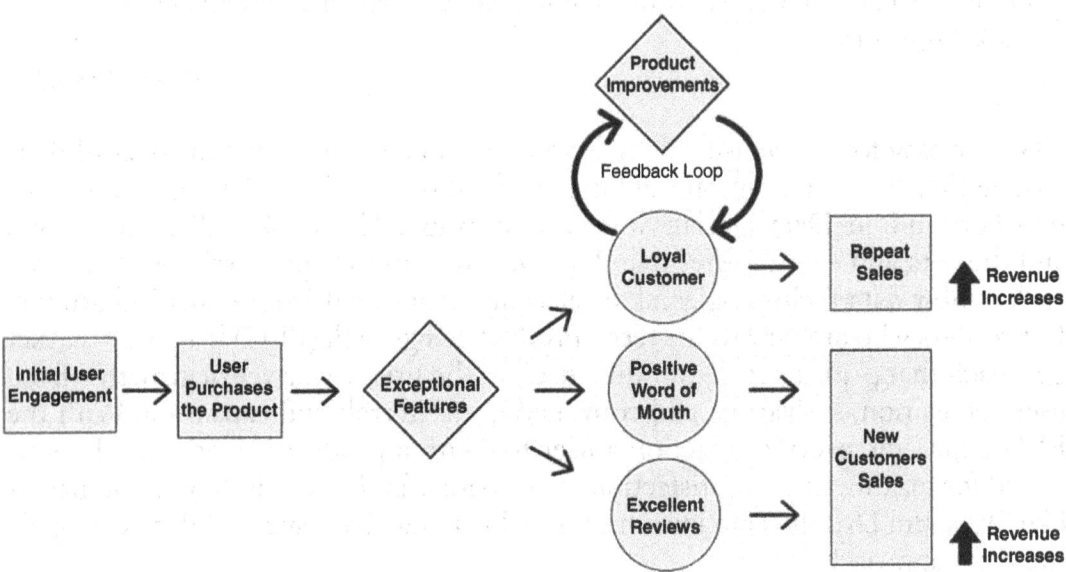

FIGURE 4.1 The basic mechanics of PLG.

These customers are often willing to provide positive word-of-mouth referrals and excellent reviews, which attracts new customers in turn. Loyal customers provide positive feedback that helps with product improvements and fuels the entire growth process. The influx of new customers, along with repeat sales from loyal ones, results in an increase in revenue. The main benefits of PLG are happier customers, lower customer acquisition costs (CAC), and more sustainable, scalable growth.

Let's look at the metrics and key performance indicators (KPIs) you need to track in order to assess the performance of a PLG strategy.

Measuring PLG Performance

As far as KPIs for measuring the performance of a PLG strategy, I suggest you track the following six categories of metrics:

- North star
- Acquisition
- Activation and engagement
- Retention
- Growth and expansion
- Referral and advocacy

Table 4.1 describes these categories a little closer.

Caution

To any data or AI start-up founder who's reading this, please take caution. While it's relatively simple for a tech start-up founder to track PLG growth metrics, you also need to know how to interpret these metrics in the context of a broader growth strategy. This type of interpretation requires a significant backdrop of education and experience in both growth and marketing. Do-it-yourself growth and marketing strategy is a recipe for disaster. My advice to founders: Hire an expert to help you with your marketing and growth strategy, if you haven't already.

Table 4.1 Metrics to Measure PLG Performance

Metric Type	Description and Benchmark Numbers
North Star Metrics that reflect revenue growth as a function of PLG strategy	I recommend focusing on Payback Period as your primary metric. While the LTV/CAC ratio has traditionally been used for tracking the long-term profitability of your customer acquisition strategies, be sure to prioritize metrics that offer quicker and more reliable insights into customer acquisition efficiency. • **Payback Period**—The amount of time it takes to recoup your investment in acquiring a customer. This is a wonderful metric for aligning marketing with product growth. • **Benchmark:** An acceptable payback period ranges from 6 months, for B2C products, to 18 months for B2B enterprise products.
Acquisition Trends and patterns that indicate the effectiveness of your initial user attraction strategies	• **Free Trial Signups (#)**—This measures the effectiveness of initial user attraction strategies. • **Website Visits (#)**—Tracks the effectiveness of online presence and marketing campaigns in driving traffic. • **Website Conversion Rate (%)**—This measures the conversion of site visitors to registered users. This is a measure of how well targeted your traffic is to the unique value proposition (UVP) of your product, and how effective your website is at converting visitors. Usually, 2%–4% is good for B2B industries and an average of 2%–5% is acceptable across all industries – but note that this doesn't take mobile apps into consideration.[1] • **Customer Acquisition Cost (CAC, $)**—This metric reflects the cost of acquiring new customers. For your company to be profitable and enjoy sustainable growth, CAC should typically be less than LTV. However, there are exceptions, such as in early-stage start-ups that are prioritizing rapid growth, companies that are operating in high-growth markets, and firms that have substantial investment backing, to name a few. For SaaS industries, the average CAC is around $702, and for B2B $536 per customer.[2]
Activation and Engagement Metrics that reflect the early interaction and engagement of users with the product	• **Free-to-Paid Conversion Rate (%)**—This metric tracks how well your funnel is converting free users into paying customers. It's a key measure of initial user activation. Usually, good numbers are 25% for opt-in trials (i.e., no payment information is required) and 60% for opt-out trials (credit card information is compulsory).[3] • **Feature Adoption Rate**—As discussed above, this indicates how frequently users are engaging with various features of the product. This reflects on product value and user activation. I recommend using a bar chart to display this metric, as shown in Figure 4.2. Having a feature adoption rate of about 28% is good for B2B SaaS companies.[4] • **Time-to-Value (TTV, #)**—This measures the speed at which users are able to generate value from your product in a self-serve environment. It's an important metric for understanding early user experience and engagement. TTV is best measured in days.

Retention

Crucial barometers of long-term success

- **User Retention Rate (%)**—This measures how well the product keeps users engaged over time, indicating long-term user satisfaction and product fit. This is a measure of the rate at which a company retains its customers over a given period of time. A high retention rate, of course, indicates that more customers are staying. It's always good to aim for a 25% or more user retention rate for 90+ days.[5]
- **Product Stickiness (DAU/MAU, %)**—This indicates how often users engage with the product, which is a key indicator of its "stickiness" or ongoing user engagement. A high DAU/MAU ratio indicates that users are returning to the product frequently, thus suggesting high stickiness. Try keeping the ratio around 13% per industry standards.[6]
- **Churn Rate (%)**—This metric tracks the rate at which customers stop using the product. It's crucial for understanding user retention challenges. This metric measures the rate at which customers or subscribers cancel their subscriptions over a given time interval. Usually, a monthly churn rate of about 4% is good for SaaS companies.[7]
- **Net Dollar Retention (NDR, %)**—While churn rate is fundamental, it only tells part of the retention story. To get an even clearer picture of your customer retention and growth, be sure you're also looking at NDR. NDR describes revenue growth from your existing customer base. It does so by factoring in upgrades, downgrades, and churn. If your NDR is more than 100%, this indicates that your expansion from upsells and cross-sells is greater than your losses from customer churn and downgrades. To illustrate, if your NDR is 110%, this would mean that your existing customers are generating 10% more revenue this period than they did last period, which, of course, is a positive indicator for product-market fit and customer satisfaction.

Growth and Expansion

These metrics are key indicators of a product's scalability and market acceptance.

- **Product Qualified Leads (PQLs, %)**—This metric identifies which percentage of leads are highly engaged with the product and are, consequently, more likely to convert. PQLs are freemium users who are interested in the product AND also actively benefiting from its use, thus indicating a higher likelihood of converting to paying customers.
- **Expansion Revenue (%)**—This measures the amount of revenue growth that can be attributed to existing customers through upselling, cross-selling, or upgrades. It's measured as a percentage of revenue expansion from your existing customer base over a given interval of time.

(continued)

Table 4.1 Metrics to Measure PLG Performance (*continued*)

Metric Type	Description and Benchmark Numbers

Referral and Advocacy
These metrics provide a window into your customer experience and loyalty.
	• **Net Promoter Score (NPS, #)**—This metric gauges customer loyalty and satisfaction, which indicates the potential for customer referrals and organic growth.
	  • NPS = 9–10: Promoters
	  • NPS = 7–8: Passives
	  • NPS = 0–6: Detractors
	
	NPS = (Total % of Promoters) ± (Total % of Detractors)
	* An average NPS score of 40 for B2B/SaaS companies is acceptable.[8]
	
	While NPS has long been the go-to metric for evaluating referrals and advocacy, it has a drawback in that it is susceptible to manipulation through how surveys are conducted. The QXScore has emerged as a newer, more powerful metric that doesn't suffer this same weakness.
	• **QXScore**[9]—QX scoring provides a more comprehensive way to track and manage customer sentiment. By measuring both quantitative metrics and qualitative feedback, the QXScore accounts for both the behavior and the attitudes of your users.
	  • Acceptable QXScore: 60–75, This range suggests that users are generally satisfied but there are areas needing improvement.
	  • Good QXScore: 75–90, A score in this range reflects strong user satisfaction and positive engagement.
	  • Great QXScore: 90–100, A QXScore in this range is excellent. This shows that users are highly satisfied, engaged, and likely to be advocates for the brand.
	• **Word of Mouth Coefficient**—By tracking customer referrals as a function of customer satisfaction, Word of Mouth Coefficient (WOM) has become a leading way to track organic growth and the effectiveness of your word-of-mouth marketing efforts.
	  • Acceptable WOM Benchmark: 0.1, 1 referral per 10 customers
	  • Good WOM Benchmark: 0.3, 3 referrals per 10 customers.
	  • Great WOM Benchmark: 0.5, 5 or more referrals per 10 customers.

Data-Driven Optimization of Product Features and User Experience

Let's take a look at some notable methods for using data to optimize product features and user experience. Table 4.2 breaks down some of the fundamental ways that data directly supports product and PLG.

A continual review of decision-support product analytics facilitates the sort of lightning-fast adjustments that you need to maintain or improve upon product performance.

Table 4.2   Data-Driven Product Functions

Function	Description
Iterative product development	An iterative approach to product development demands that you focus on continuously collecting and analyzing user interaction data to identify areas for improvement that you can use in prioritizing development efforts on features that offer the most value to your users.
Analyzing feature usage	Feature usage data clearly shows which features are being used the most and which are underutilized. The feature adoption chart shown in Figure 4.2 illustrates an effective way to communicate such findings.
A/B testing for continuous improvement	Implement A/B testing to experiment with different versions of product features or user experiences. A/B testing is helpful in refining features, as well as the overall messaging and workflows to optimize the product for maximum user satisfaction and conversions.
Integrating user feedback data	By actively collecting and analyzing qualitative and quantitative user feedback, you're able to make prescient, data-informed recommendations for product improvements. Incorporating user feedback into the product development process helps ensure that the changes are in line with user expectations and needs.
Performance monitoring and optimization	Continuously monitor product performance metrics to verify whether optimizations are having the desired effect on user experience and engagement. Use analytics to track KPIs such as user retention rates, session lengths, and conversion rates.

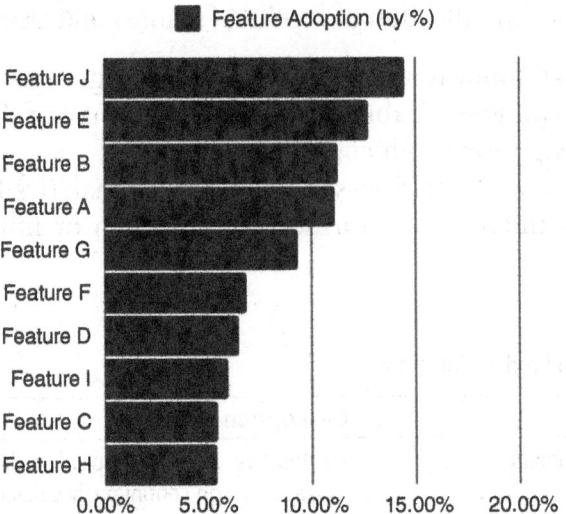

FIGURE 4.2 A simple feature adoption chart.

The Role of Analytics and ML in PLG

Product analytics provide insights into users' interactions, preferences, and behaviors. Without them, any PLG strategy is dead on arrival. By meticulously analyzing product data, you'll uncover the patterns and trends that you need in order to tailor your product so that it meets the evolving needs of users.

Remember that user engagement is key. The right analytics solution enables you to monitor how users interact with the product in real time. At a minimum, you should be tracking:

- Which features are most used
- How often the product is accessed
- The pathways users take within the application

These insights enable you to truly understand what users value the most about your product.

To illustrate, imagine that your product analytics show a particular feature being more frequently used than others. In this case, you'd probably want to make recommendations on ways to further improve this feature to drive even more growth, or on how to develop related features that amplify this existing user satisfaction and engagement.

Product analytics can be broken cleanly into two categories:

- Descriptive and diagnostic
- Predictive and prescriptive

Let's take a look at both.

Descriptive and Diagnostic Analytics in PLG

Descriptive and diagnostic analytics implement tracking, data visualization, and reporting to provide visibility into how users are engaging with your product and ways in which to improve that engagement.

For example, if you're tracking the pathway that users take within an application, you'll then have concrete details on the pages that users are frequently visiting, the order in which users are interacting with pages (or features), and the back-and-forth that's happening between different components of your application. These insights can then help you improve your UI design, resolve areas where your users are getting stuck or confused, and identify what features they like and dislike. Mixpanel is a powerful tool for tracking user interactions within your application.

Tip

Most software users are concerned about their privacy nowadays. With solutions like Fathom and Umami, you can preserve your users' privacy, while still generating the product analytics you need to support PLG.

Analytics are also helpful in identifying and grouping users based on their preferences and behavior patterns, which are indicated within interaction data. By segmenting users in this way, you'll be able to identify and validate distinct user personas. Subsequently, you can target these personas with personalized experiences and solutions to better meet their specific needs and preferences. This is a traditional approach to personalization, but later in this chapter, I'll share automated ML-Driven methods for achieving even more efficient growth results from a personalization strategy.

Driving PLG with Predictive and Prescriptive Analytics

Predictive and prescriptive analytics are subsets of data analytics that deploy ML to forecast future user behaviors based on historical data or real-time data. Prescriptive analytics provide suggestions for improvements based on those predictions. Oftentimes, there's confusion between the two terms, so I'll illustrate with a quick example here. Let's say an ML model predicts that there will be a massive influx of patients based on historical data—perhaps the time of the year along with recent cases. So, this is a classic example of predictive analytics. Prescriptive analytics goes a step further. It answers the question "What next?" by suggesting a series of actionable steps based on pre-set rules. So, in our case, the model will also inform you on the series of steps you can take to streamline patient admissions.

From a PLG perspective, the goal of predictive and prescriptive analytics is to improve growth while optimizing for spend. These types of analytics are useful for informing product development, optimizing marketing strategies, and improving customer support.

To illustrate how these analytics are helpful, imagine you're using an analytics tool to predict churn. Predictive insights generated by the tool indicate a high likelihood of churn for a certain segment of users, Segment III. On top of this, the tool also generates prescriptive insights that suggest reasons behind this churn for each user in Segment III. With the knowledge of who these at-risk users are and the probable reasons for churn, you can then make recommendations for proactive measures for re-engaging these users.

Tip

To re-engage users who are at risk for churn, consider sending them targeted messaging or personalized incentives. You can do this using a PLG-focused marketing automation solution, like Humanic AI, that leverages generative AI and individual AI agents to guide your users toward the goals you intend for them.

By building your PLG strategy on solid analytics, you're able to make evidence-based recommendations for future product improvements. Data-informed, continuous feedback loops will help you evolve your product in tandem with changing user needs and requirements—which is really important given the speed at which user preferences change.

AI and ML Tools for PLG

Product managers and internal stakeholders utilize a range of AI tools to analyze data and improve decision-making processes related to product strategy. When used effectively, these tools are also powerful drivers of PLG. The process from tool to tangible growth results generally looks like this:

1. **Use of AI-enabled tools**—Product managers and internal stakeholders employ AI-powered analytics tools to efficiently process and interpret large datasets. These tools provide trends, predict user behaviors, and identify areas of the product that need improvement.

2. **Analysis of relevant data sources**—Product managers and stakeholders develop insights into user sentiment and behavior over time by using AI-enabled tools to generate insights from customer relationship management (CRM) data as well as various types of survey data, including NPS, customer satisfaction surveys, and product feedback surveys. These insights shed light on how users are interacting with the product and how they feel about it.

3. **Feedback communication**—These insights are communicated to the development team in order to inform the team members about what aspects of the product are working well and what aspects need refinement.

4. **Response by the development team**—Based on this feedback, the development team makes necessary adjustments to the product. These adjustments could involve tweaking existing features, adding new functionalities, or removing features that aren't adding value. The goal of such changes is to improve the overall user experience.

5. **Improved PLG**—This improved user experience directly contributes to PLG. After all, a product that meets user needs in an effective manner is likely to attract more users, retain them longer, and encourage positive word-of-mouth. With the user at the center of its development, this cycle of feedback and improvement helps to evolve and improve the product on a continual basis.

General

AI and ML Tools for PLG

The following is a list of AI and ML tools that are useful for driving PLG:

- **Customer data platforms (CDPs)**—These platforms consolidate data from multiple sources in order to build comprehensive customer profiles.

These profiles help teams understand customer behavior across different touchpoints, thus enabling better personalized marketing and product development. More on this in Chapter 5.

- **Predictive analytics tools**—Tools like SAS, IBM SPSS, Humanic AI, and Altair RapidMiner use ML to predict future behaviors based on historical data. These predictions inform decisions about product changes or marketing strategies to improve user engagement and satisfaction.

- **Natural language processing (NLP) tools**—AI tools that utilize NLP, such as MonkeyLearn or Lexalytics, can analyze text from customer feedback surveys, social media posts, or product reviews to gauge sentiment, extract themes, and identify customer pain points.

- **Advanced business intelligence (BI) tools**—Advanced BI tools like Tableau, Looker, and Microsoft Power BI offer AI features that help product leaders visualize complex data, uncover trends, and deliver actionable insights, without needing to delegate this analysis work to an analyst.

- **A/B testing platforms**—Tools like Optimizely and VWO use AI to manage and optimize A/B tests. This, in turn, helps teams determine the most effective product changes based on user responses.

- **User behavior analytics tools**—Platforms like Mixpanel and Amplitude employ AI to analyze user actions within an app or on a website. The insights these tools generate help product teams understand which features are most and least engaging in order to identify areas for improvement and drive growth.

- **Voice of customer (VoC) tools**—Medallia and Qualtrics utilize AI to analyze customer feedback at scale. This helps companies rapidly identify common issues and trends in customer needs and expectations. More on VOC is coming up in Chapter 6.

Traditional Personalization Solutions

Traditional personalization solutions depend on static rules and classifications, like:

- **Rule-based recommendations**—An example of a rule-based recommendation is, "if a user interacts with a particular product, then recommend a predefined set of additional products to them." Static rules are not great for personalization because they do not adapt to the evidence-based preferences of users as they interact with the product.

- **Manual segmentation**—Manually assign users to broad segments with the assumption that all members of the same segment will appreciate the same features. These broad segments often fail to capture individual nuances and preferences, which, in turn, leads to less effective personalization.

With ML-Driven recommendation engines, however, you're able to deploy dynamic, automated, personalized recommendations that aren't limited to such curated lists or large segments. Say hello to extremely granular segmentation that adapts to each user on an individual basis!

ML-Driven Hyper-Personalization

Think about it. We've already had recommendation engines driving mind-boggling growth rates for entertainment and e-commerce platforms for more than a decade. Platforms like Spotify recommend music to their users all day, every day. You go to listen to a new song that's been recommended to you by the platform and lo and behold, the song exactly matches your mood and personality. It's easy to shrug such a thing off as happenstance, but is it really?

Truth be told, recommendation engines and deep data partnerships are behind most of the hyper-targeted recommendations you're getting from platforms like Facebook, Netflix, Spotify, and Amazon. There's a lot that goes on in the background to make this happen. Refer to Chapter 3 to quickly recall how Spotify is using its "Discover Weekly" feature to drive PLG. Figure 4.3 shows

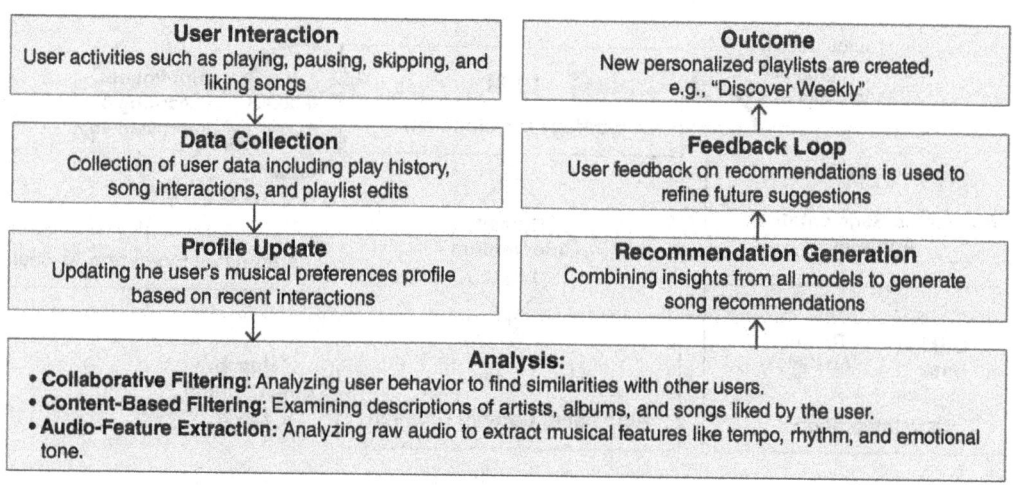

FIGURE 4.3 How Spotify uses recommenders to drive PLG.[10]

how Spotify uses recommendation engines to capitulate PLG via the "Discover Weekly" feature.

Driving PLG with Foundation Models

Out on the very leading edge of PLG, we have LLM-driven applications that are globally changing the game for SaaS companies. Case in point, Humanic AI.

Humanic AI is a marketing activation platform that has redefined the landscape of PLG by seamlessly integrating product analytics with advanced generative AI. Unlike traditional marketing automation platforms, Humanic is heavily focused on two main PLG stages: user activation and free-to-paid conversions. By connecting with your product analytics tools and marketing platforms, Humanic leverages LLMs to automatically generate micro-cohorts and create custom-tailored activation strategies in real time.

As shown in Figure 4.4, Humanic's platform doesn't just predict user behavior—it also leverages LLMs to dynamically assemble personalized marketing content and sequences based on real-time data. These assets, including multi-step email campaigns, are crafted and refined by the AI to nudge users toward the next stage of their journey, in turn, significantly reducing friction in the buyer journey. While the AI handles much of the heavy lifting, human experts have allotted spaces to step in order to review and refine the strategies and marketing creative. This protects brand cohesiveness while maximizing impact.

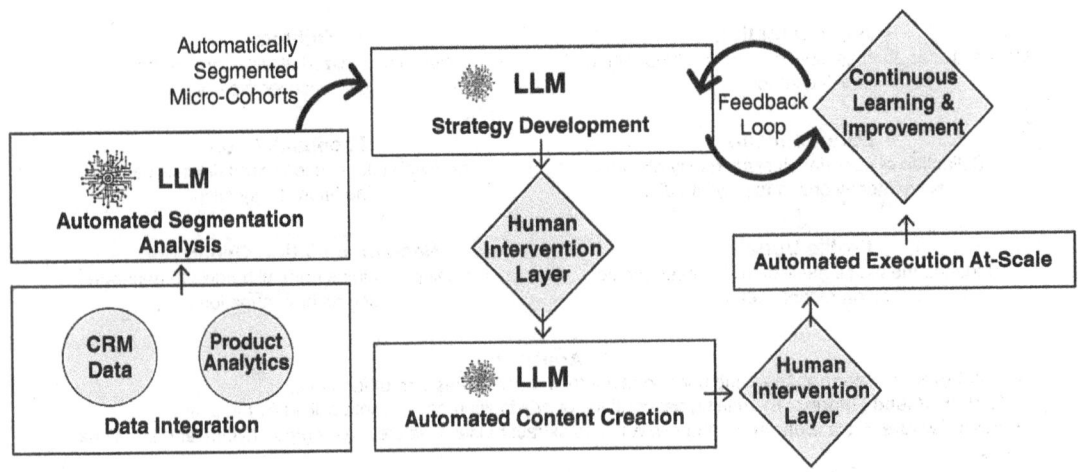

FIGURE 4.4 How Humanic uses LLMs to drive PLG.

This innovative combination of data-driven insights and generative AI allows Humanic to deliver a highly personalized user experience, driving deeper engagement, more conversions, and improved customer loyalty over the long term. By leveraging LLMs to automate both strategy development and execution, Humanic empowers its customers to drive more powerful PLG results by scaling their activation efforts in a systematic manner.

To be perfectly honest, the way that Humanic is leveraging foundation models to drive PLG is unprecedented. To say that the market is nascent is a massive understatement. Many of the potential applications of LLMs in PLG strategies are still largely theoretical or in the early stages of experimentation and development. This is particularly true of applications that would involve highly sophisticated and context-sensitive interactions. While some components of these applications are being actively developed and tested, the full realization of LLMs' potential in these areas is not yet a widespread reality.

That said, the power of LLMs in PLG is absolutely ripe for development. As quickly as this space is evolving, I'd be remiss not to discuss at least a few potential applications of LLMs in PLG.

Consultative Conversations

Imagine integrating LLMs into e-commerce platforms. Users could describe what they are looking for in natural language—for example, "*a lightweight, waterproof hiking jacket.*" The LLM could then interpret the full context of the query and suggest products that more accurately match these specific requirements. This type of interaction could easily mimic a consultative conversation with a knowledgeable store owner, thus elevating user satisfaction and engagement.

Dynamic Personalization and Recommendations

Beyond simple search, LLMs could dynamically adapt to ongoing user inputs within a session. For instance, if a user adjusts their query from "*hiking jackets*" in order to include "*matching shoes,*" the model could contextually understand the relationship between these items and make combined recommendations. This ability to understand and react to concatenated user queries could transform the users' shopping experience into a highly personalized dialogue with the product. Compare this with today's traditional search on e-commerce platforms, and you'll be able to appreciate how much better such searches will get after LLMs are integrated.

Intelligent Customer Support and Retention

In a SaaS environment, LLMs could analyze natural language customer feedback, support tickets, and interaction logs in order to more effectively assess behavior and sentiment. This could enable more sophisticated customer retention strategies, by enabling things like the identification of at-risk customers based on their interactions and sentiment. Similar to the way that Humanic AI works, LLMs could then assist in generating personalized messages or offers that cater to the specific needs and preferences of these users, which would increase retention and decrease churn.

Real-Time Feedback Analysis and Product Adaptation

LLMs could be used to continuously, automatically analyze user feedback across various channels to derive insights about user satisfaction and product issues. This continuous feedback loop could inform product development, in turn, allowing teams to make swift adjustments to directly address user needs and improve the overall product experience.

Clearly, LLMs hold promising potential to revolutionize aspects of PLG by offering more nuanced and intelligent user interactions and analytics. These are yet the early days. The journey from potential to effective implementation will involve considerable exploration and development, and this process is not without its challenges.

If you're actively experimenting with using LLMs in PLG, be sure to exercise caution during product development by putting the following best practices into place:

- **Data privacy and compliance**—Be sure to follow the data protection laws that are relevant to your jurisdiction and implement strong security measures to protect your customers' data.

- **Bias and fairness**—Check for any bias in the model output, especially if an end-user is directly using your LLM chat interface to get output. You'll need to check for and mitigate any kind of bias related to race, gender, class, religion, ethnicity, and age.

- **Transparency**—Maintain transparency about how the foundation model is making decisions.

- **Human in the loop**—Always keep humans in the loop and make sure to have the final say when it comes to making decisions—be those related to model output, user experience, or personalization.

Don't worry, I'll discuss the need for this in greater detail in Chapters 7 and 13.

At this point, we've had a thorough look at PLG and how the use of AI is driving bottom-line revenue growth. Chapter 5 looks at different strategies you can use to leverage data and AI technologies in growth marketing for your company and why growth marketing is a perfect companion to your PLG strategy.

Notes

1. Geckoboard. (2024). Website Conversion Rate. https://www.geckoboard.com/best-practice/kpi-examples/website-conversion-rate/
2. Userpilot. (August 11, 2023). Average Customer Acquisition Cost: Benchmark by Industry and How to Improve It. https://userpilot.com/blog/average-customer-acquisition-cost/
3. Userpilot. (November 15, 2021). SaaS Conversion Rate- Industry Average and 10 Tactics on How to Improve Yours. https://userpilot.com/blog/saas-conversion-rate/
4. Earlynode. How to Increase Feature Adoption in SaaS – The Complete Guide. https://earlynode.com/product-management/increase-saas-feature-adoption
5. Geckoboard. Retention Rate. https://www.geckoboard.com/best-practice/kpi-examples/retention-rate/
6. Arora, P. (March 25, 2024). The Top 10 SaaS Metrics of 2024 with Benchmarks. https://www.klipfolio.com/blog/top-saas-metrics-benchmarks
7. Recurly Research. What is a good churn rate? https://recurly.com/research/churn-rate-benchmarks/
8. Raileanu, G. (March 29, 2024). What Is a Good Net Promoter Score? (2024 NPS Benchmark). https://www.retently.com/blog/good-net-promoter-score/
9. User Testing. (June 1, 2021). Introducing our holistic score for measuring user experience: QXscore. https://www.usertesting.com/blog/qxscore-for-measuring-user-experience
10. Velardo, V. (February 11, 2019). Spotify's Discover Weekly explained–Breaking from your music bubble or, maybe not? *Medium.* https://medium.com/the-sound-of-ai/spotifys-discover-weekly-explained-breaking-from-your-music-bubble-or-maybe-not-b506da144123

Recommended Reading

Yousuf Bhaijee. How to Calculate Your Word of Mouth Coefficient. https://brian-balfour-s5lh.squarespace.com/blog/how-to-calculate-your-word-of-mouth-coefficient

5

Amplifying Growth Marketing Outcomes with Data and AI

My dream is that every person in the world will have their own Apple computer.
To do that, we've got to be a great marketing company.

– Steve Jobs

Speaking from the perspective of a fractional CMO who supports B2B tech start-ups and scale-ups, firsthand experience has proven to me that generative AI is transforming the marketing function more dramatically than any other. While every industry is experiencing rapid transformation, the content-heavy nature of the marketing function means that the sector is especially affected by AI content generation. I'm not the only one reporting this fact. In 2023, 64% of marketers openly acknowledged that AI is of extreme importance to their success in the next 12 months.[1]

Growth marketing is nothing new; its data-intensive approach to marketing has been around since the early 2000s. A lot has changed in growth marketing since those early days when the notion of applying big data and analytics to marketing really took hold. In this chapter you're going to see some of the most novel and cutting-edge ways that you can leverage data and AI in marketing to drive exponential business growth.

Starting first with strategy, then with campaign optimizations, and lastly, your ongoing marketing activities, let's look at how you can quickly harness data and AI technologies in your marketing to drive substantial growth for your company.

AI- and ML-Driven Marketing Strategy Support

There are two main routes by which you can leverage ML and AI to drive growth by improving marketing on a strategic level:

Marketing strategy development support—Decision-support to better inform your strategy

Marketing strategy executional support—Automation-support in the execution of your strategy

Decision-Making Support for Marketing Strategy Development

Truth be told, you'd be leaving a lot on the table if you only use generative AI models for content generation purposes—a topic we'll explore in the latter half of this chapter. What most people don't realize is that LLMs can amplify the effectiveness of your marketing strategies, too, but not in the way you think they would. To fully understand this point, you need to know how LLMs work from a user perspective and how you can go about accessing each of their different modalities.

While an LLM is an amazing resource for content generation and synthesis, its most valuable feature is the reasoning engine it uses to support these tasks. Via prompt engineering, you can access a reasoning capacity that's higher than that of many humans.

Tip

Although you should never trust an LLM to generate accurate content or predictions, if you have a ground source of truth from which to validate, then you can use LLMs to decrease the cognitive overwhelm that often comes with strategy development work.

Figure 5.1 shows just a few of the ways that LLMs support data-driven marketing strategy development.

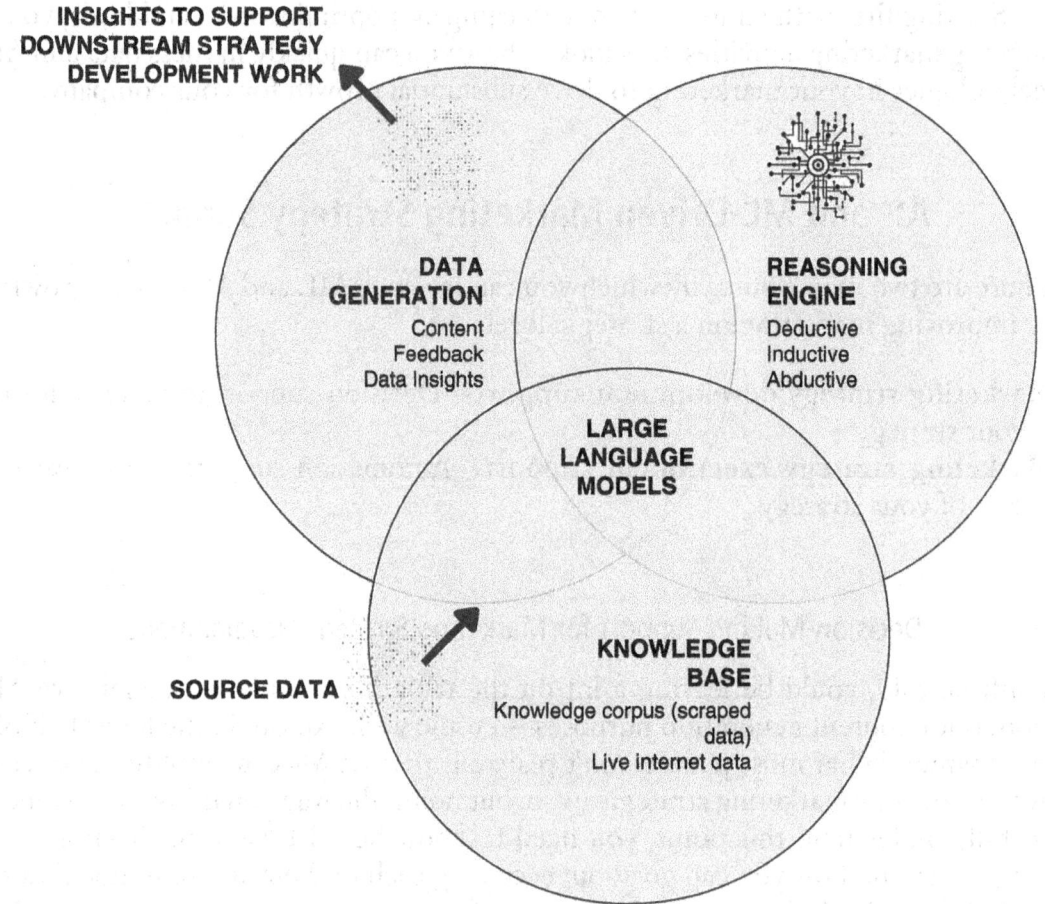

FIGURE 5.1 LLM support of the marketing function.

Warning

While you could use an LLM to synthesize the marketing characteristics of your brand and produce a marketing strategy, that's a really bad idea. Similar to how you should never take financial advice from an LLM, protect your marketing ROI by always putting your marketing strategy and leadership requirements in the hands of a proven expert.

I would never rely on—or advise relying on—strategic advice that's been auto-generated by AI. The safe bet is to use an LLM to synthesize data and conduct preliminary market research. All marketing strategies should inevitably be

Table 5.1 AI-Enabled Decision-Support for Marketing Strategy Development

Strategy	Description	Tools
Content strategy	Say hello to market research automation! Predict future content resonance by analyzing current trends from publicly available internet data, social signals, and content performance metrics. It helps leaders adapt their content strategy to consumer interests or better engagement.	Talkwalker, Brandwatch
Influencer marketing strategy	Evaluate the potential ROI and relevance of influencers based on past performance data, audience demographics, and engagement rates. It makes data-driven decision-making in influencer partnerships easier.	Favikon Upfluence, Brandwatch
Marketing mix strategy	Use advanced analytics and AI to allocate the marketing budget across channels and campaigns to maximize ROI and efficiency.	Pecan AI, Proof Analytics

reviewed and approved by a marketing expert who has the experience that's needed to access feasibility, risks, and the viability of alternative approaches.

Fundamentally, LLMs in marketing strategy serve a decision-support role. Their real value is in providing marketing leaders with forward-looking predictive trends around which to develop strategy. Historically, marketing departments were completely reliant on a data team to produce predictive insights for them, but with recent advancements in AI, there are many new and promising alternatives. Table 5.1 shows just a few of the ways that AI is improving the ROI of time and resources spent on marketing strategy development.

Once you have a strategy in place, you'll be ready to execute. You'll probably be happy to hear that generative AI models dramatically improve the efficiency of many executional marketing requirements as well.

AI-Assisted Marketing Strategy Execution

Beyond decision-support for marketing strategy development, there are a plethora of clever ways for you to leverage ML and AI to automate the execution of your marketing strategy in real time. This usage of data and AI would fall into the growth marketing category of use cases because data technologies are being used to execute within the marketing function.

To see how this works, let's use pricing strategy as an example. You'll recall that back in Table 3.3, I mentioned that dynamic pricing strategy is a prominent data-intensive growth marketing use case. Let's look under the hood at how that actually works.

A traditional pricing strategy relies on simple, time-based, or rule-based adjustments that you can implement using tools like Microsoft Excel or QuickBooks. While traditional pricing strategies have long been effective for revenue optimization and growth, if you really want to maximize profitability while maintaining competitive pricing for your customers, you should explore what's available via dynamic pricing.

ML-Driven dynamic pricing applications consider a multitude of real-time factors, including inventory levels, competitor pricing, and demand fluctuations. Each of these elements is dynamically analyzed in real time, allowing for agile adjustments of prices in response to market conditions. Figure 5.2 illustrates how this would work at a high level.

Dynamic pricing is prevalent across retail and e-commerce. This is a reflection of the highly competitive nature of these markets and the need to adjust prices in real time based on consumer demand, inventory levels, and competitor pricing.

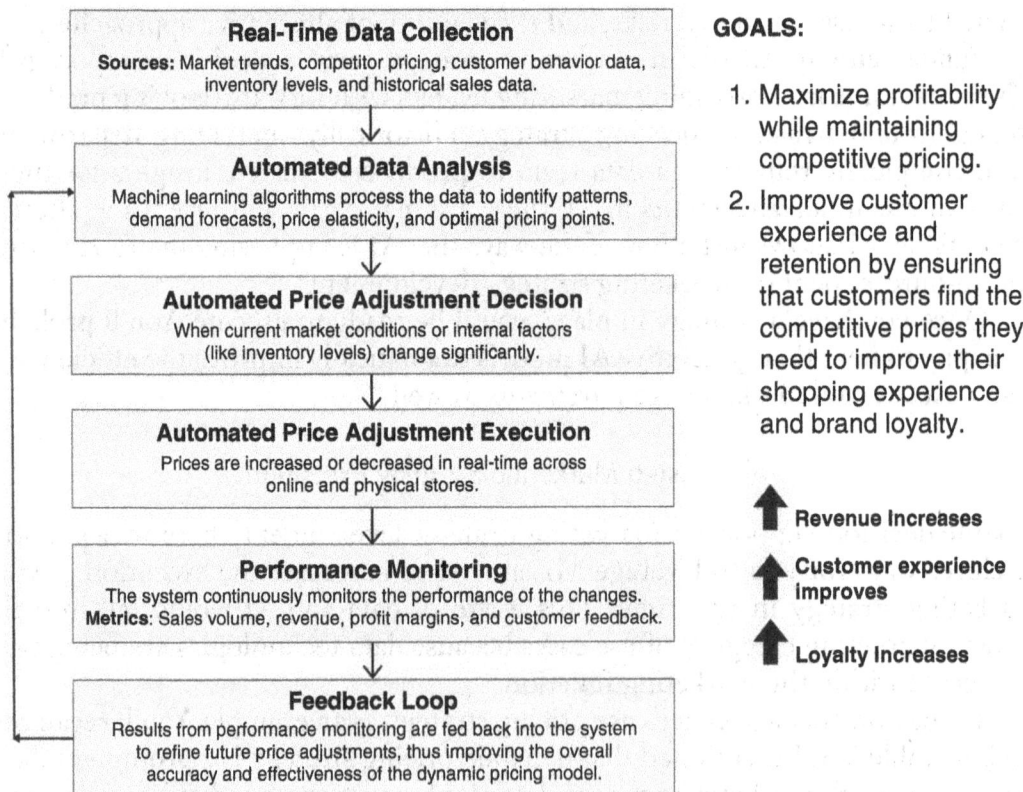

FIGURE 5.2 An example of dynamic pricing for a large-scale retailer.

Popular tools to facilitate dynamic pricing for retail and e-commerce companies include Competera and Feedvisor.

Dynamic pricing is increasingly being adopted across other industries, including airline and travel, hospitality, entertainment (such as is the case with event ticketing), automotive, chemical, manufacturing, utilities, and others. For example, Model N's Revenue Cloud offers dynamic pricing solutions to help companies in pharma, medtech, high tech, and life sciences to increase their top-line revenue, improve profit margins, and decrease revenue leakage.

Now that we've explored how predictive analytics and AI are useful in supporting the development and execution of your marketing strategy, let's look at how you can use them to improve the performance of your marketing campaigns.

Segmentation and Campaign-Level Optimizations

Segmentation and personalization are some of the most prominent growth marketing use cases. For good reason, you can't optimize at scale unless you have clean segments and clear targeting.

Tip

First segment, then optimize.

Let's look at how advancements in AI are driving more powerful outcomes in growth marketing via segmentation and campaign-level optimizations.

Customer Segmentation, Targeting, and Personalization

In Table 3.3, I mentioned a customer segmentation use case that involved using ML to segment customers and tailor marketing efforts to hyper-targeted groups based on their buying behavior, history, and preferences. While that approach may sound innovative to people who are not intimately involved with the marketing function, segmentation based on demographic and historical purchase data is actually an established use case. This capability is available to marketers in a variety of established marketing applications. Let's look at some of the more novel ways that advancements in AI are helpful for increasing customer engagement by enabling even more dynamic, predictive, and deeply personalized marketing.

Using AI products that deploy complex ML models to analyze vast datasets, you can algorithmically identify specific customer segments based on various factors, including behavior, preferences, and potential future actions. This is now achievable at a level of precision and adaptability that was previously unfathomable to most marketers.

If you remember, Chapter 4 discussed "granularity" as a major factor in segmentation and personalization. With more precise, accurate, and nimble customer segments, you're able to:

- Tailor your marketing campaigns more effectively, so that your messaging and offers more deeply resonate with each segment. This helps with higher engagement and conversion rates.

- Optimize your resource allocation and direct marketing resources to the channels and segments that are most likely to yield positive outcomes. This increases marketing efficiency.

- Predict market trends from your customer data and adapt. By adapting your marketing strategies to evolving customer preferences and behaviors, you can protect your brand relevance and competitiveness on a proactive, ongoing basis.

Tip

If you're looking for the deeper, predictive segmentation capabilities that are only available through the use of AI and ML, I encourage you to explore the solutions that are available within the customer data platforms, mParticle and Segment.

Warning

Whenever you're using predictive analytics to segment people based on customer data, you must be extremely careful that you are not propagating harmful bias. If done wrong, you can put your company at risk for lawsuits and reputational damage due to discriminatory practices or breaches of regulatory and legal requirements. Chapter 13 provides direct, actionable guidance on how to assess AI ethics and compliance.

With clean customer segments in hand, you'll be ready to use these insights to build and refine your marketing campaigns for maximum effectiveness and efficiency.

Table 5.2 Predictive Analytics for Common Types of Marketing Campaigns

Use Case	Benefit	Tool
Email marketing campaigns	The predictive analytics that are typically built into email marketing solutions enable you to predict the right time to send emails, determine which customers are most likely to engage with them, and modify your content accordingly by analyzing past customer behavior. This can increase your email open rates and conversions.	Mailchimp, HubSpot
Customer retention campaigns	Data-driven customer retention campaigns identify customers who are at risk of churning and develop targeted, automated messaging campaigns and offers to retain them by analyzing customer interaction history and other relevant data. You can also identify "churn drivers" for each customer (or a segment of customers) and tune your messaging accordingly.	Akkio, Optimove
Product recommendations campaigns	E-commerce platforms and retailers often use predictive analytics to fuel their recommendation engines. Such recommenders analyze past purchasing behavior, browsing history, and customer preferences to anticipate future buying behavior. This helps brands personalize product recommendations and increases the likelihood of purchase. Revisit the Spotify use case in Chapter 4 to understand this better.	Glood Product Recommendations (for Shopify), Adobe Power Sensei (for Magento sites)
Social media marketing campaigns	Your social media strategies should be directly informed by insights derived from predictive analytics. The tool will analyze social media trends, customer sentiments, and engagement patterns automatically and return predictions to help you enhance your brand's social media activities. Examples of predictions include insights into effective content types, posting times, and channels for targeting specific audience segments.	Emplifi, sproutsocial
Lead generation and nurturing	Your lead generation and nurturing strategies should also be driven by predictive analytics. You can optimize your current campaigns and identify new potential leads based on characteristics of high-value existing customers by using ML to score your leads and predict which are most likely to convert. This works much better than the explicit lead scoring method that requires you to manually define the variables/features that lead to better scoring for your customers.	Marketo Engage, Salesforce Pardot

Campaign-Level Optimizations

Using AI and ML, it's possible for advertisers to increase the efficiency of their ad campaigns significantly. The DoorDash case study in Chapter 3 exemplified this. But predictive analytics are useful for optimizing a wide variety of campaigns, beyond just the advertising use case. Table 5.2 shows common ways in which predictive analytics drive growth marketing outcomes on the campaign level.

Now that you've seen how predictive analytics are helpful in optimizing your marketing campaigns, let's look at how you can leverage AI to streamline your ongoing marketing operations.

Driving Efficiency Across Ongoing Marketing Activities

When it comes to generative AI, one of the lowest hanging fruits is to use it to streamline marketing activities and increase the bottom-line revenue they generate. By "ongoing marketing activities," I'm referring to executional marketing tasks that must be carried out on a continual basis in support of your marketing strategy, like content marketing, social media marketing, and even customer service as it pertains to the marketing function. Basically, any ongoing marketing activity that is required to maintain and grow a brand's awareness, engage with its audiences, foster its customer relationships, and drive conversions over time would fall into this category.

Using AI to Decrease Content Marketing Costs

Imagine that your content marketing strategy involves publishing weekly content drops where you'll post a video on YouTube, and then distribute that video via your blog, social media channels, and email channel. Let me show you a process that my team and I have used dozens of times, both to produce content for our channels and to produce sponsored content to build awareness for my brand partners.

Here's how you, too, can use generative AI to achieve a dramatic reduction in content development costs and time.

1. **Outline development**—Assuming you've already developed an editorial calendar, you know (1) what the topic for this drop should be, and (2) the SEO keyword around which you need to optimize. Head over to your favorite content generator and use those parameters to do content research and generate a blog draft.

2. **Written content generation**—Once you've refined the draft to your liking, use the tool to generate a 1,000-word blog post in one click. Also, generate the SEO-optimized metadata for the post.

3. **Video recording and editing**—Take that blog post and repurpose it into a script for a YouTube video. Record the video, then edit it using an AI-enabled video editor. With this type of video editing tool, you'll automatically get a video transcript that you can use to edit the video as simply as if you were editing a Word document. Produce a version of the video for YouTube and then break up its most valuable parts into smaller TikTok style videos for distribution on social media.

4. **Visual content generation**—Take the metadata that you got in step 2 and use it to prompt an image generator to generate images that match the topic of your post. Let the best image serve as your blog feature image.

5. **Social media and email copy creation**—Bring your finalized video transcript into a copy generator and use it to generate social media captions and email copy to promote the content drop in just one click.

6. **Publish**—Migrate, SEO-optimize, and publish your video on YouTube. Then migrate your blog copy, the YouTube video embed, the blog post metadata, and your feature image to your website. Humanize the content, configure your SEO settings, and hit the 'publish' button to publish the SEO-optimized blog post on your website.

Tip

Always fact check and humanize any AI generated content before publishing. Consumers are very likely to turn away from brands that don't add a deep layer of human oversight to their content.

Granted, with the preceding process, graphics development and social media scheduling work will still need to be done manually, but you can see how the workflow has been greatly improved by the use of generative AI. Done manually, the process above would cost between $500 and $1,000 and would generally take a team about 2 weeks to complete. A reasonable budget for such a workflow would be at least $4,000 per month. Now the entire process could theoretically be handled by one person in a few hours per content drop, for only the cost of their time and a tool budget of ~$100 per month. At scale, you can see how dramatic the savings could be.

AI marketing start-ups are shipping incredibly powerful tools for content creators and marketers, but the ecosystem is neither mature nor stable. To safeguard the relevance of this book over the long haul, I've moved my AI marketing tool recommendations online. If you're interested in using the exact tool stack that I use to execute the preceding workflow, you can access those details for free at www.data-mania.com/book.

Improving Content Marketing ROI with Advanced Generative AI Tools

Traditional social media marketing techniques can be expensive and time-consuming. But with AI, the process is moving toward democratization, where an individual or a smaller team can quickly use the workflow described previously to deliver upon a weekly publishing schedule. Let's discuss how you can use retrieval-augmented generation (RAG) to improve upon the quality of your AI generated content in order to further lower the amount of time and effort that is required by team members to fact check, relevance check, and humanize marketing content.

I'm currently in the process of building a strategy for creating hyper-targeted marketing content, so I'll share with you a peak under the hood. Figure 5.3 is a workflow diagram that shows how to construct a RAG-powered content generator, where the RAG component can be run in something as simple as a custom GPT by OpenAI.

By using RAG to create content in the manner shown above, you'll reduce the occurrence of model hallucinations while also producing content that is both up-to-date and much more precisely and accurately targeted to the people in your audience and their pain points. This way you can use AI to generate content that very much resonates with current trends and audience interests.

Tip

From a tools perspective, the preceding workflow is low cost and easily accessible. You can use ChatGPT as the content generator and a custom GPT as the RAG element.

Now, let's take this example one step further by looking at how you can leverage AI agents within the content marketing workflow for yet even more efficiency.

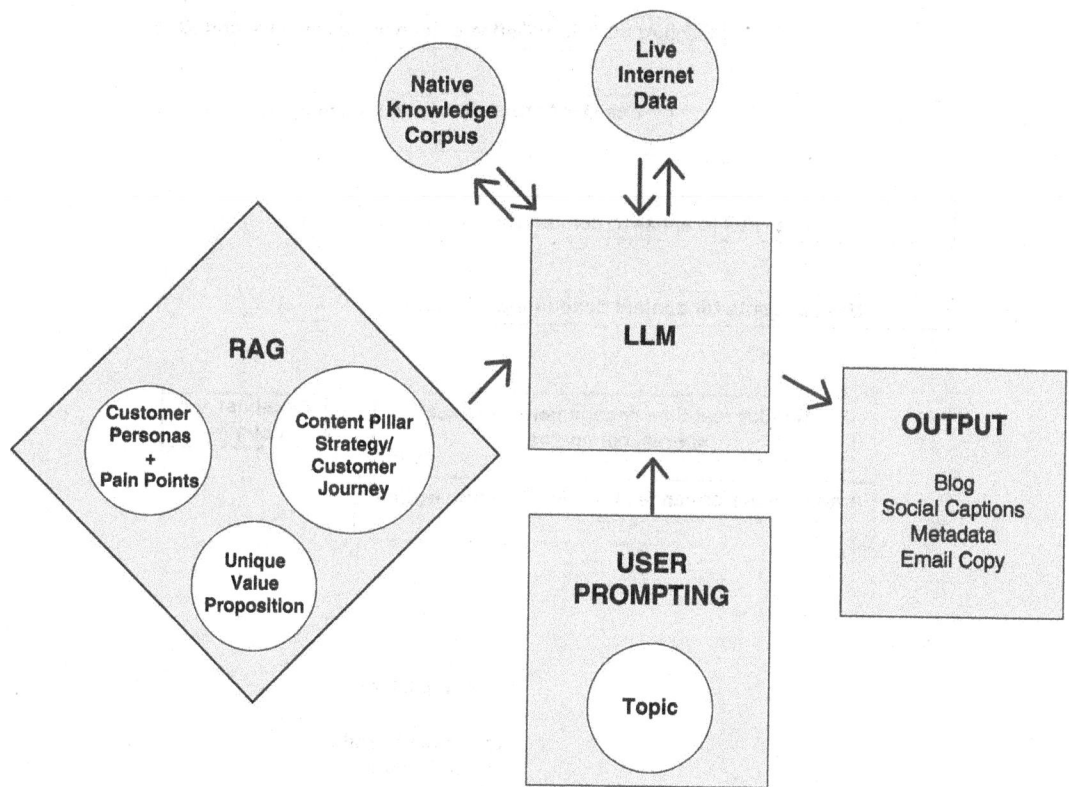

FIGURE 5.3 RAG-powered content creation.

In Figure 5.4, you can see an entire automated social media marketing workflow that takes you through every layer of the management process, from content creation to publishing and refinement, all in an automated manner.

While the idea of using AI agents to schedule posts and analyze channels might sound like a far-off future, the fact is that these tools exist and are commercially available today. I'm not clear on how compatible such tools are with the terms and conditions of most social media platforms, so I'll refrain from providing more details—but, just know, if it feels like you're interacting with an AI, you probably are!

Tip

Always have a team of professionals who are responsible for overseeing and refining the output of AI models, both to humanize it and to remove biases, if any. Letting an AI do a complete takeover of your social media accounts is currently a recipe for disaster.

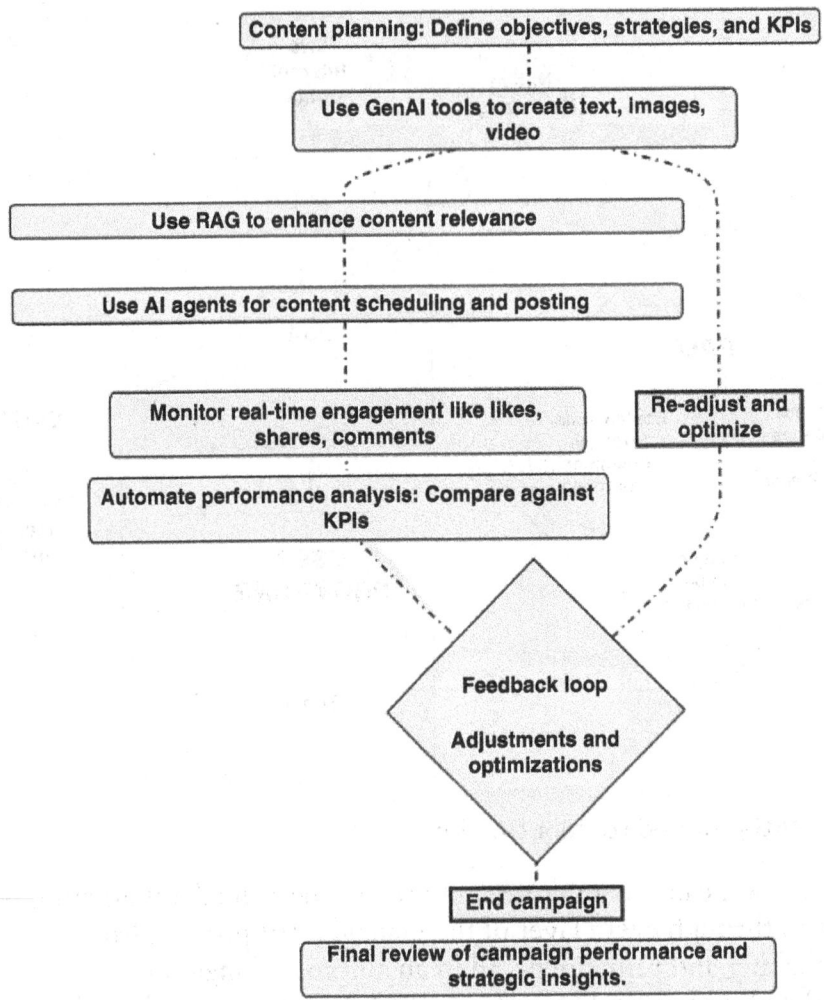

FIGURE 5.4 Conceptual schematic for a RAG-powered AI tool that automates social media marketing management.

While we're talking about social media marketing and content automation, let me introduce you to a powerful tool called Predis.ai. Just to test the tool, I created an account and provided it with my website URL. Within less than one minute, it had read my website and produced the social media graphic and caption shown in Figure 5.5. Pretty impressive!

Equally impressive is the growing trend and development work that's driving huge advancements in the field of AI-driven marketing automation. For instance, over at HuggingFace Spaces for marketing automation, you can find all sorts of

FIGURE 5.5 End-to-end content creation automation by Predis.ai.

marketing-related use cases for generative AI. These HuggingFace Spaces allow developers from all around the world to make the best use of foundation models by quickly developing wrapper applications atop and then publishing them for public good. In the coming years, we'll see much more of this type of open-source generative AI tool development that will eventually give way to tremendous progress in this space overall.

Decreasing Customer Service Overhead with RAG and AI Chatbots

The use of AI in customer service is nothing new. That said, earlier applications were usually rule-based systems that had no real understanding of the human language and context. They'd produce robotic-sounding messages over and over again, even if you rephrase your question in a different format. Traditional AI chatbots are pretty annoying from a user perspective.

But now, with advancements in generative AI, we've seen phenomenal progress in this area. I estimate that by using RAG powered AI chatbots, you can decrease your customer service headcount by 90%. Before getting too excited about the business benefits though, make sure you read to the end of this section, where I share my personal experience and why such an application could be egregiously costly to your business's bottom line.

Figure 5.6 illustrates what a customer support bot powered by RAG might look like under the hood. Let me explain with a hypothetical example. Let's say you bought an electronic item and there seems to be a problem with it. The process goes like this:

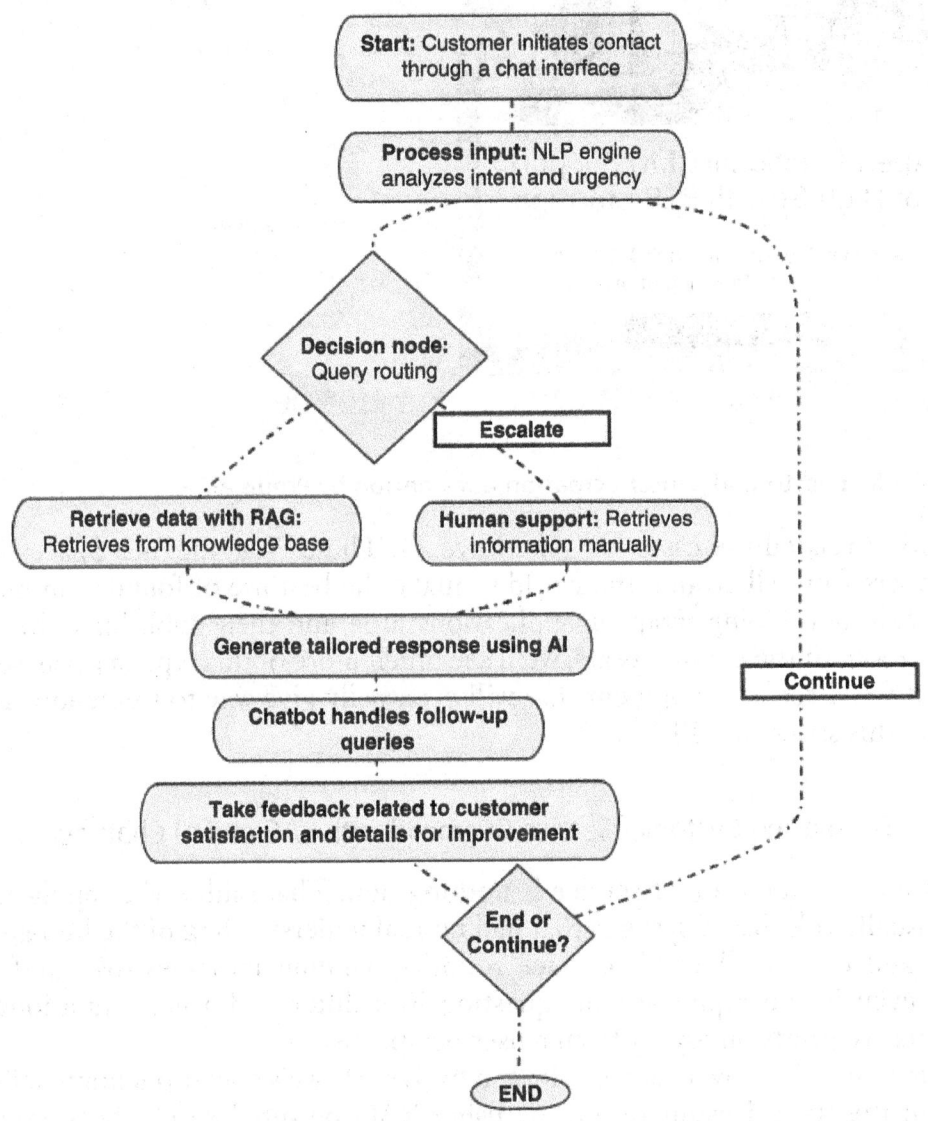

FIGURE 5.6 Use of RAG-powered AI chatbots for more efficient and accurate customer support.

1. You'll start by reaching out to customer care on the provider's website. You open a live chat and describe the issue.

2. The bot asks you for the order number and then lists all the items you've recently purchased.

3. Once you've clicked on the item in question, the bot assesses the concern while also taking into account your tone and urgency as well.

    (a) Based on this, if the issue is serious or requires expert support, the bot will redirect the chat to a live customer agent who then takes it forward. Interesting to note here, the live support agent also uses AI to generate quick replies.

    (b) If the issue is simple, say, a commonly occurring software glitch, for example, then the RAG-powered AI agent quickly pulls details about this from its source data and then curates the information to resolve your issue.

This kind of tool or chatbot can be deployed across multiple channels, including mobile applications, social media, and websites. It's scalable. Even small and mid-size businesses can use this tool to handle simple queries, so their customer support team can work on more complex queries or issues. As an added benefit, these AI agents learn continuously from user feedback and interactions, which will improve their performance even more over time. Some notable tools that have been working in the space are LiveChatAI, your GPT.ai, and Conversica.

When you're able to quickly resolve and close tickets quicker with AI chatbots, you might have happier customers. Not to mention that, with this newfound efficiency you can redirect even more resources into bettering your product, which in turn leads to higher customer satisfaction levels and overall revenue growth!

All this being said, there is growing unrest among us humans about the need for more transparent and ethical use of AI. Too much societal change too quickly is good for no one. To provide just a small example of how an AI chatbot might do you more harm than good, I'll share a story about a customer service exchange I had recently. I was on a webchat seeking customer support for a website issue. The provider did not disclose that they were using generative AI to power their chatbot, which is both unethical and now against the law, according to the EU AI Act. Had I not been an AI expert myself, I would have never known I was chatting with a bot. Yes, the responses were smooth, helpful, and accurate, but I immediately asked to be handed over to a person. Truthfully, the exchange diminished my trust in the provider.

Caution

Yes, you can use RAG and GPT-4 APIs to quickly offload about 90% of your customer service work, but I'd caution you to consider the ethics of that choice and make every effort to protect your brand reputation by always disclosing to your users if and when they're interacting with an AI agent.

Now that you've seen some of the incredible products and services that are built from effective data and AI strategy, I want to provide you with some small input on go-to-market considerations for commercial data and AI-driven products. We'll look at these next, in Chapter 6.

Note

1. Kaput, M. (August 29, 2023). The 2023 state of marketing AI report, In: *Marketing Artificial Intelligence Institute*. https://www.marketingaiinstitute.com/blog/2023-state-of-marketing-ai-report

CHAPTER

6

Validating Product-Market Fit for Commercial Data and AI Products and Services

The only thing that matters is getting to product-market fit.

– Marc Andreessen

The market for data and AI innovation is moving faster than any one person can keep up with. In order for a company to see any chance of survival or penetration with data and AI products and services, market validation and product-market fit (PMF) must be non-negotiable priorities. Tech start-ups experience the highest failure rates across all industries—and within this sector, AI wrapper start-ups are especially vulnerable due to an absence of robust competitive barriers. Product-market fit and market validation provide the level of security that's prudent to de-risk investments by qualifying that a solution indeed solves a real and pressing need within a viable market. This chapter guides you through the process to validate your data or AI product idea before making the decision to invest substantial resources.

While this book is almost exclusively dedicated to supporting the strategic needs of in-house data and AI solutions, as a fractional CMO for B2B tech start-ups, I'd be remiss not to provide preliminary recommendations for those readers who want to use the approach shared in this book to develop a commercial data or AI solution and take it to market. If you're bringing a new product or service to market, one of the first things you need to do to protect your investment of time and capital is to build and execute a strategy for achieving PMF. Much like how a "line of best fit" shows the relationship between data points in a dataset, PMF describes how well a product meets the needs of its market. Without PMF, most products struggle to gain traction in the market, whereas with PMF, products tend to easily drive revenue growth by naturally attracting and retaining loyal customers.

PMF strategies are one of the more popular types of strategies I deliver for my early-stage start-up clients, so I have a lot to say on this topic. Since we only have one chapter to cover it though, I need to present you with a high-level approach and only the most broadly relevant details you need for building such a strategy. The chapter begins by exploring the reason why many data and AI start-ups fail, then presents a high-level road map for achieving PMF, and, lastly, digs deeper into some of the more powerful details to support you in the process.

Identifying Reasons Why Most Tech Start-Ups Fail

The average business failure rate is 50% within the first five years, according to Bureau of Labor Statistics data.[1] For VC-backed tech start-ups, that number is even higher. However, if we look at the failure likelihood of AI wrapper start-ups, then we're facing a cataclysm. As of 2023, the tech industry has the highest rate of start-up failures in the United States.[2]

An AI wrapper start-up is a company that builds its entire product or service offering around an LLM, simply by building a user interface, adding unique features, or integrating the model into specific applications. These ventures are at risk for many reasons, but the most glaring is that these businesses are generally not defensible, which is why most VCs are steering clear.

Note

Data start-ups and AI wrapper start-ups are not in the same category when it comes to failure risk. Data-intensive start-ups and professional services firms have been around for decades. The demand for data management, predictive analytics, business intelligence, and machine learning solutions is not going anywhere. Additionally, customers and users increasingly expect that generative AI capabilities will be integrated into their products and services. Among these, the transformative "prompt and receive" SaaS feature is becoming a standard across almost every industry. Not catering to this expectation would massively compromise your competitiveness.

A fundamental prerequisite for building a defensible start-up is to have a validated market and a solution that effectively satisfies the needs of that market. In fact, the validation of both your market and your PMF is an ongoing necessity that supports every aspect of building and scaling a successful, defensible start-up. This process ensures that the business is aligned with real market demands and customer needs, both of which are fundamental to maintaining a competitive advantage and achieving long-term success.

Let's look a little deeper at how to validate the market and PMF for any new data or AI offer.

Tip

Market validation and PMF are as important to established businesses as they are to early-stage start-ups. Any time you're considering bringing a new offer to market, you need to validate before building.

Market validation is a process used to test the viability of a product or idea in a specific market, whereas PMF is more specifically focused on ensuring that a product satisfies the needs of its target market. Figure 6.1 illustrates a generalized

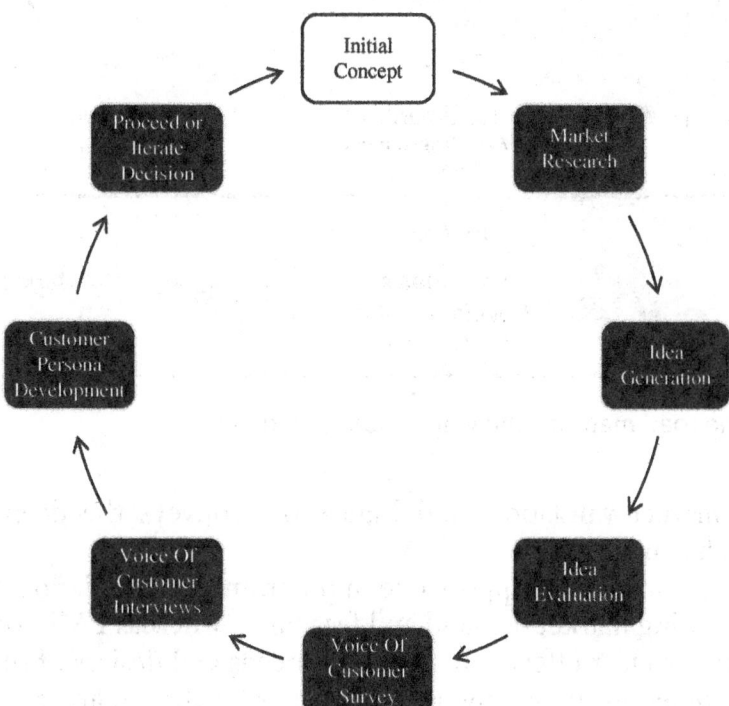

FIGURE 6.1 A market validation flowchart.

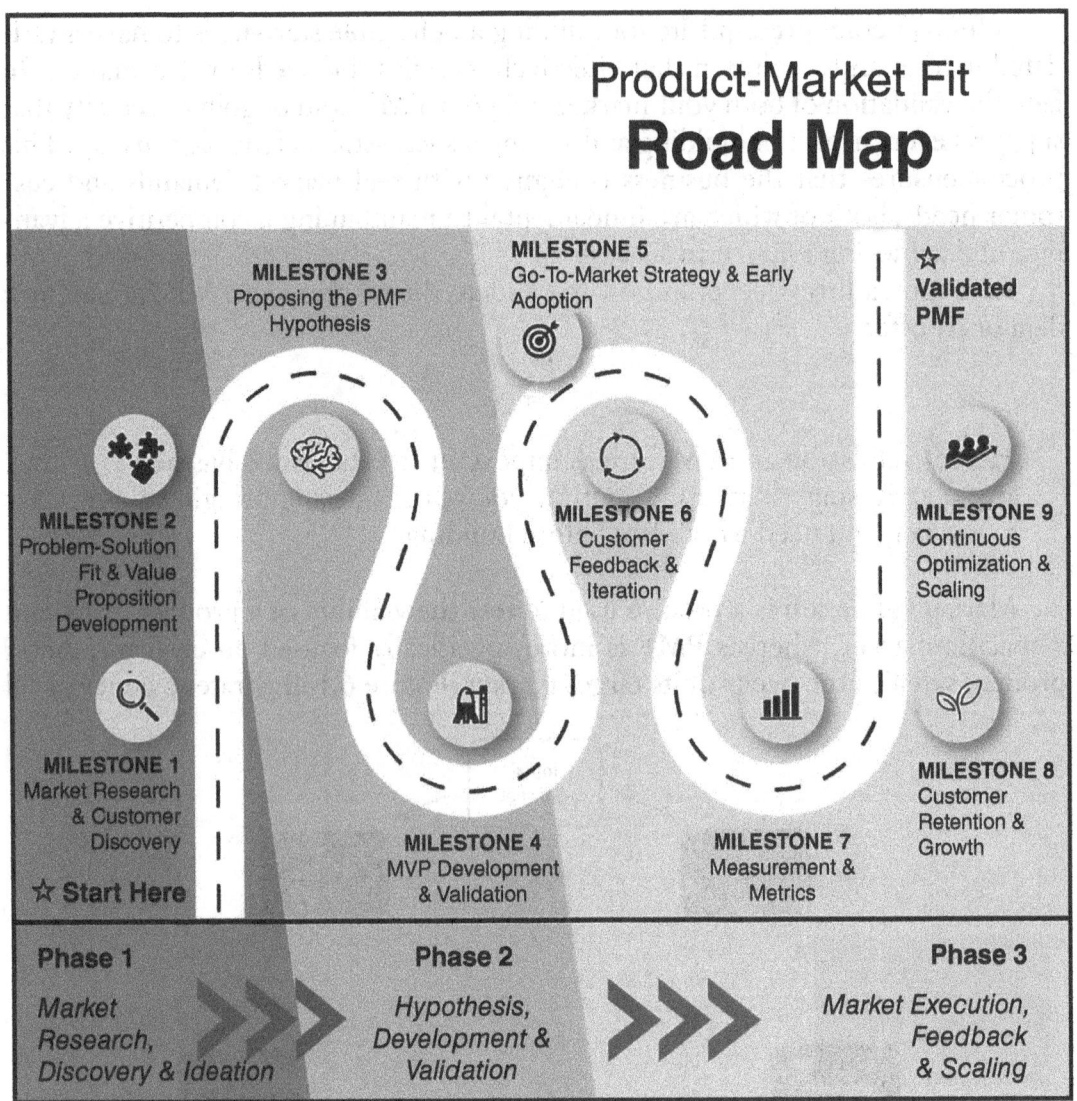

FIGURE 6.2 The road map to achieving product-market fit.

view of the market validation, and Figure 6.2 conveys the deeper intricacies involved in achieving PMF.

While these processes support one another, market validation focuses more heavily on assessing market demand and feasibility, whereas PMF focuses on validating that the product effectively meets the needs and desires of the target market. PMF is generally more involved and lengthy than market validation, but market validation is indispensable as a first step to achieving PMF.

Achieving Product-Market Fit

PMF doesn't have to be the nebulous monster some early-stage startup founders make it out to be. There is a fairly cut-and-dry blueprint for achieving it, but the problem is that most early-stage founders don't have that blueprint when they begin building. Figure 6.2 breaks the process into nine achievable milestones.

As you can see, I like to take a three-phase approach to validating PMF. Let's explore each phase in greater detail.

Executing Market Research, Discovery, and Ideation

This phase involves surveying the market landscape, identifying customer needs, and ideating upon potential solutions that address those needs. The process involves the following two parts:

1. **Market research and customer discovery**—Conduct in-depth market research to understand the market size, trends, and dynamics. Within this research, be sure to conduct competitor analysis and collect Voice of Customer (VOC) feedback to identify customer pain points, desires, and expectations. We'll look at VOC in greater detail later in this chapter.

2. **PMF and value proposition development**—Based on research findings, develop a problem-solution fit matrix that aligns potential product features with customer needs. Refine this with VOC feedback to ensure that the product directly addresses the most significant customer pain points you've identified during customer discovery.

Developing and Validating a PMF Hypothesis

This phase involves developing a hypothesis that details the conditions under which your product will achieve PMF, followed by validating this hypothesis through MVP development. This process involves the following two parts:

1. **Proposing the PMF hypothesis**—Formulate a specific, measurable, and testable hypothesis that outlines the conditions for achieving PMF. Within this hypothesis, detail target segments, key features, and expected market reaction. Align your team on these focus areas and document the hypothesis clearly.

2. **MVP development and validation**—Develop an MVP that addresses the core customer problem with only the most essential features. Make sure you validate this MVP by collecting feedback from early adopters to verify whether it resonates with your target audience.

Executing in the Market, Iterating on Feedback, and Scaling

This phase involves launching the product, gathering feedback, iterating based on this feedback, and eventually scaling the product. This process involves the following five parts:

1. **Go-to-market strategy and early adoption**—Develop a go-to-market strategy that is informed by market research as well as your customer personas, and that targets early adopters. Be sure to tailor your messaging to resonate with the pain points and needs of these early users.

2. **Customer feedback and iteration**—Systematically collect customer insights through surveys, interviews, and analytics. Use this feedback to identify trends, issues, and areas for improvement. Then, based on that feedback, iterate on the product to move closer to achieving PMF.

3. **Measurement and metrics**—The following are some metrics and benchmarks you can use to assess PMF.

    (a) **Net Promoter Score (NPS)**—We discuss NPS in Chapter 4.
        1. Range: –100–+100
        2. Good PMF indicator: 50+
        3. Excellent PMF indicator: 70+
        4. Interpretation: An NPS above 50 suggests that your product is delivering significant value to customers and that these customers are likely to recommend the product to others.

    (b) **Customer Satisfaction Score (CSAT)**—CSAT measures how satisfied your customers are with your product, based on their direct responses to survey questions.
        1. Range: 1–5 or 1–10
        2. Good PMF indicator: 4+ (on a 5-point scale) or 8+ (on a 10-point scale)
        3. Interpretation: High CSAT scores indicate that your product is meeting or exceeding your customers' expectations, which is a positive indicator of PMF.

    (c) **Daily Active Users vs. Monthly Active Users (DAU/MAU)**—This ratio quantifies how frequently users are engaging with your product. High ratios here suggest that users are engaging with your product frequently, that the product is solving a problem for them, and that the solution is good enough to justify repeat usage.
        1. Range: 0–100%, with 100% indicating that all monthly users are active on a daily basis.

2. Good PMF indicator: 20%+ is often a good sign of engagement, particularly for B2B products. For consumer-facing (B2C) apps, a DAU/MAU ratio of 50%+ is excellent and suggests strong PMF.
3. Interpretation: A high DAU/MAU ratio suggests that users find your product valuable enough to use it frequently. What constitutes a "good" DAU/MAU ratio varies depending on the nature of the product.

(d) **Churn rate**—This metric describes the percentage of customers who stop using your product in a specific time interval, where high churn indicates potential issues with the product's UVPs, usability, or market fit.
1. Good PMF indicator: <5% monthly for B2C, <2% monthly for B2B
2. Interpretation: Low churn rates indicate that customers find ongoing value in your product. High churn suggests potential issues with PMF. Please note that, what qualifies as a "good" churn rate varies significantly with both industry norms and the type of subscription model.

4. **Customer retention and growth**—Develop marketing strategies for nurturing early adopters and converting them to loyal customers. Focus on upselling, cross-selling, and expanding within these existing segments in order to maintain high customer satisfaction and user retention.

5. **Continuous optimization and scaling**—Establish a continuous feedback loop for collecting ongoing customer insights. Regularly iterate on the product as you develop strategies for scaling. Be sure that you're keeping an eye on market conditions and competitor activities so you can adapt the product strategy as needed.

Warning

Achieving PMF is not a one-and-done accomplishment. Once you've validated PMF and are starting to grow, it's vital that you continue monitoring market conditions and checking back to make sure you haven't lost PMF due to some underlying changes in the market. To adapt the product's value proposition, features, and go-to-market strategies in response to market changes, be sure you're validating PMF on an ongoing basis.

Common Pitfalls When Working to Achieve PMF

It's always preferable to avoid making mistakes, rather than having to fix them after the fact. I've seen many founders who, without the benefit of a resource like this one you're reading now, have faced challenges when bringing their solutions to market. These challenges often result in premature investments into go-to-market strategies that are more effective after validating PMF.

To help you navigate these potential pitfalls, I've detailed some of the key areas where it's important to proceed with caution:

- **Premature scaling**—Scaling strategies are exciting, but if they're executed prior to validating PMF, they can lead to wasted resources and missed opportunities to iterate and refine your product. Take care that your scaling efforts are grounded in solid market validation.

- **Ignoring negative feedback**—All feedback, especially negative feedback, is worth its weight in gold. It's understandable to feel defensive but using this feedback to refine your product is an indispensable part of aligning it with the needs of your users. Without such refinements, PMF can remain elusive.

- **Mistaking initial traction for PMF**—Early adopters can be a fickle bunch. They're often excited to tinker and play with a product, even when they don't actually need that product to solve one of their urgent and pressing needs. For this reason, early adopter enthusiasm doesn't always translate to broader market appeal. It's important to validate their willingness to pay so you have some certainty that the enthusiasm translates into long-term value for a wider audience.

- **Emphasis on vanity metrics**—While it's tempting to focus on impressive numbers, be sure to prioritize metrics that reflect real user engagement and value delivery. Doing so will paint a clearer picture of your product's true market fit.

- **Feature creep**—It's common to want to add new features, especially in uncertain times. That said, it's important to make sure any new feature directly addresses user needs while enhancing your core value proposition. Adding too many features too soon can dilute your focus and confuse users.

- **Neglecting the business model**—Your business model should be capable of satisfying your revenue goals for the company. Even if users love your product, you want to have a clear path to monetization that supports the sustainable growth of the company.

- **Failing to iterate quickly**—If you're slow to integrate user feedback, this can translate into missed opportunities and an overall loss of market share.

- **Targeting too broad a market**—In the wise words of Sudha Murty, "If you try to please everyone, you will please no one." The fastest route to PMF is for you to find, and build for, a target market positioned in a financially viable niche of high demand and low supply. Start with a focused niche and then iterate with research and experimentation.

- **Insufficient customer research**—Decisions based on assumptions or personal inclinations often lead to costly mistakes. Ground your product decisions in thorough customer research and real user data to avoid these pitfalls.

- **Pivoting too quickly or too slowly**—Pivoting is a big decision that requires a delicate balance. To avoid veering off course, I suggest you use quantitative methods and seek expert advice before deciding if it's the right time to pivot.

Now that you've got a bird's eye view of the PMF validation process and its pitfalls, let's look at some of the activities that will serve you well in developing a strategy for achieving and maintaining PMF.

Executing the Fundamental Tenets of PMF

There are two core activities upon which PMF validation happens. Those are market research and customer persona development. Let's look at each in detail.

Conducting Market Research

Market research is the indispensable basis upon which all phases of the PMF journey are dependent. Market research embodies the following core activities:

- **Market sizing and trend analysis**—This is where you research the market and collect quantitative and qualitative data points that inform your understanding of the market needs and whether your solution meets those needs.

- **Competitive analysis**—This is where you analyze competitors to identify market gaps, assess their strengths and weaknesses, and uncover opportunities to differentiate your product.

- **Voice of customer feedback**—This involves collecting direct feedback from potential customers through surveys, interviews, and other methods to understand their pain points, preferences, and expectations.

- **Focus groups**—This is where you gather small, targeted groups of potential customers to discuss and provide feedback on your product concepts, features, or marketing messages, allowing for deeper insights into customer perspectives.

Table 6.1 Free or Low-Cost Sources for Market Research

Category	Resource
Market research and competitive analysis tools and sources	SEMrush, Similarweb, Google Trends, Google Search
Social media platforms	Twitter, LinkedIn, Facebook Groups, Reddit, Instagram, TikTok
Marketplaces and peer-to-peer review sites	Acquire.com, Amazon, Course Hero, Upwork, G2, Capterra

Generally, you want your products and services to be positioned in an area of high and rising demand with only a moderate degree of competition. Market research is a prerequisite to helping you gain an advantageous position within the market. After performing market research, you will have generated:

- **Qualitative and quantitative findings**—This information will be used to support or disqualify the viability of your preliminary ideas.

- **New ideas for features, products, or services**—Formulate these based on what you learn about the market and how competitors are serving it.

Be sure to do research within each of the categories listed in Table 6.1. Each category will provide you with its own unique type of information about your market.

Manually scavenging through treasure troves of data is a tiresome but indispensable part of this process. The good news is that new generative AI solutions can make this work a lot faster and more efficient. If you're interested in leveraging a generative AI solution that's custom tailored for market research and competitive analysis needs, then be sure to check out Crayon, an intelligence platform that utilizes generative AI to uncover layers of the competitive landscape that may not be visible through traditional research methods alone. Other generative AI solutions that are helpful in market research include general LLMs like GPT-4, Claude, and Perplexity.

Validating a Market-Ready Solution with VOC Feedback As mentioned earlier, to fully validate market readiness for your solution, you need to conduct VOC surveys and interviews, as well as build customer personas. Between each step, you should continually analyze and evaluate the data you collect from your potential and existing customers. This process is iterative, so expect to return to earlier stages on an as-needed basis as things evolve.

At a high-level, the process goes like this:

1. **Customer surveys**. Conduct surveys from people who match your customer personas.

2. **Analyze and assess**. Analyze the survey results holistically to identify key trends and findings within the body of research.

3. **Identify**. Look for a handful of individuals within the responses who seem like they're the closest fit to your customer personas. You'll be able to identify that by analyzing their responses and comparing them to those of others surveyed.

4. **Interview**. Contact those individuals and request that they join you for customer interviews.

5. **Document**. After voice of customer interviews (VOC), you would again analyze and evaluate interview responses. Based on those findings, you would then build documentation to support your customer personas.

Note

In my experience, about 10–20% of survey respondents will stand out as being an exceptional fit for interviews. Your mileage will vary, but as long as your surveys generate high-quality and relevant feedback, you're on the right track.

Let's look at this process in greater detail.

Conducting VOC Surveys   The purpose of VOC surveys is to gather insights directly from your customers and leads in order to drive more effective service or product development. VOC surveys also foster stronger customer relationships that ultimately drive revenue growth.

As a rule of thumb, the more substantial the investment or the higher the risk associated with your project or product, the more critical and detailed your VOC efforts should be. For projects with significant investment requirements, make sure to:

1. Capture a broad spectrum of feedback across diverse channels to support you in generating actionable feedback.

2. Establish a response system for promptly addressing feedback in order to mitigate risks.

Note

If you have an early-stage or pre-revenue start-up, then you may be able to get by with finding just 50–100 targeted respondents to complete your VOC survey. The thing that matters most here is that your respondents are relevant, meaning they're actually lookalikes to the customer personas you have in mind for your product or service idea.

When conducting VOC surveys, be sure not to tell people what you have in mind for them with respect to your product or the service ideas. Leave your questions open-ended in order to gather information about their needs and pain points without creating any bias with your ideas about a solution. This type of bias will decrease the effectiveness of this process. Regarding what types of questions to ask in a VOC survey, some should be open-ended, and others should require categorical responses (e.g., "yes or no" or "on a scale of 1–10").

Bonus resource

With this book, I'm providing my voice of customer kit, which includes voice of customer survey questions, as well as scripts to help you connect with the right people whom you need to complete the survey. These are available for you to download for free at www.data-mania.com/book.

Performing VOC Interviews   The purpose of VOC interviews is to gather a deep and qualitative understanding of the needs, pain points, and preferences of people who are represented by your customer personas. The insights you garner will support you in driving better targeted product or service improvements that increase customer satisfaction and loyalty. Although VOC interviews can be wearisome, they pay off in multiples by allowing you to converse with customers about their pain points and solution needs.

Bonus resource

With this book, I'm providing customer interview questions and a customer persona template. These are available for you to download for free at www. data-mania.com/book.

When selecting individuals for VOC interviews, your selection criteria should account for the depth and relevance of their potential insights, in addition to their fitness to your existing customer personas. Again, don't tell respondents anything about the solution you have in mind for them because this will create bias in their responses.

VOC interview questions should be open ended. The interview is meant to be a conversation between you and the individual so you can develop a deep understanding of their needs, their pain points, and what they've tried in the past to solve the problem that didn't work. Phrase your interview questions with enough context such that respondents provide answers that are generally relevant to your solution space. That said, also leave things open enough for them to share insights you can use to improve your product or service development.

Tip

As you conduct these interviews, solution ideas are going to start jumping out at you. Jot those ideas down and keep going. The key here is to move through this as quickly as possible and not get stuck in idea limbo-land.

Building Your Customer Personas

Another fundamental thread that weaves the PMF process together are your customer personas. You need to align your customer personas with the evidence you've gathered from market research, VOC surveys, and VOC interviews. As shown in Figure 6.3, your customer persona documentation should represent a comprehensive understanding of the target customer's behaviors, needs, and motivations. This ensures the relevance of the solution you're developing while also setting the stage for solid customer engagement and retention.

Bonus resource

I've developed a customer persona worksheet to guide you through the process of collecting details on your customer personas. It's available for free at www.data-mania.com/book.

You can find the customizable customer persona template shown in Figure 6.3 at www.data-mania.com/book.

After conducting VOC surveys and interviews, it's time to distill your insights into comprehensive customer personas. When developing customer personas for AI and data products, you need to dig a lot deeper than basic demographics, and

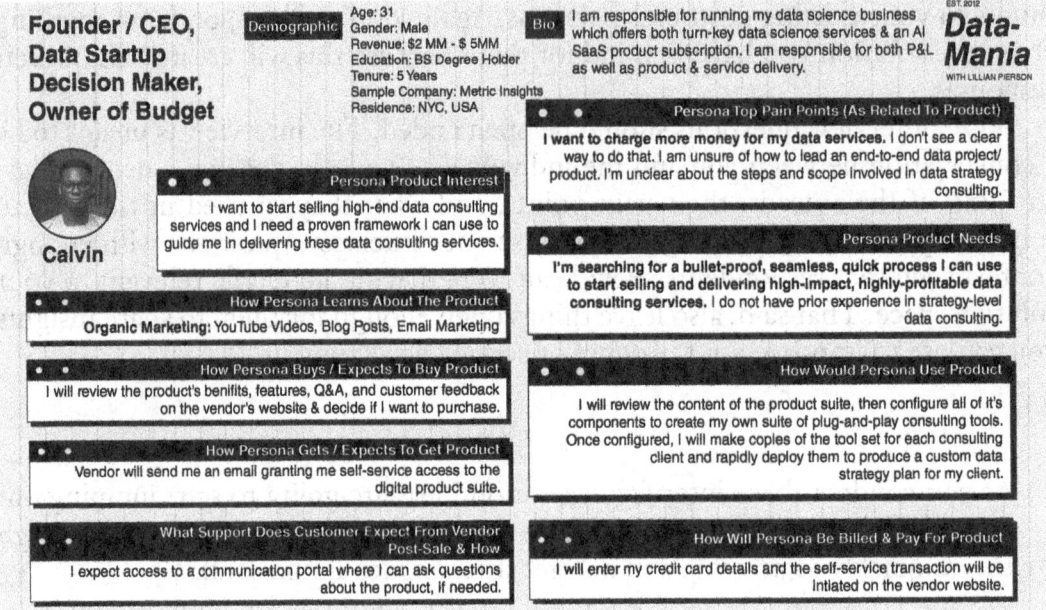

FIGURE 6.3 A high-level example of customer persona documentation.

really take the time to map out customer preferences as they relate to the solution. Consider these elements:

- **Technical proficiency**—What's the persona's comfort level with advanced technology? How proficient are they with data?

- **Data environment**—What types of data do they handle, and how is it managed within their organization?

- **Decision-making process**—Who holds the influence over purchasing decisions for AI or data tools?

- **Current workflow**—How do they currently carry out the tasks that your product will be optimizing?

- **Pain points**—What specific challenges are they facing that your product can solve?

- **Success metrics**—How do they gauge success in their role?

- **AI attitudes**—What's their perspective on adopting AI? Are there specific concerns or areas of excitement?

- **Learning style**—What's their preferred method for learning about new technologies?

For example, here's a more detailed persona for a data analytics product:

An Example of a Customer Persona for a Data Analytics Product

- **Name**—Sarah Thompson
- **Role**—Marketing Director at a mid-size e-commerce company
- **Age**—38
- **Technical proficiency**—Moderate—comfortable with basic data analysis tools but not deeply technical.
- **Data environment**—Works with customer purchase data, website analytics, and social media metrics, all scattered across various platforms.
- **Decision-making process**—Influences decisions but needs CFO sign-off for larger investments.
- **Current workflow**—Spends hours every week manually gathering data from different sources and combining it into spreadsheets for analysis.
- **Pain points**—Struggles with time-consuming data collection, difficulty spotting trends across datasets, experiences a lack of real-time insights.
- **Success metrics**—Focuses on increasing conversion rates, customer lifetime value, and ROI on marketing campaigns.
- **AI attitudes**—Excited about the potential of AI but wary of the learning curve and has concerns about data privacy.
- **Learning style**—Prefers hands-on learning and video tutorials over lengthy manuals.
- **Key quote**—"I know there are valuable insights hidden within our data, but discovering these insights feels like searching for a needle in a haystack."

Generally, you want to develop 2–4 customer personas who seem extremely relevant for your product or service. For those individuals, you need to start thinking about their expectations with respect to the solution. Write a narrative about how the person is actually going to use and interact with your product or service and use this narrative to inform your development requirements.

You'll also want to create customer journey maps for each persona starting all the way from the awareness to the post-purchase onboarding, activation, and advocacy phases. This will go a long way in helping your development and marketing team identify key features and strategies for each phase.

Lastly, you want to get clear on how the person will pay for the product or service. These channels must, of course, be prepared in advance of taking your product or service to market. You should align payment options with the expectations of people who match your customer personas, so document those expectations first, then build. Once you've documented your customer personas, share the documentation with your development and marketing team, as well as any relevant stakeholders. This will establish clarity to support their executional requirements for product marketing moving forward.

Note

Although I've described the market validation and PMF process in a linear manner, it's not actually a linear process. Establishing market validation and PMF require you to iterate back to earlier steps based on new insights.

Note

The customer persona documentation I've discussed is extremely high-level. For product and marketing strategy development purposes, you'd be wise to go into a lot more detail.

Exploring Powerful Practices within PMF Strategy Development

As someone who's helped 100s of tech companies, from the IBMs and SAPs to the early-stage VC-backed and bootstrapped technical founders, to bring their products and services to market, I want to leave you with a few of my favorite approaches that you can leverage on your own journey toward PMF.

Proposing a PMF Hypothesis

When you're preparing a PMF hypothesis in Part 3, it will serve you well to take the time to identify your unfair advantages. You also need to take a numerical approach to offer idea assessment before selecting one as the basis of your PMF hypothesis. Let's look at each of these in greater detail.

Identifying Your Unfair Advantages   An *unfair advantage* is a unique characteristic or asset that cannot be easily replicated or matched by competitors. Some types of unfair advantages are relevant to all business models, whereas others are relevant only to either products or services. I'll provide starter ideas for all three categories.

Unfair advantages that are relevant to both SaaS start-ups and technical professional services firms include:

- **Expertise in a niche market**—Do you specialize in a specific sector or technology that few competitors have mastered to the same degree? Think LLM fine-tuning or a product for AI explainability!

- **Proprietary technology**—Have you already developed unique algorithms, platforms, or software functionalities that are patented or difficult for competitors to replicate? Have you built custom, in-house technology tools or platforms that improve the efficiency or effectiveness of your solution?

- **Exclusive partnerships**—Do you have any exclusive agreements with key players (e.g., for integrations or data sharing) that enhance the capabilities of your solutions while locking out competitors?

- **Cost advantage**—Are you able to leverage technology, automation, or economies of scale to offer your solution at a lower price point than competitors can feasibly match?

- **Data monopoly**—Do you have access to, or control over, unique datasets that can be used to improve your solution, better understand your customer needs, or offer personalized experiences?

- **Patents and intellectual property**—Are you holding any IP rights that cover critical aspects of your solution and deter competitors? Are you holding patents or IP rights that underpin your methodologies, processes, or the technologies you implement, thus establishing a legal barrier of entry?

- **Regulatory compliance and security**—Are you able to provide superior compliance with industry regulations and standards, or unparalleled data security? Does your team have an unparalleled understanding of complex regulations in specific industries or geographies where most struggle?

- **First-mover advantage**—Are you able to be the first to offer a specific type of SaaS solution in a niche market?

- **Vertical integration**—Do you have control of more of the supply chain or related services than do your competitors?

- **Community engagement**—Do you have a strong, engaged community of users who can contribute to growth and adoption?

If your company is a tech consultancy, on the other hand, and you're working to bring a new service to market, the following unfair advantages can serve as powerful differentiators:

- **Elite talent**—Do you employ leading industry experts, thought leaders, or individuals with rare skills that increase the quality and innovativeness of your services?

- **Customer network**—Do you already have an extensive network of loyal customers and advocates that can serve as a base for referrals and testimonials?

- **Global delivery model**—Do you have a robust, global delivery model that ensures consistent service quality across geographies? This can help you cater your services to multinational clients.

Your unfair advantages represent your most marketable assets at this time. They lay a solid foundation for market research, go-to-market strategy, and PMF overall. Make sure you're clear on yours.

Using Numerical Methods to Select an Optimal Product or Service Idea
Now, I want to show you how to use numerical methods and your market research findings to select an optimal product or service idea. To do that, you need to assess your ideas against critical go-to-market considerations to select the most viable one for further validation.

To assess your offer ideas, you want to take an evidence-backed, quantitative approach to evaluate between competing offer ideas you've generated. For this I recommend you lean into the market research you've already collected and score out your ideas using a multi-criteria decision matrix like that shown in Table 6.2.

Evaluate the soundness of your offer ideas against one another by assigning the idea a score between 1 and 10 for each of the following go-to-market criteria (where 1 represents least favorability, and 10 represents maximum favorability).

- **Price point**—What's the highest price a person is willing to pay for this offer? Higher price points are more favorable. This determines the pricing strategy for the offer, which impacts its positioning in the market, perceived value, and target customer segments.

- **Urgency**—How urgently do people need this product or service? Greater urgency is more favorable.

Table 6.2   A Simple Multi-Criteria Matrix for Selecting Optimal Product or Service Ideas

Criteria Score on a Scale of 1 (Unfavorable) – 10 (Very Favorable)	OFFER IDEA 1 Offer Description	OFFER IDEA 2 Offer Description	OFFER IDEA n... Offer Description
Price point			
Urgency			
Time-to-market			
Upfront capital cost			
Delivery cost			
Customer acquisition cost			
Maintenance cost			
Market size			
Uniqueness			
Total score (Σ) =			

- **Time-to-market**—What's the timeline for development to launch? This influences the product's relevance upon release and the company's ability to capitalize on current market trends or gaps. Smaller time-to-market is more favorable.

- **Upfront capital cost**—What's the initial investment required to develop and launch the offer? Lower upfront capital costs are more favorable.

- **Delivery cost**—What are the expenses associated with distributing the product or service to customers? This influences the choice of distribution channels and overall pricing strategy. Lower delivery costs are more favorable.

- **Customer acquisition cost**—What's the cost of acquiring a new customer? This is important for planning marketing and sales strategies, and estimating the profit potential of the offer. Lower customer acquisition costs are more favorable.

- **Maintenance cost**—What are the ongoing expenses to support the offer post-launch? This affects long-term profitability and customer satisfaction. Lower maintenance costs are more favorable.

- **Market size**—What's the total potential sales opportunity for the offer? This is crucial for assessing the viability of the product and setting realistic sales targets. Larger market size is more favorable.
- **Uniqueness**—How unique is this offer from similar offers on the market? More uniqueness is more favorable. This is essential to positioning, marketing, and the ability to capture market share.

Bonus resource

My interactive start-up idea selector tool is available for you to download for free at www.data-mania.com/book. You can use it to help you assess your offer idea.

Tip

At this stage you've already done a lot of research, so you should have ample evidence to support the scores that you assign your ideas. If, however, you find you are lacking data to support your scoring on a particular criterion, then you may need to go in and do some more targeted research.

After performing this evaluation, select your top three offer ideas while keeping in mind the following factors:

- **Lower-third ideas**—If the idea scores out in the lower-third of all your ideas, it's not likely to be viable.
- **Middle-third ideas**—If the idea scores out in the middle-third, proceed with caution. With ideas in this category, it's likely that you'll be able to get some traction, but it's going to take a lot of work.
- **Top-third ideas**—If the idea scores out in the top-third, it could be a home run. Make the most of these ideas.

Tip

If you're unable to find three viable ideas, consider starting the entire ideation process from scratch by revisiting your customer concept.

Identifying the Most Viable Offer Idea

After assessing the viability of your offer ideas, go back and do some additional research to get a more concrete estimate for the market size of each of them. For this, you're just reconfirming the viability of these ideas while also gathering a little more information about which one might be the most viable of the three.

Simple ways to do this include brainstorming what Google Search keywords are a fit for your offer ideas. Gather data that demonstrates adequate search volume for those keywords using both SEMrush and Google Trends. Look at the 10-year, the 12-month, and the 5-year Google Trends snapshot to see if those are relevant. Be sure to take screen grabs and make notes.

Caution

Before building anything, always make sure there's a really solid market for what you plan to offer, and that there are enough people in that market with enough demand and urgency to support your new solution. If you can't find any competitors who are serving your target market with similar offers, that probably means there is not enough market demand to support your offer.

Use your market research findings to refine and select the single most viable offer idea. Document that idea and prepare yourself for the work that's required to clarify and validate a PMF hypothesis.

After having completed the steps outlined in this chapter, you'll be prepared to develop a market-validated solution that sets you up for PMF success. Now that you've seen how to de-risk your development by validating the market and PMF, Chapter 7 offers a primer on how to safeguard against ethical and reputational risks that are inherent to data and AI solutions.

Notes

1. Parker, E. (October 23, 2023). What Percentage of Businesses Fail? (2024). https://clarifycapital.com/blog/what-percentage-of-businesses-fail
2. Howarth, J. (November 3, 2023). Startup Failure Rate Statistics (2024). https://explodingtopics.com/blog/startup-failure-stats

The Data & AI Trifecta: Ethical Considerations, Deployment Tactics, and Competitive Analysis

7

Complying with Regulatory and Ethical Standards

The potential benefits of artificial intelligence are huge, so are the dangers.

– Dave Waters

Your company's compliance with data laws, regulations, and ethical standards is of paramount importance. This chapter presents a high-level overview of imperative standards, as well as a primer on ethical considerations you should be aware of when building with foundation models. In Chapter 13, you learn how to go about evaluating your company's current state compliance with relevant legal and regulatory frameworks.

The Standards

The passage of increasingly restrictive regulations is a natural consequence of the rapid advancement of AI and data-intensive technologies. People can and should be protected from the irresponsible usage of data and AI systems. This section looks at a few of the broader regulatory requirements that all leaders and data professionals should be aware of.

Requirements for Businesses Serving the European Union

When it comes to protecting the rights of its citizens, the European Union leads the way. With its Artificial Intelligence Act (AI Act) and General Data Protection Regulation (GDPR), there is no region of the modern world where it's safer to be "human" in the age of data and AI.

Note

Although the laws outlined in this section are valid only within the European Union, they apply to all companies doing business there, regardless of where those companies are headquartered.

Before getting into the nitty-gritty of laws and regulations, let's play a fun game called "This, Not That." Table 7.1 provides "this, not that" pairs of scenarios, practices, or configurations: one that aligns with best practices and regulatory requirements ("this"), and one that falls short or violates them ("not that").

Now that you can see a few scenarios that illustrate what compliance done right looks like within the EU, let's dig into the regulations.

On 13 March 2024, the European Parliament announced that it had passed a new law mandating the ethical use of AI: the AI Act.

Table 7.1 This, Not That, of Data and AI Compliance

This	Not That	Regulatory Requirement
An AI system designed to support cognitive behavioral therapy is used under the guidance of a licensed therapist, with explicit user consent.	A manipulative AI tool changes user behavior in a harmful way, such as by increasing addiction to an online platform.	Artificial Intelligence Act
A credit scoring AI system transparently uses financial history data, with users' consent, to assess creditworthiness.	An AI system assigns social scores to individuals based on their online activity and personal associations, impacting their access to services.	
AI is used for biometric verification at border controls, with strict regulations and oversight.	Real-time remote biometric identification systems are deployed in public spaces without clear legal basis or safeguards.	

This	Not That	Regulatory Requirement
A social media platform promptly deletes users' profiles and all associated data upon request, without undue delay.	An online retailer keeps customer data indefinitely, even after requests for deletion, and uses that data for future marketing needs.	General Data Protection Regulation (GDPR)
A website asks for explicit consent to track cookies with a clear explanation of what data is collected and for which purposes.	A website assumes consent by default, using pre-checked boxes for data collection without explicit user approval.	
A cloud storage provider allows users to easily export their data in a commonly used format at no extra cost.	A fitness app locks in user data, preventing or complicating the process of moving data to another service provider.	

Artificial Intelligence Act[1]

The AI Act is a landmark legal regulation that requires AI systems used within the EU to be safe, ethical, and transparent.

- The rights of individuals:
  - AI applications that are considered a threat to people's safety or rights are banned. These include manipulative cognitive behavioral tools, social scoring systems, indiscriminate biometric identification, and real-time remote biometric identification systems (with limited exceptions for law enforcement under serious conditions).
  - AI systems that interact with humans must adhere to stringent transparency requirements that make users aware of the fact they are interacting with AI, including AI chatbots and deep fake content generators.
- Obligations of providers and users:
  - All systems deemed "high-risk AI" must undergo thorough, ongoing risk assessments, maintain high-quality datasets, ensure transparency, and incorporate human oversight. These include AI applications in critical public service areas like healthcare, education, and border patrol.

(continued)

(continued)

- General purpose AI systems, like generative AI models, will face additional regulations depending on their applications. There's an ongoing debate on the exact obligations, especially for high-risk categories.
- Penalties for non-compliance:
  - Fines up to €30 million, or
  - 6% of the company's global turnover, whichever is higher.

Back in 2016, the EU also passed the data protection law, GDPR. You may have heard of it. It's the regulation that cost Meta Platforms (aka, Facebook, Instagram, and WhatsApp) €1.590 billion in fines in 2023 alone.

General Data Protection Regulation[2]

The General Data Protection Regulation (GDPR) is an EU-wide data protection law that changes the way personal data is handled across various sectors. It gives individuals in the EU more control over their personal data, while placing strict obligations on businesses and organizations that process it.

- Rights of individuals:
  - Clear consent is required for data processing.
  - Access to personal data by the individual must be made available.
  - Rights to rectify, erase ('right to be forgotten'), and port data.
  - Ability to object to data usage, especially for profiling purposes.
- Obligations of businesses:
  - Implement robust security measures.
  - Appoint a Data Protection Officer in certain cases.
  - Notify authorities of data breaches.
  - Provide transparent information provisioning about data processing.
- Penalties for non-compliance:
  - Fines up to €20 million, or
  - 4% of global annual turnover, whichever is higher

Now let's turn to the data laws and regulations that govern business operations within the United States.

Requirements Within the United States

Being the capitalist society that it is, the United States is considerably less restrictive than the EU. That said, there are still some laws that data professionals and leaders of data-intensive companies should be familiar with.

California Consumer Privacy Act of 2018[3]

Under the California Consumer Privacy Act of 2018 (CCPA), California residents have powerful rights over their personal data. This regulation gives consumers the right to be informed, to delete, and to opt out of the sale or sharing of their personal information. It also lets them correct inaccuracies and limit the use of sensitive data. Businesses, including data brokers, must comply with these consumer rights and disclose details about their privacy practices.

- Potential penalties for non-compliance:
  - Up to $7,500 for each intentional violation
  - Up to $2,500 per infraction for other types of violations

Note

Although the CCPA is a state law, it applies to all companies doing business in California. If there's any chance whatsoever that your company has customers residing in California, you'll want to make sure that you're adhering to CCPA requirements.

Health Insurance Portability and Accountability Act[4]

The Health Insurance Portability and Accountability Act (HIPAA) of 1996 is a US law that protects sensitive medical information. The Act upholds the confidentiality and security of patients' health information and establishes

(continued)

(continued)

guidelines on how healthcare providers, insurers, and other related entities must handle and protect sensitive personal health data.

- Potential penalties for non-compliance:
  - Civil penalty per violation: $127–$63,973* per violation (with an annual cap of $1,919,173 as of 2024)
  - Criminal penalties: $50,000 and up to one year in prison

HIPAA laws only really affect companies that deal with people's health and medical data, but there's also the Gramm-Leach-Bliley Act that protects an individual's financial data.

Gramm-Leach-Bliley Act[5]

The Gramm-Leach-Bliley Act (GLBA) of 1999 mandates that financial institutions ensure the confidentiality and protection of consumer data. It applies to banks as well as any other type of company that provides financial products or services, including loans, investment advice, or insurance. This act introduces strict rules on how personal financial information should be handled and shared.

- The obligations of businesses:
  - Financial institutions must provide clear and conspicuous communication to their customers about their information-sharing practices. They must offer customers the option to opt out of information sharing with non-affiliated third parties.
  - Companies must implement a written information security plan that outlines how the company protects clients' personal information.
  - Financial institutions must protect against "pretexting," which is the practice of obtaining personal financial information under false pretenses, including through fraudulent access to data systems.
- Potential penalties for non-compliance:
  - Civil penalty per violation: The minimum civil penalty for GLBA violations can include fines of up to $100,000 per violation for financial

institutions. Additionally, directors and officers of the company can be held personally liable, with fines up to $10,000 per violation.[6]
- Criminal penalties: Substantial fines and up to five years in prison.

Note

The data strategy you develop should ultimately support a data or AI solution that strictly complies with applicable laws and regulations. At the very least, this compliance will prevent damage to your company's reputation while maintaining trust with clients and partners.

Early Regulatory Compliance Considerations

Chapter 13 offers a deep dive into how to go about assessing your organization's current state regulatory compliance. At a high level, this process involves:

1. Mapping the regulatory landscape to understand the legal and regulatory environment your organization operates within
2. Reviewing existing data policies and procedures for compliance
3. Conducting interviews with key stakeholders to gain a holistic view of how data-related legal and ethical responsibilities are managed
4. Identifying gaps and risks in your company's current practices
5. Documenting all findings in a detailed report to guide future compliance

Don't worry—you're not expected to go back to school to get a law degree in order to do this. Think of yourself as the leader here, where you're calling on subject matter experts to execute the work plan elements as needed in order to facilitate the development of a high-ROI data strategy.

Warning

Do not attempt to conduct legal matters on your own. This is one place where you definitely need the support of credentialed experts who have a solid knowledge of the current data regulations and guidelines as they apply to your industry.

Stakeholder discussions are one thing you are absolutely responsible for as the leader in this data strategy development project. There is no such thing as over-communication. Beyond the procedural stakeholder interviews discussed in Chapter 13, you should be seeking ongoing communication with your stakeholders at all points in the development process. Let me provide you with some food for thought as compliance-relevant conversation starters:

- With respect to data regulations and laws, are you aware of any requirements that your business unit is routinely monitoring to stay in compliance?

- Are there regulations or laws that you worry might be applicable but have been omitted from procedural consideration within the organization?

- With respect to data processing, usage, and storage, what best practices have been handed from the top down to your business unit? Does your unit operate within compliance with those practices? Or, are there areas that you feel are no longer relevant and should be updated?

- How prepared do you feel the organization is to respond to non-compliance issues in the worst-case scenario?

- Are you aware of actions that the organization is taking to improve its satisfaction with data privacy and compliance requirements?

Adherence to ethical principles should also be considered sooner rather than later.

Ethical AI Should Be Top of Mind

The results of an AI gap analysis paint a picture of your organization's readiness for ethical AI deployment. By identifying these gaps early, you can either fix them or select use cases that won't be affected by these gaps. This proactive approach can help you build trust and minimize the risks associated with AI projects.

Chapter 13 provides extensive instructions on how to conduct an AI ethics gap analysis. For now, suffice it to say that this process involves:

1. Surveying ethical AI baselines to establish benchmarks
2. Assessing regulatory compliance
3. Evaluating accountability structures within your organization
4. Examining AI explainability to ensure decisions are transparent
5. Checking for bias mitigation procedures to avoid ethical vulnerabilities

6. Identifying training needs to ensure staff are equipped to handle ethical issues related to AI

7. Evaluating the alignment of potential use cases with established AI ethics measures

A meticulous approach like this helps you identify gaps in practices and infrastructure, prioritizing their resolution, and ultimately ensuring that your AI use cases align with ethical principles.

Whether you're in strategy development mode or not, your organization and its business units should always be prepared for an AI ethics gap analysis. To that end, make sure to encourage technical teams to always document each step of an AI model's lifecycle—from its development until its deployment. Ideally, this documentation will be sufficient to explain the data sources used for the development of the AI model, the design/architecture of the model, the output validation process, and, ultimately, the way the model makes decisions.

It can also be helpful to establish periodic technology audits that can help you get a better picture of the data sources you're using, the algorithm or logic behind different implementations, the outputs (and therefore the correctness) of the AI models, and the reliability of the AI systems you have in place.

Implications When Building with Generative Models

As you may have surmised from the previous discussion about the AI Act, if your potential use cases revolve around the use of generative models, then you'll need to exercise extra caution. You'll need to make sure that the use case you choose—and subsequently implement—goes beyond meeting the requirements of the EU's AI Act. You need to future-proof it by taking measures to ensure that the solution you build aligns with the principles of trust, transparency, and ethical consideration. Though I'll cover principles and design considerations for ethical AI extensively in Chapter 13, let me give you a brief introduction of the do's and don'ts with regards to use cases that involve generative AI.

Generative AI is as alarming as it is inspiring. As of 2024, the volume of AI-generated disinformation, especially deep fake images concerning elections, rose by an average of 130% per month on platforms like X (formerly Twitter). This is only going to get worse in the coming years.[7] There's also an increase in misinformation on social media channels, with more than 63% of X users having reported encountering deceptive and misleading content as well as dubious claims.[8] While other social media platforms may be politically slanted in other directions, similar misinformation issues are present there, too.

What does this have to do with AI strategy? A lot, actually. If your potential use cases involve supporting the output of AI-generated content, then you'll need to tread extremely carefully—knowing that it's your responsibility to make sure your users are protected from any kind of generative model mishaps—misinformation, deep fakes, and intellectual property (IP) violations among others.

Tip

If one of your potential use cases aims to help people generate AI content— whether that be audio, images, text, or videos—then, now while you're in the planning stages, make sure you're considering legal risks that arise due to potential bias, misinformation, IP infringement, or lack of transparency caused by your solution. Although the users that generate questionable content are not without responsibility, legal remedies will be sought from the company that facilitates the transgression.

FIGURE 7.1 Stable Diffusion's output for the one-shot prompt "AI start-up founders" as of March 2024.

Ethical Bias

Generative models can sometimes propagate and amplify existing biases. For example, Figure 7.1 shows what was generated by Stable Diffusion when prompted to generate images of "AI start-up founders."

Personally, I don't find that group to be fairly representative of diversity in gender and ethnicities. That's my subjective opinion. Maybe you think that the image is an accurate representation of what "AI start-up founders" look like. Your opinion is no more or less valid than others. My point here is that generative AI has the propensity to further propagate harmful, biased stereotypes that disadvantage members of minority populations.

Misinformation

Sometimes, a generative AI model makes claims that are simply not true. In other words, claims are not supported by facts. This is what we call *model hallucinations*, and they're especially problematic when the prompts are related to healthcare, financial advice, politics, or education.

The type of misinformation that results from model hallucinations can have serious consequences, such as providing false pretenses that mislead people when they go to make life-altering decisions like:

- Making investment choices
- Seeking medical advice
- Voting for a particular political party

This problem can be somewhat mitigated through the use of retrieval-augment generation (RAG), as discussed in Chapter 2. It's also possible, however, that the model doesn't understand prompt context very well and ends up pulling and aggregating information from different sources. In this case, the output might give the illusion of the response being 100% accurate when, in fact, the truth is more nuanced.

For example, when asked, "Is Ozempic effective for losing weight quickly and safely?," the model might generate data by referencing trending blogs and opinion pieces to show that indeed the medication is safe and effective for weight loss. But you and I both know that, ideally, an informed decision of whether to take medication should always be made by consulting a doctor, looking at peer-reviewed papers, and studying documentation regarding its side effects. Young people or users who are new to generative AI technologies have a propensity to believe the model's response without second thoughts. This risk must be accounted for within a data strategy.

Intellectual Property Infringement

Almost all AI companies are choosing to ignore the copyright and IP infringement risks that are inherent in the products they're monetizing, but in the long run, that's not a prudent choice.

Using the same example—where a user asks an LLM, "Is Ozempic effective for losing weight quickly and safely?"—imagine though that the user writes a secondary prompt to get the model to generate content on a very specific topic around which very little source data exists. For example, the prompt might say, "Tell me about the long-term studies related to Ozempic safety." If the content that's generated from this prompt is almost an exact replica of a copyrighted work it was derived from, then who's liable? Right now, AI companies are acting as judge and jury over the matter. In fact, to protect its investment into Copilot and the Azure OpenAI Service, Microsoft has introduced the Copilot Copyright Commitment[9] wherein, so long as the user adheres to the required guardrails and content filters that are integrated within the products, then Microsoft promises to defend commercial customers against copyright infringement lawsuits and cover any adverse judgments or settlements.

Warning

IP laws don't care whether a piece of content is directly lifted from a copyright owner or whether an LLM generated the copyrighted piece verbatim. The laws still apply, and if your use case involves generative AI, then you'd be wise to take caution.

Lack of Transparency

As of 2024, there are no proven tools that can shed light on the transparency and interpretability of AI systems. Much research and development is currently underway to develop tools that can answer questions like:

- How does the model reach a specific conclusion?
- What are the primary or core features that contribute to what the model ultimately outputs to the end user?

- What's the precedence of these features?
- How does a change in prompt influence the model's output?

These problems are deeply associated with the lack of transparency and explainability inherent to generative AI models. When there's no way of knowing why a model outputs what it does, it becomes really difficult to debug issues related to a model's behavior and output in different scenarios. When you're building a data product that utilizes a generative model, this can be one of the major pitfalls.

Note

In Figure 13.1 of Chapter 13, I've laid out some common ways to attempt to establish explainability for generative models and LLMs in particular. Chapter 13 also takes a quick look at different real-world case studies related to AI bias and its far-reaching consequences for society at large.

Ultimately, when working with use cases that revolve around the use of generative AI models, the onus is on you to make sure you're not prioritizing quick success over responsibility. Make it a point to discuss the consequences of AI bias and misinformation with your team. Help them establish systems that uphold the core values of trust, responsibility, and transparency for AI models.

With data and AI compliance having been thoroughly introduced, Chapter 8 looks at some strategies for successful AI deployment, how you can choose the right technology stack for your use case, and the common obstacles you'll likely encounter while doing so.

Notes

1. EU AI Act: First regulation on artificial intelligence (December 19, 2023). https://www.europ arl.europa.eu/topics/en/article/20230601STO93804/eu-ai-act-first-regulation-on-artificial-intelligence
2. European Council: The general data protection regulation (January 11, 2024). https://www.consilium.europa.eu/en/policies/data-protection/data-protection-regulation/
3. California Consumer Privacy Act (CCPA) (March 13, 2024). https://oag.ca.gov/privacy/ccpa
4. Summary of the HIPAA Privacy Rule (October 19, 2022). https://www.hhs.gov/hipaa/for-professionals/privacy/laws-regulations/index.html
5. Gramm-Leach-Bliley Act. https://www.ftc.gov/business-guidance/privacy-security/gramm-leach-bliley-act

6. CPAs and the Gramm Leach Bliley Information Safeguard Rules - https://www.picpa.org/articles/cpa-now-blog/cpa-now/2022/03/14/cpas-and-glba-information-safeguard-rules

7. Wiggers, K. (March 6, 2024). Political deepfakes are spreading like wildfire thanks to GenAI. https://techcrunch.com/2024/03/06/political-deepfakes-are-spreading-like-wildfire-thanks-to-genai/

8. Zipdo (June 14, 2023). Social media misinformation statistics: slide deck. https://zipdo.co/statistics/social-media-misinformation/

9. Smith, B. (September 7, 2023). Microsoft announces new Copilot Copyright Commitment for customers. https://blogs.microsoft.com/on-the-issues/2023/09/07/copilot-copyright-commitment-ai-legal-concerns/

Recommended Reading

European Commission (June 7, 2022). High-level expert group on artificial intelligence. https://digital-strategy.ec.europa.eu/en/policies/expert-group-ai

8

Practical Tactics for Successful AI Deployments

The most powerful tool we have as developers is automation.

— Scott Hanselman

Now that you've had a glimpse of regulatory compliance requirements and implications when building with ML or generative models, let's explore the dynamics where the rubber meets the road. In this chapter, you're going to see powerful executional-level strategies for successful AI deployments in the real world, as well as obstacles that you're likely to encounter along the way.

As you read this chapter, keep in mind that I am simply presenting practical deployment considerations you should be aware of before attempting to build an AI strategy. Although I reference the need for you to plan and prioritize throughout this chapter, I'm not leaving you to figure out how to do that on your own. In fact, the remainder of this book is dedicated to walking you step-by-step through the entire process of applying the knowledge shared in this chapter and those prior in order to build a data or AI strategy that drives business growth in a powerful manner.

Setting the Stage for AI Deployments

"AI deployment" refers to bringing models into production. The fact is, the deployment of ML models and foundation models usually falls under the same large AI umbrella, but there are major differences between them.

- **Building with ML models**—Right off the bat, ML models are always designed for specific tasks like classification, clustering, forecasting, prediction, etc. This is the traditional type of AI deployment we've all come to know and love.

- **Building with foundation models**—With foundation models, we're talking about building predictive applications by leveraging pre-built generative AI models that have already been trained on a huge corpus of data. In some cases, this data is multimodal, meaning that it consists of a variety of formats like text, image, audio, and video. With foundation models, you'd typically be fine-tuning for specific use cases, but these models should also be able to perform a wide range of general tasks. The magnitude of size and scale of foundation models differentiates them from traditional ML models in terms of resource requirements and scalability.

Note

Multimodal data is both consumed and generated by foundation models, where multimodal LLMs like GPT-4 have the ability to process, interact, and generate all the above data types.

- **Building of generative AI models**—If you're already out there building LLMs, image generators, audio generators, or video generators, then I'm going to take a wild guess that you're not reading this chapter. This type of transformative development work is incredible, but it falls outside the scope of what we discuss in this book.

The AI discussion is getting more nuanced by the day.

Note

For this chapter, I'll refer to ML model deployment as "AI deployment," and I'll point it out explicitly if I'm discussing an AI deployment that involves building applications with generative models. Despite their differences, many best practices for ML deployment will also hold true for generative model deployment.

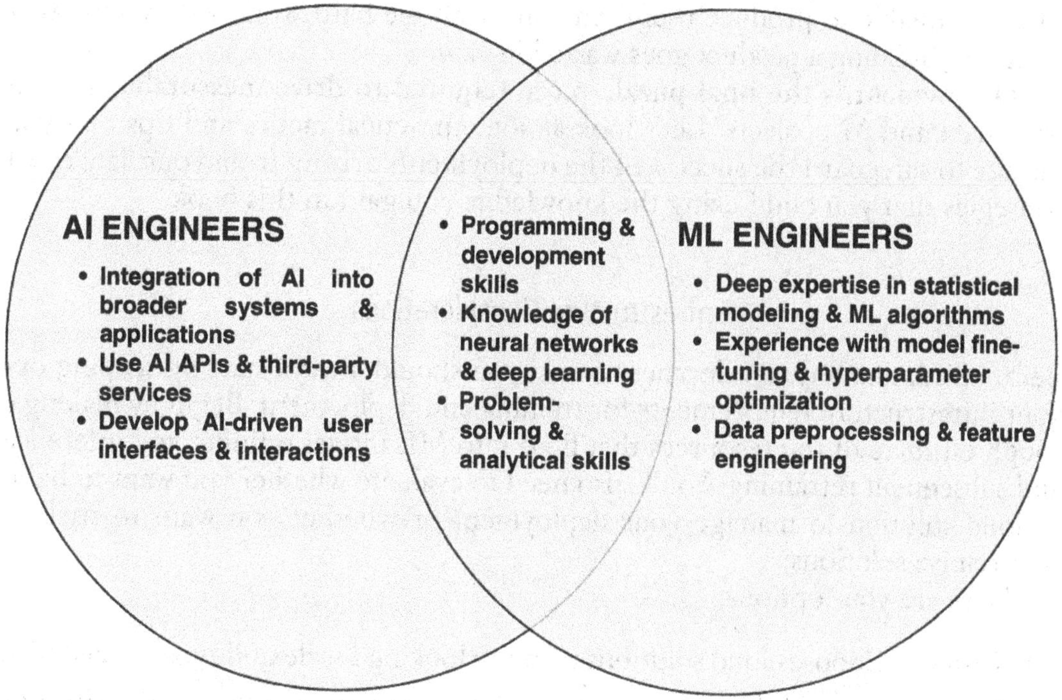

AI ENGINEERS

- Integration of AI into broader systems & applications
- Use AI APIs & third-party services
- Develop AI-driven user interfaces & interactions

- Programming & development skills
- Knowledge of neural networks & deep learning
- Problem-solving & analytical skills

ML ENGINEERS

- Deep expertise in statistical modeling & ML algorithms
- Experience with model fine-tuning & hyperparameter optimization
- Data preprocessing & feature engineering

FIGURE 8.1 ML engineers vs. AI engineers.

While it's true that fullstack developers can use APIs to build light-weight predictive or generative features, to build an application that's heavily powered by foundation models, you'll generally need to hire an AI engineer or an ML engineer, or both. Figure 8.1 illustrates what you need to know about the differences between these roles.

Depending on your organization's structure and the complexity of the project, the distribution of tasks between AI and ML engineers will differ between companies.

Important Considerations When Deploying AI

In my experience as a consultant, one thing consistently rings true: teams excel at every step of the ML model-building process except deployment. They tend to find it difficult to bring the solution together and package it effectively for third-party use. This is problematic for many reasons, the most obvious being that, when a team is unable to produce useful outcomes, all the hard work and expense that went into building a product goes wasted in vain.

Deployment is the final puzzle piece required to drive measurable growth from data and AI projects. Let's look at some practical tactics and tips that you can use to safeguard the success of the deployments arising from your data or AI strategies that you build using the knowledge you gain in this book.

Infrastructure Considerations

Before initiating any development work, you should always start by scoping out your infrastructure requirements for training and deployment. Begin by making a rough estimate of the resources that'll go into ML model training and inference and subsequent retraining. You'll also need to evaluate whether you want to build a cloud solution to manage your deployment or whether you want to stick to on-premise solutions.

Here are your options:

- **Cloud**—Choose cloud solutions if you're looking for flexibility and scalability.
- **On-premise**—If data security and connectivity are a concern, go with on-premise solutions. This will require a significant investment in hardware such as GPU and servers, network infrastructure, storage, and security.
- **Hybrid**—Consider a hybrid solution as well. This may look something like training your ML model using cloud resources like Google's A2 VM or AWS EC2 and then deploying your model using on-premise resources. (This config would save you money on expensive GPUs, by the way.)

When deploying a solution, you'll also need to consider the following rules of thumb:

- **Simplicity**—You want to facilitate simpler management of the ML model.
- **Consistency**—There should always be consistency in the environments across which the models run.
- **Reproducibility**—Deterministic models are non-random mathematical models, the outcome of which are precisely determined by known relationships between variables. The models are reproducible, meaning that anyone should be able to run them repeatedly and always get the same results. To achieve reproducibility, use containerization and orchestration.

Tip

You can use Docker for packaging the ML model and its dependencies into a container that'll run reliably across different environments. Kubernetes is a great tool for orchestration, where you can manage the configuration, coordination, and scaling of the containers on a very large scale across clusters to ensure reliability.

Strategies for Deploying ML Models

The process of deploying ML models should be seamless, and it should be designed such that it doesn't affect third-party performance. There are several techniques available to help you facilitate this when deploying your ML models for third-party usage. The following are some of the more popular strategies you'll want to consider:

- **Shadow evaluation**—With shadow evaluation, you run a new model in parallel to an existing one, but you don't use the output of this new model—be it classification, clustering, or prediction.

- **A/B testing**—With A/B tests, half the requests would go to one model and the other half to another model. You'll see which ones work better in a real-world scenario using the metrics that you have selected for evaluation.

- **Multi-arm bandits**—This is just like A/B testing, but instead of deciding on a model at the end, you decide it on the fly based on its performance.

- **Blue-green deployment**—With blue-green deployment, you have two identical production environments, and you gradually shift the traffic from one environment (say, blue) to another (green). If the model doesn't perform well at a later stage, you can always roll back to the original (blue) production environment.

- **Rolling deployment**—In this approach, you gradually replace instances of the old model with the new version, allowing both versions to run in parallel. This process involves incrementally updating instances until all are running the new model. This method helps in minimizing downtime and allows for testing the new model's performance and stability as it progressively takes over from the old one.

- **Re-create strategy**—This deployment approach involves completely replacing the old model with a new version, which results in significant downtime. This method is typically used when there are major changes in the model's architecture or when a complete retraining of the model is necessary. During the deployment, the old model is taken offline, and the new model is launched. During the transition, you'll experience a disruption of service until the new model is fully operational.

If you want a risk-free testing of new models without affecting your current operations in any way, then choose shadow evaluation. Alternatively, A/B testing lets you directly compare two models with real user traffic to determine the better performer. The multi-arm bandits method is a much more dynamic approach but works very similar to A/B testing except that you're deciding which model receives more traffic based on how it's performing in a live setting.

In my opinion, you should stick to blue-green deployment if you need high availability and a reliable fallback option. But if your scenario requires even small amounts of downtime, then stick with rolling deployment. The re-create strategy model is only really helpful if you're doing major updates as previously described.

Continuous Monitoring and Maintenance of ML Systems

To manage ML systems in an effective manner, you'll need to devote ongoing attention to their performance and reliability. Let's look at some key strategies for maintaining these systems.

Monitoring Model Performance   It's really important for you to monitor the performance of ML models over time using predetermined metrics, such as accuracy, precision, recall, or other domain-specific metrics. Model performance may deteriorate over time, which can be due to several factors, including data drift. Data drift occurs when there are changes in the underlying input data, leading to model outputs that are no longer accurate or relevant.

Regular monitoring helps you to identify these issues early so that you can make timely adjustments or retrain the model. This is one way to make sure that your model remains effective and accurate. Always account for these changes to maintain the reliability and usefulness of your ML system.

Managing Resource Utilization   Another factor that's commonly overlooked is the variation in resource utilization over time. Teams should regularly evaluate whether resource usage is increasing. If it is, then you need to determine whether this increase is due to issues like memory leakage or inefficiencies in model architecture. Such considerations directly impact the cost efficiency and scalability of ML systems.

Tip

If you're facing performance issues with your model, you need to take a look at the bottlenecks. Start by logging the key areas to identify where resource utilization is at its maximum. Optimization techniques that you can try include compression techniques like quantization or pruning. Quantization is where you reduce the model's numerical precision and pruning is where you remove unimportant parameters to simplify the model. Resource leaks are another cause of performance issues. If you notice resource leaks, they can be due to memory leaks, unclosed database connections, or orphaned processes in some cases.

Ensuring Model Maintenance   Model maintenance is another core component that you must address. To accommodate for data drift that's caused by changes in data distribution, label drift, and other real-world scenarios, you need to plan to periodically retrain the model using both new and existing data. Additionally, if there is an increasing demand, adjustments may need to be made to the data pipeline to handle this influx in an effective manner. If you introduce new data that differs substantially from previous sets, you'll need to fine-tune the model with the new dataset.

Note

User feedback is an important driver for model retraining. Incorporating feedback can help in aligning the model more closely with user needs and expectations.

Security and Compliance Considerations

As mentioned in Chapter 7, there's a possibility that an ML model's output has confidential information or perpetuates bias. This risk becomes much more pronounced in the case of foundation models, where there's a high risk of bias or misinformation in the model output. To mitigate these risks, you need to address the following issues in your model training and deployment activities:

- **Encryption**—If the inference of the model contains any kind of sensitive information, you'll need to flag and either remove that information from the training set or use differential privacy methods that add noise to the query results and by doing so, add a layer of obfuscation and privacy to individual entities represented in the source data.

- **Anonymization**—Consider implementing k-anonymity and l-diversity to anonymize personal information. k-anonymity protects anonymity by ensuring that each individual's data is indistinguishable from at least k-1 other individuals, while l-diversity does so by ensuring diversity of sensitive attributes within each group.

- **Compliance**—Stay updated on the latest compliance guidelines, such as data privacy laws in your jurisdiction and make provisions for model retraining, if that's required.

The preceding issues are more common in generative models than in ML models, but similar issues can also arise in ML model deployments. Prevention is better than cure. The issues are best resolved in the initial stages of model training instead of waiting until they appear later on. I'll cover security measures in greater depth in Chapter 13.

Note

Model inversion attacks are becoming an increasingly popular way for hackers to extract and infer personal information from a model's output through techniques like reverse engineering. In this case, you can use federated learning during the model training process. That is, instead of sending the data to the learning algorithm, you'd do exactly the opposite by sending the learning algorithm to various decentralized data sources. With this approach, the model learns on each of the local data and then all the learnings are appended to the global model.

Model Explainability

Model explainability is an increasingly popular topic today because, well, we need to be able to understand what prompted an AI model to output a certain result, or to make a specific "decision." When you're able to trace the output of the model back to the data source or a specific instance of labeled data, you can identify which parameters caused it to output a specific result.

Teams often fail to address model explainability early on during the pre- and post-deployment phases. Failure to address explainability factors early on in a deployment results in much more complex problems when building with foundation models. This is because foundation models typically behave in nonintuitive ways. We'll look at model explainability for ML models and LLMs in much more detail in Chapter 13 and then go through some tools you can use to address the model transparency issue in Chapter 17.

Choosing the Right Technology Stack for Your Deployment

Always pre-plan your entire tech stack before you journey into the model building and deployment phase. Be sure to make plans for your user interface and backend components while you're at it. While there's no one-size-fits-all stack that'll give you the best performance, efficiency, and scalability, there are some proven and tested combinations. Let's take a look at a few common types of tech stacks and how you can go about choosing between them.

Lightweight Web Applications

If you need to build lightweight applications like recommendation systems, predictive systems, or chatbots for customer support, then you may want to consider using the following technologies:

- **Frontend**—HTML, CSS, JavaScript with frameworks like React or Vue.js for interactive UIs
- **Backend**—Flask or Django
- **AI/ML frameworks**—TensorFlow.js for browser-based model inference and scikit-learn for basic ML models
- **Deployment**—AWS Elastic Beanstalk for easy scaling and management

Enterprise-Level Scalable Applications

If you need to build complex enterprise applications for object detection in real time, health monitoring, or predictive maintenance for a shop floor, then you might want to consider using the following technologies:

- **Backend frameworks**—PyTorch with TorchServe for efficient model serving
- **Containerization**—Docker for containerizing applications and Kubernetes for orchestration
- **Cloud services**—AWS SageMaker, Azure ML, or Google's Vertex AI for managed ML services with scalability and integration options
- **Data processing**—Apache Kafka for real-time data streams

Remember that enterprise-level scalable applications require a lot of computing power for model inference. Enterprise-level applications may also be real-time applications that have strict requirements around processing time and require close to real-time inferencing to be able to operate. This is especially true of object detection-based use cases in real time.

Object detection applications are heavyweight and need scaling with changing needs, so the preceding stack will support them more effectively than would traditional on-premise solutions and monolithic architectures.

Mobile Applications

If you need to build mobile applications for simple tasks like image recognition, speech recognition, music recognition, or other daily use products, you may want to consider using the following technologies:

- **Mobile development framework**—Swift for iOS, Kotlin for Android, or Flutter
- **AI frameworks**—TensorFlow Lite or Core ML for iOS to get a low latency
- **Backend**—FastAPI for lightweight scalable backend
- **Deployment**—AWS Amplify or Firebase for easy deployment

Internet of Things

If you're looking to build Internet of Things (IoT) solutions for predictive maintenance in manufacturing, inventory management, or industrial automation, you may want to consider using a specialized stack like one of the following:

- **Edge AI frameworks**—TensorFlow Lite for edge devices
- **Hardware**—Raspberry Pi and NVIDIA Jetson for edge devices
- **Connectivity**—AWS IoT Greengrass or Azure IoT Edge for managing deployments

Note

The preceding stacks are purely based on my experience working on different projects. However, you'll need to make your own decisions based on your use case, user requirements, and other important factors like scalability, performance, and budget. I'll show you how to do this in the chapters that follow.

Generative AI Applications

If you're looking to get some experience building with foundation models, you could build some fun applications with PartyRock from AWS. Later, when you have more experience, you can try the ChatGPT Playground by OpenAI. Then you can consider publishing your work on Hugging Face Spaces.

Cost Considerations: Build vs. Buy

Several cost factors come into play when you're deploying your AI model for external use. Your decision between a cloud, on-premise, or hybrid solution relies on the factors at the beginning of this chapter. You'll also want to consider:

- **Budget**—What capital is available to allocate toward development?
- **Speed**—What inference speed will be required? Do you need real-time responsiveness, or can your application tolerate some delay?
- **Scalability**—To what extent must your solution scale?

Table 8.1 highlights some cost factors associated with AI deployment and how you can decide between options.

Table 8.1   Cost Factors Associated with AI Deployment

Cloud	On-Premise	Hybrid
Infrastructure Cost Factor		
Scalable and flexible Can become expensive with more usage Follows a pay-as-you-go model **Cost: $$$$**	Very high up-front investment in hardware, server, storage, and network Cost-effective in the long-term unless there's a significant change in requirements Complete control over pricing and usage **Cost: $$**	Best of both cloud and on-premise solutions to use on-premise resources for data storage (ensures privacy) and using cloud solutions/ resources when you need additional computing power. **Cost: $$$**

(continued)

Table 8.1   Cost Factors Associated with AI Deployment (*continued*)

Cloud	On-Premise	Hybrid
Compute Resources Cost Factor		
Get access to advanced hardware resources based on your needs Save money on spot instances (unused instances that cost way less than on-demand instances) but with reduced reliability **Cost: $$**	Significant investment will go into GPUs/TPUs, but you'll have complete control over usage without worrying about instances not being available—which can happen in the case of cloud solutions sometimes if a specific GPU is in high demand for example. Based on future needs, you may have to keep upgrading your infrastructure to accommodate. **Cost: $$$$**	You can prefer using on-premise solutions for normal usage and switch over to the cloud when the demand is high to run model inference and pay only for the resources you've consumed. **Cost: $$$**
Data Storage Management Cost Factor		
Pay-as-you-go format for data storage as well. Your costs will go up with higher data volumes, but it's flexible. Though cloud solutions are very secure, you may be working with highly sensitive information where you'd like to implement your own data policies. **Cost: $$$**	The initial investment is large, and it's less flexible if there are more data storage requirements at a later stage. Choose this if you work with highly sensitive data. **Cost: $$$$**	Though this is complex to implement, you can place less sensitive data on the cloud and highly confidential data on-premise and operate based on your requirements. **Cost: $$$**
Scalability Cost Factor		
You can scale the solution based on your needs, but the costs will increase significantly. **Cost: $$$**	You'll need to invest further each time based on your needs, which can become expensive over time. **Cost: $$$**	You can run sensitive operations on-premise and general tasks on the cloud. **Cost: $$$**

Speed and Efficiency

When it comes to the speed and efficiency of AI deployments, there are quite a few set-in-stone strategies that can guarantee success. One such strategy is to implement a continuous integration and continuous deployment (CI/CD) pipeline to streamline your testing and deployment process.

Continuous integration ensures that code changes made by any team member are automatically verified through a suite of predefined tests. These tests may include unit tests, integration tests, and any other custom tests that you have specified. So, the model will be evaluated on a validation dataset (or unseen data), and the results will then be compared against a set of performance metrics to make sure it meets the threshold values you've defined. This process helps maintain the integrity and functionality of the project as it evolves.

If all the tests are successful and the conditions are met, then this model is automatically deployed to a staging environment. This means you're saving time that would have otherwise gone into manually performing all these steps over and over again. This process is risk-free as you'll be able to roll back to a previous version if something goes wrong.

Deploying AI with Agile and DevOps Principles

Agile and DevOps principles are the cornerstone of software development, and it can be beneficial to adapt the same philosophy for AI deployments. Let's extend these five core principles to cover key considerations in AI deployments:

- **Iterative development and continuous feedback**—Agile methodologies propose frequent iterations of development that allow for continuous feedback and adjustments. This is really important for AI deployment, which often requires you to adapt to problems like data drift and model degradation.

- **Collaboration**—DevOps focuses on collaboration between developers, operations, and quality assurance teams. In our case, this means data scientists, AI researchers, and IT operations teams who are working together to successfully deploy and maintain AI models in production environments.

- **Automation**—By automating the deployment pipeline as much as possible, you can reduce errors and delays. When deploying your model, you'll want to focus on automating data ingestion, model training, testing, and the rollout of models to production.

- **Continuous monitoring**—DevOps relies on monitoring to ensure software performance and health. In the same manner, AI deployments can benefit from monitoring model performance, data quality, and predefined metrics.

- **Scalability**—DevOps principles dictate that you have a plan for the scalability of your AI application and that you remain continually equipped for its future needs.

Table 8.2   Common Pitfalls Related to AI Deployment and Best Practices

Pitfall	Best Practice
Deploying manually	Use the CI/CD principle. You can use GitLab CI/CD for continuous integration and Jenkins X for continuous deployment.
Lack of a deployment strategy	Consider different strategies listed in this chapter to choose one that seamlessly switches usage from the old to the new model without or with minimum downtime.
Failure to monitor the ML system	Define a full-fledged strategy to monitor hardware and resource consumption, implement a feedback loop, and address model degradation due to data drift by continuous monitoring and retraining/fine-tuning. You can use Prometheus for system monitoring and then link with Grafana for visualization of the logged data. You can use Kubeflow Pipelines for automated model retraining.
Lack of scalability	Build an architecture that you can scale easily based on your demand. The best way to go about this is to use a cloud solution that'll give you the flexibility to scale up or down based on current demand.
Ignoring security and compliance	Consider three core factors throughout the entire AI life cycle: security, privacy, and compliance. These issues are best addressed in the earlier phases.
Not deploying with proper testing and validation	Conduct extensive testing on real-world datasets in the testing environment before deploying the model for external use.

Common Pitfalls and Best Practices

Model deployment can be challenging for a wide variety of reasons, including, but not limited to, the complex nature of changing input data, the resource utilization conundrum, the lack of a proper strategy in place, and changing security and compliance guidelines. Table 8.2 lists some common pitfalls you might encounter and how you can navigate them with ease.

Considerations When Building with Foundation Models

While it's true that most of the advice I've provided for ML deployment will also apply when building with foundation models, there are additional factors you should keep in mind when working with foundation models.

Practical Tactics for Success in the Deployment of Foundation Models

You might wonder how these tactics are any different from the ones that we've already seen. Trust me, when you're working with foundation models/generative models, you'll want to be extra careful! It can be like playing with fire, especially when it comes to AI ethics, compliance, and security.

These additional strategies will help you identify whether there are any risks associated with your development from its inception, so you don't end up spending loads of money and resources on a project that was doomed from the start. By making sure you have a basic understanding of foundation models and their implications in deployment, you are doing due diligence before getting involved.

Build Scalable and Flexible Infrastructure Foundation models are computationally much more expensive than traditional ML models due to their size and the complexity of operations, so you'll have to make additional considerations when you're deploying one for external use. Remember, you'll need to be able to handle multiple inference requests at once from multiple users. My advice of using cloud solutions stands true for these use cases—especially because making provisions for on-premise infrastructure can be very expensive

Be Wary of Model Bias Chapter 7 discussed how generative models amplify the bias that's inherently present in the training data. Once the model is deployed, your end users would typically prompt it with their queries, and you should ensure that the model's output is fair and responsible. You'll learn about different ways of doing this in Chapter 13.

Address Model Security Adversarial attacks (like model inversion attacks) are much more common in the case of foundation models due to their inherent black-box nature. This also makes it notoriously difficult to determine and address points of exploitation. So, you'll need to have strong security measures throughout the AI life cycle.

Ensure Compliance With several data privacy laws, such as GDPR, HIPAA, or CCPA, and the implications of generative models with respect to intellectual property infringement (see Chapter 7), your company needs a strong ethics and compliance team. When building with foundation models, it also becomes increasingly important to monitor and log model outputs in order to find areas of noncompliance and potential problems.

Implement Continuous Monitoring   Continuous monitoring of generative models (or foundation models) can palliate some issues such as bias, misinformation, breach of privacy, and IP infringement issues. Though you can use tools like Fairlearn to help improve the fairness of AI systems, I always advocate for human intervention in these cases. With the aid of AI tools, once deployed, a team can regularly determine if the model's output is in violation of the rules established around bias and misinformation, and then flag them for further analysis.

Considerations When Deploying Retrieval-Augmented Generation

In Chapter 2, you learned about LLMs and customizing their knowledge base using RAG. What I didn't mention there was that, to be successful with RAG, you need a solid strategy for selecting reliable information sources. With RAG, the quality of your information sources directly impacts the accuracy and reliability of the content that you generate. It's the principle of garbage in, garbage out.

As mentioned in Chapter 7, the data sources you use can significantly impact the output of the model. So using high-quality input data (with regular audits) gets you output based on credible and trustworthy sources. Having a well-defined strategy for selecting these sources can minimize the risk of misinformation or biased content in the model's output. This improves the user experience, satisfaction, and, most importantly, trust.

My three favorite best practices for selecting reliable information sources to improve RAG performance are as follows.

Chunking and Indexing with Advanced Retrieval

This best practice involves preprocessing data through chunking. *Chunking* is the process of breaking down text into manageable segments for storage in embedding vectors. This involves using indexing methods, such as using multiple indexes for different user questions and guiding them to the right index using an LLM.

The following advanced retrieval methods are useful for improving the retrieval process outcomes:

- **Cosine similarity**—By measuring the cosine of the angle between vectors to determine their similarity, this method is helpful for locating documents that are contextually similar to the query.

- **BM25**—By probabilistically ranking documents based on the frequency and distribution of query terms within them, this method improves the relevance of documents returned.

- **Custom retrievers**—Custom retrievers are tailored to specific datasets or user needs, and generally improve the precision and relevance of query results.

- **Knowledge graphs**—By capturing and quantifying relationships between entities within a dataset, knowledge graphs provide semantic context that significantly improves retrieval accuracy and relevance.

You can improve the accuracy and relevance of the gathered information by reranking these results and using query transformations.

Employing Domain-Specific Pretraining and Fine-Tuning

This best practice focuses on tailoring the AI's training to specific domains by extending the original training data, fine-tuning the model, and integrating it with external sources of domain-specific knowledge.

Domain-specific pretraining involves building models that are pretrained on a large data corpus that represents a wide range of use cases within a specific domain. Fine-tuning these models on a narrower dataset that's tailored for more specific tasks within the domain tends to improve RAG performance and also reduces the limitations associated with parametric knowledge (e.g., context inaccuracy and the potential for generating misleading information).

Improving RAG Performance by Integrating with Non-Parametric Knowledge

The third technique addresses the limitations of LLMs by combining their parametric knowledge with external, non-parametric knowledge from an information retrieval system. Passing this knowledge as additional context within the prompt to the LLM can help you significantly limit hallucinations and increase the accuracy and relevancy of responses. This approach updates the knowledge base without changing the LLM parameters, so you can provide responses that cite sources for human verification. This is increasingly popular with GPT-4, Perplexity, and Bing, where you'll also get the sources that the model referred to generate the response. We'll see some instances of using RAG-powered AI tools for search in Chapter 9.

Together, these three best practices improve the accuracy, reliability, and context relevance of responses generated by RAG systems.

Now that we've explored one of the trickiest areas yet, AI deployment, we can move on to Chapter 9, where we'll review the details that will help you build your AI strategy from scratch.

Recommended Reading

SWYX & Alessio (June 30, 2023). The Rise of the AI Engineer. *Latent Space Substack.* https://www.latent.space/p/ai-engineer

PART

The Technical Foundation
for Growth

CHAPTER

9

Surveying Your Industry and Organization

If you want to understand today, you have to search yesterday.

– Pearl Buck

Thus far you've learned volumes about data strategy in general, and its specific role in leveraging data and AI to drive business growth. You've seen a handful of use cases that illustrate the power of data and AI in accelerating growth. You've learned the foundational knowledge about AI ethics and deployment that you need to build and oversee the execution of data and AI strategies.

Now, it's time to dig into the nitty-gritty details that are involved in actually building an enterprise data or AI strategy from scratch. If you recall the STAR Framework that I introduced in Chapter 2, we're now entering the "Survey" pillar of that framework. This is where you'll survey your industry and select the use cases that are likely to offer the highest ROI given your organization's current state.

Generative AI-Powered Market Research

Before looking at the requirements involved in tech assessments and use case evaluation, I want to take a small detour to help you streamline the market research work I'll be prescribing in the second half of this chapter. In Chapter 2, you learned of numerous uses for RAG-powered LLMs. Of those, you'll recall a use case where you can get LLMs to return up-to-date information directly from the internet, complete with reference sources to boot. I'd like to point out how you can use this feature to your advantage in the market research required to identify relevant use cases and case studies for your data strategy.

Traditionally, when looking for use cases or case studies, you'd have to start by browsing the internet. While this manual research method is slow and lends itself to vast omissions, it was the only research method available to most people in years past. Of course, more effective research methods have been around for years, but it was mostly only market research experts who knew how to utilize those.

Exploring the Benefits of Generative AI-Enabled Research

The good news is that, with advancements in generative AI, everyday people have access to much more effective research results, without being required to take a course on market research. Table 9.1 details the benefits associated with using generative AI for market research.

Table 9.1   Traditional Internet Research vs. Generative AI-Enabled Research

Traditional Browser Search	GenAI-Enabled Search
Search browsers rely on keywords and phrases that are input by the user. These search terms often require multiple manual refinements for best results.	LLMs interpret context and nuance from the users' prompts in order to enable more accurate responses to complex queries.
Users must sift through search results manually to find the most relevant information.	LLMs with internet access provide synthesized summaries of the most relevant and current sources, with links to those direct sources.
Search results are ranked based on algorithms that may prioritize popularity or paid placements over relevance.	Internet-enabled LLMs do not have forced algorithmic ranking of search results and instead prioritize the direct relevance of findings to the user based on their prompt.

When it comes to using generative AI for market research, I can vouch for the quality of the GPT-4, Perplexity, and You.com tools.

Never entirely rely on an AI search engine for your research. These tools should only serve as a starting point for your survey. Think of these research results as a gentle footing upon which you'll further build your research. Make sure to double-check the references that these tools provide. AI models frequently hallucinate and return completely made-up information that looks legitimate.

With generative AI-enabled market research, you'll spend much less time on the searching bit, so you can allocate more time toward actually learning from the research papers, case studies, and journals that have been automatically returned to you by the tool.

Companies that offer AI search engine products need to make money, too. To incentivize paid subscriptions, these companies will either not include access to the internet in their free versions or they'll use a lower quality LLM for searching live internet data. In the former case, the tool may return outdated results, depending on what the cut-off date for the model is. In the latter case, the results returned by the tool will often be irrelevant to your needs. For detailed research of use cases and case studies, consider purchasing the pro version of generative AI tools that offer internet access.

Demonstrating Generative AI-Enabled Market Research

Let's quickly look at how to use common generative AI research tools. The following example shows a prompt you can use to research use cases for analytics and AI in the healthcare sector.

Use Case Research Prompt

"Give me a list of two use cases for data analytics and AI in the healthcare sector from the period of 2020–2024.

(continued)

(continued)

Requirements:

- Research results must originate from work done in the U.S.A.
- ONLY provide reputable sources, blogs, and reports.
- ALWAYS provide the reference links that go with any results that you return."

Figure 9.1 shows the results that (paid) GPT-4 returns when prompted with the above.

And Figure 9.2 shows the results from the same prompt when using the free version of Perplexity.

If you study the results carefully, I'm sure you'll find reasons that support the opinion that the paid version of GPT-4 provides better research results than the free version of Perplexity. If you were to pay to upgrade to Perplexity Pro, however, you can expect the tool to provide improved results.

Lastly, I want to show you how to take the results from GPT-4 and further narrow them down so you can dig a bit deeper.

Use Case Research Refinement Prompt

"Of the results returned above, please provide more specific studies that meet the following requirements.
   Requirements:

- The topic MUST be about the use of generative AI in the healthcare sector and its implications.
- Sources must ONLY be from reputable scientific journals or research papers.
- The results must have been published between 2020 and 2024."

⑤ **ChatGPT**

Here are two use cases for data analytics and AI in the healthcare sector in the U.S.A. from 2020–2024, with the reference links included:

1. **Generative AI for Caregiver Assistance and Healthcare Operations:**
   - **Use Case**: Development and implementation of AI tools such as MedLM and Vertex AI Search, created by Google Cloud, for aiding caregivers in healthcare organizations.
   - **Impact:** These generative AI tools are designed to alleviate administrative burdens, help clinicians find information more efficiently, and reduce the cognitive load on healthcare providers by assisting with clinical documentation and analysis of medical results.
   - **Example:** HCA Healthcare is using generative AI to enhance nurse handoff processes, and Mayo Clinic has implemented gen AI-based enterprise search to improve access to healthcare information.
   - **Reference:** Google's blog on AI in healthcare in 2024.
2. **Real-Time Alerting and Predictive Analytics for Clinical Decision Support:**
   - **Use Case:** Use of Clinical Decision Support (CDS) systems equipped with real-time alerting and predictive analytics to offer immediate medical data analysis and guidance for healthcare practitioners.
   - **Impact:** Real-time data collected from wearable devices is utilized to alert medical staff to significant health changes in patients, allowing for timely medical intervention. This approach supports remote patient monitoring and helps in preventing emergency incidents.
   - **Example:** Collaboration between Blue Cross Blue Shield and Fuzzy Logix used big data analytics to identify potential opioid abuse risk factors, enabling preemptive healthcare measures.
   - **Reference:** Datapine's compilation of big data healthcare examples.

FIGURE 9.1 Using GPT-4 for market research.

Figure 9.3 shows the output from this refined prompt.

This review can serve as a comprehensive resource for understanding the state-of-the-art applications, challenges, and future directions of generative AI in healthcare.

As you can see in Figure 9.3, GPT-4 used the refinement prompt to successfully dig deeper and narrow down its output to a more specific subset. Now that you know how to use generative AI to lighten the load of your market research, let's move on to the data strategy development activities that are required for you to properly survey your industry and current state organization.

Conducting a Quick Tech Assessment

Before you jump into building a strategy, it's essential to get a snapshot of where your organization currently stands in terms of technology. This will inform your strategy and help you choose the most appropriate use cases on which to focus.

✳ **Answer**

Use Case 1: AI-Powered Diagnosis and Treatment Recommendations

AI has been successfully employed in the healthcare sector for diagnosis and treatment recommendations, outperforming human diagnostic accuracy and suggesting evidence-based treatment options. Machine learning algorithms analyze vast amounts of patient data, enabling early and accurate diagnoses [1][4]. This technology has been particularly beneficial in areas like medical imaging analysis, where AI-powered systems can quickly and accurately analyze MRI scans, ultrasounds, and other medical images, aiding in early and accurate diagnoses [4].

Use Case 2: AI-Driven Patient Data Processing and Remote Patient Assistance

AI has been instrumental in automating administrative tasks and digitizing medical data, allowing healthcare professionals to focus on critical cases and improving patient care and accessibility [1][4]. Telemedicine powered by AI enables real-time consultations and preliminary diagnoses, enhancing healthcare accessibility, especially in remote areas [1][4]. AI-driven patient data processing has also led to the development of AI-powered chatbots that can assist patients with self-diagnosis or support doctors in diagnosis, providing personalized care and reducing costs [2].

References:

[1] https://tateeda.com/blog/ai-in-healthcare-use-cases

[2] https://research.aimultiple.com/healthcare-ai-use-cases/

[4] https://gloriumtech.com/top-5-use-cases-for-ai-in-healthcare/

FIGURE 9.2 Using the free version of Perplexity.ai for market research.

🌀 **ChatGPT**

Here is a specific study that meets the criteria provided:

Study Title: A Comprehensive Review of Generative AI in Healthcare.

- **Authors**: Yasin Shokrollahi, Sahar Yarmohammadtoosky, Matthew M. Nikahd, Pengfei Dong, Xianqi Li, Linxia Gu
- **Submitted**: October 1, 2023
- **Abstract:** This review paper provides an extensive overview of the applications of generative AI models, specifically transformers and diffusion models, in healthcare. These models are applied in medical imaging, protein structure prediction, clinical documentation, diagnostic assistance, radiology interpretation, clinical decision support, medical coding, and drug design. The paper discusses how these applications have significantly improved clinical diagnosis, data reconstruction, and drug synthesis. It also addresses current challenges and proposes future research directions.
- **Reference:** arXiv:2310.00795v1

FIGURE 9.3 GPT-4 output from the refinement prompt.

To initiate your data strategy planning efforts, you need to do a quick tech assessment, wherein you'll readily identify what technologies are available within your organization to support the implementation of new data-intensive use cases. This is a simple three-step process: inventorying your current technologies, assessing their capacities and limitations, and inventorying your current state data skillsets and resources.

Inventorying Your Current Technologies

The task at hand is to make a list of all tools, technologies, platforms, and hardware that your organization currently uses. Examples of such technologies include those related to cloud platforms, data analytics tools, CRM systems, and ML systems.

Note

The thing to keep in mind here is that you don't need an exhaustive list of every single technology, but you should capture key technologies, especially those related to data management, predictive analytics, and AI.

Assessing Your Technologies' Capacities and Limitations

For each technology, jot down its primary function, capabilities, and known limitations. For example, if you were assessing the capacity and limitations of PowerBI, then you might say something like this.

"The primary function of PowerBI is that it's a business intelligence tool built for visualizing data and sharing insights across an organization or by embedding them within an app or website.

The capabilities of PowerBI include:

- **Data visualization**—PowerBI provides robust data visualization tools that allow for the development of a wide variety of charts and dashboards.
- **User-friendly interface**—The interface is intuitive and this makes it easier for people with limited technical skills to create basic reports and dashboards.
- **High scalability**—PowerBI is capable of handling large datasets without a hiccup, thus making it suitable for both small and large enterprises.

Its limitations include:

- **Learning curve for advanced features**—While basic functions are easy to grasp, the advanced features involve a significant learning curve.
- **Cost**—The basic version is free, but advanced features and the ability to share dashboards peer-to-peer requires a paid license.
- **Data refresh limitations**—The free version of PowerBI has limitations on how often you can refresh the data."

As you can see, this quick assessment example provides an overview of Power BI's strengths and weaknesses, which can then be used to inform decisions on whether it would be suitable for a potential use case you're evaluating within your data strategy planning process.

Inventorying the Current State Data Skillsets and Resources

Make a list of the human capital your organization currently has available to execute any potential data strategy requirements. Quickly list all the skills that you believe they have to support your project.

Keep it simple. There's no need to survey or interview team members at this time. In this stage, you are just making a quick estimate of current state capabilities.

Also, list all the different data resources that your company currently has available to leverage in a new data project. Look for quick wins in terms of time-to-value. If you have clean datasets that are ready to go, those represent a definitive advantage over messy datasets that will need to be cleaned and reformatted.

When creating a quick catalog of data resources, it often helps to list resources according to category. For example, first, create a list of the structured datasets that are available, followed by unstructured, and then semi-structured. Working in this way helps to force your memory into recalling items you might otherwise forget.

Spend about 45 minutes completing this task. You'll refer back to the documentation you produce here as you proceed through the rest of the data strategy building process.

Next, we'll look at case study research, then use case research, and then request for information.

Identifying Appropriate Case Studies

Case studies provide context, inspiration, and proof of concept for the data initiative you're planning. They show practical applications of data or AI in addressing issues like the ones at hand within your organization. They underscore the practical challenges and benefits of different approaches. Consequently, when you review case studies in the manner described below, you'll develop clear and articulate insights to guide your data strategy development.

Case studies also provide evidence to support your plan and convince stakeholders of the value of your initiative. They help to demonstrate that your ideas are both theoretically sound and that they've been successfully implemented in practice.

My objectives for you in this section are three-fold:

1. Learn how to research relevant case studies online.
2. Identify and categorize the business objectives of each case study.
3. Learn to extract valuable information from case studies to inform your data strategy.

Researching Case Studies

Using traditional research methods, or the generative AI research method shown earlier in this chapter, you'll need to conduct market research around case studies that are relevant to your current state organization.

Best practices for this research include:

- **Sources**—Search for case studies from reputable sources, such as industry reports, academic journals, and highly credible blogs.
- **Keywords**—Use keywords that are relevant to your project and industry. For example, if you're focusing on data analytics in healthcare, keywords might include "*healthcare data analytics case study*" or "*patient data analytics.*"

Tip

Make sure that the case studies are recent enough to be relevant to your current project.

Categorizing Cases by Business Objectives

After you've identified interesting case studies, you need to categorize them according to their primary business objective. Table 9.2 describes types of business objectives that are typically served by case studies and use cases.

Extracting Information from Case Studies

For a case study to be useful, you should be able to extract from it the following four elements:

- **Situation summary**—This describes the context in which the business found itself before implementing the solution.
- **Challenges**—This describes the obstacles and issues the business was facing.

Table 9.2   Case Types by Business Objective

Case Type	Business Objective
Operational improvements cases	Improving operational efficiency
Marketing improvements cases	Growing and improving marketing ROI
Decision-support cases	Improving decision-making across the company
Data monetization cases	Monetizing data resources, technologies, or skill sets
Finance cases	Improving financial data analysis or driving other fiscal improvements
Product growth cases	Optimizing product features, improving user experience, and driving growth

- **The solution**—This provides a detailed explanation of the data strategies and technologies employed to address the challenges.

- **The results**—This describes quantifiable metrics or qualitative outcomes showing the impact of the implemented solution.

If a case study doesn't provide this level of detail, it's too general and should be discarded. Try to identify at least five potential case studies before moving on to use case research.

Once you've looked at potential case studies, you've already done a substantial amount of research and in-depth analysis on what is or is not possible. Now, it's time to look into use cases to learn more about how particular data solutions were successfully deployed in the past. Your findings here will further guide your design and strategy development.

Researching and Identifying Appropriate Use Cases

In addition to case studies, we'll be utilizing use cases as strategic templates for potential data initiatives you may want to consider implementing. This research helps you evaluate and select potential use cases for your organization's current capabilities and objectives in order to drive both immediate and long-term business growth.

Having clearly defined use cases is helpful in several ways:

- It allows you to align your data initiatives with business goals so every data-related action contributes to broader organizational objectives.

- It informs the requirements for technology, tools, and methodologies. Each use case requires unique types of data, levels of data quality, and analytical techniques. You need to know how feasible a use case is for your organization based on its current state capabilities.

- It helps set the scope for necessary data governance and management policies to ensure data privacy, security, and compliance with regulations.

Let's look at how to identify, categorize, and extract insights from use cases, which will be valuable to your own data strategy planning. The process and best practices involved in researching use cases are almost identical to those involved in case study research. The steps are as follows:

- **Use case research**—Refer to the previous section on researching case studies for my recommendations on conducting use case research.

- **Categorization by business objectives**—Once you've found potentially helpful use cases, it's time to categorize them by their primary business objectives. Refer to Table 9.2 for classifications of cases by business objective.

- **Extracting useful information**—For a use case to be beneficial to your data strategy, you must be able to identify the following six elements:
  - *Actors*—Who are the main parties interacting with the system?
  - *Pre-conditions & post-conditions*—What must be true before and after the use case is executed?
  - *Main success scenario*—What is the primary pathway for fulfilling the use case's objectives?
  - *Industries* and *functions*—Which industries and business functions are impacted by or involved in this use case?
  - *Business use case diagram*—Do you have enough information to at least create a diagram that visually represents the flow and interactions of the use case?
  - *Technology specifications*—Do some research into the organization and try to identify the technical requirements, such as platforms, software, or hardware that's utilized in support of each use case.

Note

Regarding technology specifications, you can often uncover this information by looking at the technology requirements that a company specifies in its position descriptions on job board websites.

Try to identify at least 10 promising use cases before moving on to the next step in this process. Once you've listed 10 use cases, you'll need to take a structured approach to gather more data that'll help inform your selection of potential use cases. Let's look at how to do that.

Warning

If you pinpointed a preliminary use case or case study earlier in this chapter, but find it lacking in the depth needed to formulate a comprehensive use case, then it's best to discard it from further consideration. While these cases may offer valuable insights into possible use cases for our data initiatives, those that lack sufficient information for even hypothetical use case development are inadequate for serving as foundational elements in our data strategy planning.

Extracting Relevant Information from Existing Documentation and Interviews

Before proceeding further into the data strategy planning process, you need to extract relevant information from existing documentation and interviews. This generally requires a simple Request for Information (RFI) from your sponsor.

In case you're brand new to the world of strategic consulting, a "sponsor" refers to an individual or group within the organization providing you the support, resources, and authority required to enable the successful execution of the data initiative you're planning.

The sponsor is typically a high-level executive or decision-maker who has a vested interest in the project's success and is responsible for championing the initiative within the organization.

An RFI to the sponsor would involve formally asking for access to existing documentation and information that is required for responsible data strategy planning. RFI responses will help you get an in-depth understanding of the organization's current data landscape, including its data sources, data management processes, and how data is currently being used in the organization.

RFI responses will also help uncover your organization's current data capabilities and limitations. This can be information pertaining to areas such as data quality, data integration, or data accessibility. Plus, these responses should provide you with the up-to-date information you'll need later in order to identify any potential legal, regulatory, or ethical issues that may lie on the horizon.

The following are some key documents and pieces of information that you should include in your RFI:

- **Mission and vision**—Clarity with respect to your organization's business vision and mission is crucial for aligning your data strategy with overarching organizational goals. These statements often provide the guiding light that informs what the business aims to achieve in the short-term and long-term.

- **Data inventory**—This is a comprehensive list of all the data assets that are available within the organization. If you haven't created this yet, it's high time for you to assemble one. Clarifying what data you have is the first step in figuring out what can be done with it.

- **Reference architecture**—This includes existing architecture diagrams or documents that show how your data systems are currently set up. Reference architecture provides a high-level view of your data ecosystem and helps you visualize how various components interact with each other.

- **Data governance, AI ethics, and data privacy policies**—These are sets of policies, procedures, and protocols that guide how data should be handled, secured, and utilized in an ethical manner. Make sure to collect any policies that pertain to:
  - Data access
  - Data quality
  - Data privacy and security
  - Data lifecycle management
  - Data compliance

Make sure you gather these policies from all parts of the organization.

- **Organizational chart**—An organizational chart provides a hierarchical structure of your organization and paints a clear picture of who is responsible for what. It's especially important for identifying key stakeholders, understanding departmental interrelationships, and knowing who to engage with during the strategy formulation.

- **Vendor list**—This is a list of all third-party vendors that provide software, hardware, or services that are related to data operations. Having this helps you identify dependencies, costs, and possible limitations or advantages that come with each vendor relationship.

- **Road maps for current projects**—You need an awareness of ongoing or upcoming projects that may intersect with your data strategy. This will help you to identify synergies, avoid conflicts, and ensure that your data strategy dovetails nicely with other initiatives.

Review all of this information before proceeding with the process of narrowing down your use cases that's presented next.

Identifying Your Best-Fit Use Cases

Let's look at how to go about identifying and selecting the top three use cases that best align with your organization's business objectives and data-related capabilities. At this point in the process, you should have identified at least 10 use cases that seem like promising fits to your organization's current needs. You've also completed an RFI and extracted findings to support your understanding of your organization's current data capabilities and limitations. You've preliminarily identified gaps and areas for improvement.

Based on the work you've done thus far, you now need to identify from your research the top three use cases that are most relevant to your business and its objectives. A use case-driven approach like this helps you prioritize your alternatives for potential data initiatives and connect them to business objectives. It'll increase the chances of successful adoption and high impact results.

Note

In this process, you're only using the use cases you've researched as references. You're not trying to replicate the use cases verbatim, as they need to be tailored to your business, its current state, and its objectives. In this process, use cases serve as clearly articulated concepts illustrating the success you're trying to emulate.

Identifying the three most relevant use cases can guide your data strategy, ensure that it aligns with business objectives, encourage stakeholder buy-in, and enable effective outcome measurements.

Note

Your evaluation at this point is cursory. You need to do your best to quickly estimate the feasibility of the use cases you're considering so you can select the three that seem most promising based on your current understanding of your organization.

After you've done some preliminary approximations to estimate which are your top three use cases, you'll next take those use cases and perform a more in-depth analysis of their feasibility in order to determine which are the most promising potential use cases for reaching your company's immediate and long-term growth targets.

Tip

The use cases you choose here should demonstrate clear business value. This will demonstrate the effectiveness of your early-stage data strategy planning process to stakeholders.

When selecting potential use cases, the goal is to zero in on three "low-hanging fruit" use cases that offer a high likelihood of quick success and clear business value. These potential use cases serve as examples to secure stakeholder buy-in for your data strategy.

Selection Criteria

For each of the 10 use cases you've deemed worthy of consideration, ensure that you analyze them based on the following key areas:

- **Business vision**—How does each use case align with your organization's mission, vision, and overarching business objectives?

- **Available data technologies**—Does your existing tech stack support the use case? Are there any gaps you'll need to address?

- **Available data skillsets**—Does your team have the skills needed for this use case? If not, consider the training and hiring that would be required.

- **Available data resources**—Do you have the data assets and computational resources needed to implement the use case?

Note

If the use cases or tech specs you are reviewing are not directly relevant to your industry or your organization's current state, brainstorm how they could be adapted to fit your specific needs.

Evaluation Steps

Once you've analyzed the use cases, it's time to evaluate them against the following factors before finally selecting a use case as one of your three potential use cases for use in further research and development.

The evaluation steps are as follows:

1. Consider the use case and your answers to the following questions:

   - **Relevance to business vision**—Is the use case aligned with your organizational goals?

   - **Relevance to data technologies**—Can your current technology stack accommodate the techniques and tools mentioned in the use case?

   - **Relevance to data skill sets**—Does your team have the know-how to implement the solutions outlined?

   - **Relevance to data resources**—Do you have similar types of data and the computational power required to execute the use case?

   - **Relevance to future growth**—Is the use case future-proof and sustainable in the long run? Would this use case create a competitive advantage?

2. Consider the technology specifications. Assess the technology needs outlined in the use case against your company's existing capabilities. This is crucial for determining the feasibility and ROI of potential use cases.

3. Declare potential use cases. If after having conducted these assessments, a use case still qualifies as a low-hanging fruit (meaning it could deliver quick wins with minimal complexity), label it as a "Potential Use Case."

For each potential use case, draft a statement defining its goals and objectives, and explains how it aligns with the organization's business objectives.

Bonus resource

Use the "Potential Use Case Documentation Worksheet" for this exercise. This worksheet is available for you to download for free at https://business growth.ai/.

Warning

If you are unable to identify three potential use cases from the collection of 10 use cases identified earlier in the process, then you need to iterate back and do further research to identify additional use cases that are relevant to your organization's needs. You should not proceed further into the planning process until you have at least three highly qualified potential use cases.

Additional Considerations for Generative AI Use Cases

Generative AI is so new that, honestly, it's pretty darn risky for you to recommend your company invest in such projects right now. There are an untold number of traditional use cases out there that have a much better track record in producing meaningful results.

This being said, business leaders tend to chase after shiny objects, so it's not unlikely for them to urgently mandate the development of a project or product built with foundation models. When considering such an undertaking, you'd use the same strategy-building process you'd take if you were developing a strategy to support a more traditional data solution. That said, it doesn't hurt for me to call out specific considerations you'll *really* want to make sure you take a good look at before making strategic recommendations for generative AI projects.

Before going too far down the path of building a strategy to support an AI solution that involves the use of foundation models, make sure you're comfortable with your answers to the following questions:

- Does the GenAI use case align with your organizational objectives? Is it sustainable over the long term?

- Does the GenAI use case augment your current processes? Is it adding more value, or can it contribute to a significantly improved user experience?

- Is the use case work feasible in light of the resources that your company currently has available?

- Can your company's existing technology stack support the GenAI use case? If not, what additional resources would be required?

- Is your company prepared to invest additional resources into deploying the data privacy and security that GenAI solutions require?

- GenAI use cases are fairly new, and there's not a lot of supportive material and talent out there for you to build off of. Are you and your superiors prepared for a long-term experimental undertaking that might not yield any useful results whatsoever?

These are some introductory questions that will set you up for the reality of building with foundation models. I'll discuss these considerations in much more detail throughout the remainder of this book. You don't need to have all the answers right away, but you should at least be paying them credence for the time being.

By meticulously following the steps outlined in this chapter, you'll be able to identify the most viable and impactful potential use cases. The level of meticulous detail here has the added benefit of helping you later build a persuasive argument for use case adoption, ensuring organizational alignment and stakeholder support. Once you have your three potential use cases, you're ready to move on to Chapter 10, where you'll dig into the assessment phase of the STAR Framework.

10

Perform a Technical Assessment

Data is a precious thing and will last longer than the systems themselves.

– Tim Berners-Lee

To select the winning use case around which to build your data strategy, you need to have clarity around your company's current data resources and technologies, as well as any opportunities or risks that are inherent to these assets. When you have a clear idea of the types of data your company works with, its sources, the ways that data is processed, the people who access different datasets, and how they're using it, then you can plan how to leverage data best to improve your company's bottom line. And how exactly do you identify areas of risk or opportunity? Via a thorough data and technical assessment, of course!

Before exploring the process involved in performing a technical assessment, consider a quick analogy to illustrate its significance. Imagine you're a homeowner, and you're inspecting your house in order to plan for renovations and maintenance. To do so, you'd begin by inspecting every room, utility, and structural element of your house. You'd want to make sure the rooms, furnishings, and appliances are all being used to their maximum potential. This will help you identify areas that are in actual need of renovation or maintenance. This could be perhaps modernizing an outdated kitchen or getting the plumbing redone. My point here is that you can apply the same analogy to a data leader who wants to take stock of their current data landscape in order to identify how they can use data resources and technologies in order to grow their company.

One key point I should mention here is that performing a technical assessment supports you in both identifying your current state needs and also any future state needs. This process goes a long way in helping you to "future proof" your company's data strategy, and it enables you to plan for scaling, thus helping you and your company stay ahead of the competition.

Evaluating Existing Data Inventory for Efficacy and Efficiency

When evaluating use cases and working to identify a winning use case for your data strategy, it's crucial to evaluate your existing data inventory for efficacy and efficiency. This supports you in building a successful data strategy by helping you optimize your data resources, establishing a foundation for data quality, and supporting you in identifying the use cases that can deliver the most immediate value.

This process involves taking stock of your existing data resources, assessing data quality, accessibility, relevancy, and how effectively data is being used in current processes. Going back to our house analogy. As part of your house renovation, you'd want to make sure every part of the house is in good condition and serves a specific purpose, right? The same can be said of data resources and the need to assess them before making data strategy recommendations.

The Importance of Evaluating Your Data Inventory

Evaluating your data inventory is a small yet crucial step that's required when assessing potential use cases. This step involves establishing and maintaining the inventory of data assets in order to make sure they are clearly documented and understood by yourself and others at your organization. There are several critical reasons you must evaluate your existing data inventory early on in your data strategy-building process.

- **Identifying data capabilities**—By evaluating your data inventory, you'll get a clear view of the type of data you have, how that data is being used in different use cases or processes, and where it can potentially add value. This helps to identify the use cases that are most feasible based on your current data.
- **Identifying data gaps**—This process can also highlight gaps in your data inventory, such as crucial data that is missing but would be necessary for the potential use cases you're considering. You'll need to address these gaps or issues before you go ahead with an implementation.

- **Assessing data quality**—The efficacy of any data-driven project is largely dependent on the quality of data across your company. By evaluating your data inventory, you can identify data quality issues and rectify them before they have a chance to impact the success of your data strategy.

- **Efficiency improvements**—Reviewing the efficiency of your company's current data usage can reveal opportunities for improvement. You may identify redundant data-gathering efforts, under-used data sources, or opportunities for automating manual data processes.

- **Identifying a winning use case**—In the context of selecting a winning use case, understanding your data inventory can help you identify which of the potential use cases can best be implemented given your existing data to provide immediate value to your organization.

How to Evaluate a Data Inventory

Evaluating the existing data inventory for efficacy and efficiency involves reviewing your data assets, their management, their usage, and how effectively they contribute to the overall business objectives. I recommend the following five steps.

Step 1: List Your Data Assets   Make a comprehensive list of all your data assets. This would be analogous to cataloging every item in your house, from furniture to appliances. This should include databases, data warehouses, spreadsheets, reports, and other data sources. For each item, document its source, who uses it, how often it's updated, its quality and reliability, and any associated costs.

Bonus resource

A sample data inventory is available for you to download for free at www.data-mania.com/book.

Step 2: Determine How Your Data Assets Are Used   The second step is to determine how each data asset is currently used. Which departments or teams access it? What decisions does it help with? What business objectives does it support? This will provide insights into the relevance and utility of each data asset. You can further bolster the insights that you get from this step by gathering feedback from different departments and teams on their everyday challenges related to data.

Bonus resource Database feeds are available for you to download for free at www.data-mania.com/book.

Step 3: Evaluate the Effectiveness of Your Data Assets   Evaluate how effective each data source is in meeting your business needs. Are the right people able to access and understand the data? Are there data sources that are duplicated or seldom used? Are there important decisions that could be better supported with data?

This step should include an evaluation of the data quality and the impact of that quality on decision-making. This step is crucial because data that is inaccurate, incomplete, outdated, or missing can cause you to miss out on trends and patterns and will impact the decisions you make.

Step 4: Evaluate the Efficiency of Your Data Processes   The fourth step is to look at the efficiency of your data processes. Are there delays in updating or accessing data? Are there unnecessary dataset duplications? Are there manual processes that could be automated? Are the data storage and management costs reasonable for the value provided?

Tip

Use process mining tools to analyze the event logs of your data systems. Doing this will help you identify whether there are inefficiencies in your data processes. You can automate repetitive and rule-based processes. For example, you could use data management systems to automate tedious tasks like data entry, cleaning, or report generation. Once you automate repetitive processes, you'll free up budget and employee hours for your team so that they can tend to more complex tasks.

Step 5: Perform a Gap Analysis   Finally, based on your evaluations, identify any gaps in your data capabilities. These gaps could include:

- Gaps in the data itself (e.g., missing data that could inform decision-making).
- Gaps in access (e.g., the right people can't access the data they need).

- Gaps in processes (e.g., inefficient or manual processes that could be automated).

- Gaps in integration (e.g., failures in bringing together data from different sources for a unified view).

- Gaps in security and privacy (e.g., vulnerabilities in the ways in which data is shared and accessed).

Then, based on your assessment of the data inventory, decide which use case seems most feasible at this time.

Note

At the end of this chapter, I've left a challenge for you to work on so you can get some practice assessing a sample dataset.

Reviewing and Assessing Existing Reference Architecture

Reference architecture is a blueprint that outlines the arrangement and interaction of your existing systems and data infrastructure, as well as standards for building scalable, reliable, and secure data management and processing infrastructures. Figure 10.1 shows an example of a reference architecture.

The reference architecture provides invaluable insights into how well your organization can support the proposed use cases. Your review and assessment of existing reference architecture is a fundamental step in evaluating use cases for a winning use case in your data strategy development.

Returning again to our house analogy, its foundation and structural integrity would be crucial factors to consider if you're planning for a renovation or extension. In the same way, evaluating existing reference architecture will help you understand if your systems are ready for new data initiatives. Failing to do this may result in inefficient processes, the introduction of additional risks, and ultimately, poor decision-making on your part.

Note

Following this STAR Framework process ensures that you de-risk your future data projects.

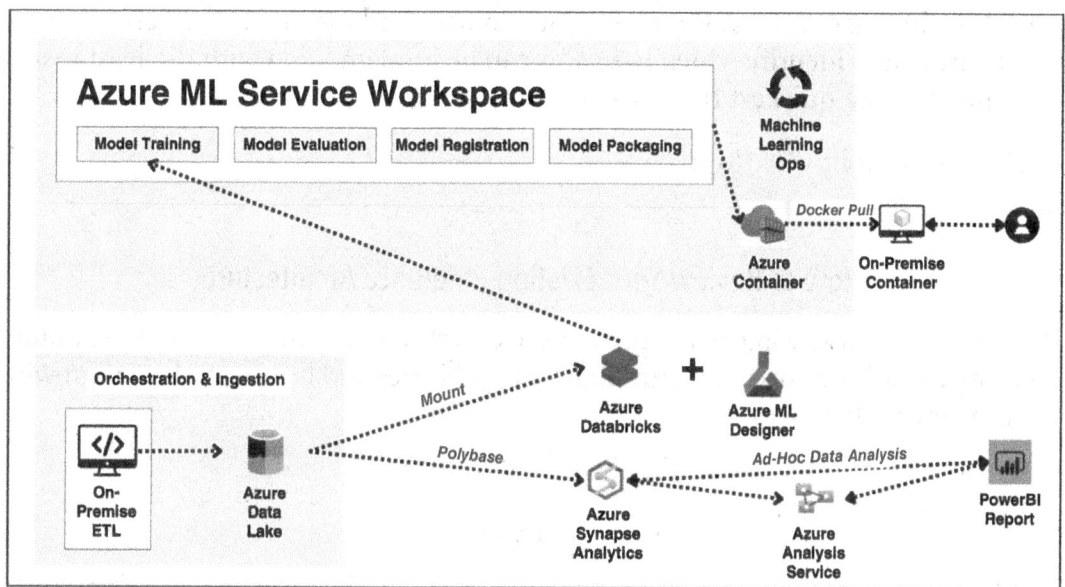

FIGURE 10.1 An example of a simple reference architecture.

The Importance of Reviewing Your Reference Architecture

Here are some reasons why it's important to assess your existing reference architecture before you plan to go forward with your selected use case:

- **Feasibility check**—Reviewing the reference architecture can reveal whether your current infrastructure can support a proposed use case. This helps you quickly assess feasibility and can save you time and resources by avoiding unworkable options.

- **Gap analysis**—An assessment of your architecture can highlight gaps or inadequacies in your systems, processes, and data flows. You can identify areas that may need to be upgraded or revamped before you can proceed with implementation.

- **Understanding impact**—By reviewing the architecture, you can assess the impact a potential use case would have on your existing systems. This provides early warnings of potential bottlenecks or performance issues. This also allows you to put risk mitigation plans in place.

- **Efficiency considerations**—Assessing your architecture often highlights inefficiencies that might hinder the success of your use case. Addressing these issues can improve the performance and outcomes of your chosen initiative.

- **Winning use case selection**—Your understanding of existing architecture helps you to identify which use cases can be implemented with the least resistance and the quickest time-to-value.

Let's look at how to do it.

How to Review Your Existing Reference Architecture

Reviewing and assessing existing reference architecture involves understanding your organization's current technological capabilities and how well they align with your business objectives.

> **Note**
>
> Before reviewing reference architecture, you should always have a firm grasp of the use cases you're considering. Chapter 9 covers what you need to know about identifying those potential use cases.

Assuming that you've got a firm handle on the potential use cases you're considering, here's a step-by-step approach that you can use to review and assess reference architecture for goodness of fit:

Step 1: Skim Your Existing Reference Architecture   Skim your existing reference architecture to ensure that you understand the individual components of the architecture, including software, hardware, data flows, and interfaces, as well as how they interconnect.

For example, Figure 10.1 illustrates a reference architecture showing the steps and services that form an integral part of building and deploying machine learning models using Azure's cloud services. When you review your existing reference architecture, you should ideally have something similar to Figure 10.1.

Step 2: Align Your Potential Use Cases with Your Reference Architecture
For each potential use case, map out how it would fit within the current architecture. Identify which components of the architecture support the use case and where modifications or additions might be necessary if you were to select that use case for implementation.

Step 3: Assess Your Architecture's Ability to Support Your Use Cases
Evaluate whether the existing architecture can effectively support each potential use case. This involves assessing whether:

- The necessary data can be accessed and processed
- The necessary operations can be performed
- The existing architecture complies with the industry regulations
- The security requirements can be met
- The architecture is scalable and flexible enough to accommodate any future growth or changes related to the use case.

Step 4: Identify Gaps in Your Architecture   Based on your findings, identify any gaps or shortcomings in the architecture's ability to support each of your potential use cases. These gaps could include, but are not limited to:

- Missing functionality
- Inefficient processes
- Scalability limitations
- Integration challenges
- Lack of disaster recovery mechanisms
- Inadequate security measures

This review and assessment should provide a clear picture of how well your organization's current reference architecture aligns with each use case. Based on your findings here, compare all three potential use cases and choose the one that's most relevant to your organization's current state and capabilities.

Identifying Major Technology Gaps Via a Preliminary Technology Gap Analysis

A technology gap analysis is the process of identifying and evaluating differences between current technology infrastructure and the technological requirements needed to achieve your organizational goals or solve specific business problems.

Identifying major technology gaps helps you evaluate potential use cases and determine a winning use case for your data strategy. Having a comprehensive knowledge of your technology gaps enables you to build a data strategy that addresses current state technology deficits while also capitalizing on your organization's technological assets. This is certain to set your project and organization up for success.

The technology gap analysis essentially involves assessing where your current technology infrastructure might fall short in supporting your potential use cases. It can help you pinpoint where you might need additional investment, reinforcement, or modification to make these use cases feasible.

The Importance of Conducting a Technology Gap Analysis

Identifying technology gaps early is key to helping you select a winning use case. Here's why:

- **Effective planning**—Identifying technology gaps allows you to itemize the resources required to implement a potential use case. It allows you to better plan and estimate the necessary investments that would be associated with the implementation of each of the use cases you're considering. Whether that means purchasing new hardware, investing in new software, or hiring experts in a certain area, you want to be aware of these requirements before deciding which use case you'll build your strategy around.

- **Risk mitigation**—By understanding where your technology may fall short, you can estimate the risk associated with each of the use cases you're considering. You want to choose a use case that is low risk and high reward. Once you've settled on a winning use case, this initial technology gap analysis will also allow you to start considering ways to mitigate the risk of your initiative failing due to inadequate infrastructure.

- **Efficient use of existing resources**—Identifying your technology gaps enables you to select the use case that most efficiently utilizes your company's resources. This ensures that all the time and money your company has put into developing and maintaining its current tech infrastructure are utilized to achieve maximum impact and ROI.

- **Winning use case identification**—The identification of technology gaps helps you determine which of the potential use cases can be implemented with minimal technological investment or adjustments. This approach allows for a quicker ROI for your organization.

How to Conduct a Preliminary Technology Gap Analysis

Now that you see why this process is vital to your ability to make an informed decision about a winning use case, let's look at how to conduct a preliminary technology gap analysis.

Tip

When conducting this analysis, make sure to consider your future needs and evolving technological requirements that are relevant to your potential use cases. For instance, if you anticipate growing users for a use case that you've shortlisted, then you'll need to consider the scalability and flexibility aspects as your future state requirements.

At this stage in the strategy-building process, you've already defined your business objectives. We covered that back in Chapter 9. Now, we're going to incorporate those objectives into a preliminary gap analysis.

Step 1: Take an Inventory of Your Current Technology   Once you have defined the business objectives, you need to take an inventory of the current technology. This includes hardware, software, data and network resources, and any other technologies that are currently in use. You also need to detail how these technologies are used, by whom, and for what purpose. You should be able to pull a lot of this information from the reference architecture, but don't stop there. Reference architectures aren't meant to be complete expansive inventories of every technology your company owns.

Bonus resource

A data use case assessment tool is available for you to download for free at www.data-mania.com/book.

Step 2: Examine Your Technology Needs   The next step is to examine each of the potential use cases to identify their unique technology requirements. This involves understanding what technologies are needed to achieve the business objectives and comparing these needs with the current technology inventory.

For example, if you're anticipating user growth and planning to include additional capabilities for your use case, you should begin by understanding the scalability of your current system and what changes you may need to make to accommodate increased growth. This can mean switching to cloud services and considering containerization technologies.

Step 3: Identify the Gaps   After identifying the technology needs, we need to identify the gaps between the current technology inventory and the technology needs for each potential use case. These gaps could be in terms of hardware, software, data, network resources, or any other aspect of technology.

> Tip
>
> Use cases are often built on technology stacks that differ from what we have available in-house. In these cases, you have to consider the various ways you can adapt the technologies you currently have available such that they achieve the same objectives as those from within the use case. You'd also want to consider the ways in which you could most efficiently adapt to meet any technology gaps that are exposed on a per use case basis.

Step 4: Prioritize the Gaps   Once the gaps have been identified for each use case, we need to prioritize them. This involves considering factors, such as the impact of the gap on the business objectives, the estimated cost of addressing the gap, the estimated time required to address the gap, and its feasibility.

Based on your technology gap analysis findings, decide which potential use case seems most feasible at this time.

Considerations for Foundation Models in Data Infrastructure

In certain cases, your potential use case may involve building with foundation models like GPT-4, Minstrel, or Claude. Even when using these models as LLM foundations, you'll still need to make provisions for a robust data infrastructure that collects, cleans, transforms, and feeds your data into them.

An example might be the super-smart LLM+RAG chatbot that we discussed in Chapter 2. This type of chatbot could be deployed within a "converse with your data" feature that you build directly into your data analytics solution. Such a feature would typically require the user to interact with a chat interface (like that within ChatGPT) to "ask questions" of the data, data that is then made available within your foundation model, a fine-tuned version, or even via RAG. A feature like this could greatly simplify the process of data analysis—no more complex SQL queries, Python scripts, or overly complicated analytics tools. Using this concept as a primary example, let's look at the factors that you'd need to consider when building a data infrastructure around a use case that sits atop a foundation model like this.

Though the foundation model is doing most of the reasoning work, the model's output (or answer) will always depend on how good your input data is. Consequently, your data infrastructure should support cleaning, pre-processing, and transforming your input data to then input it into the model.

Warning

The above reflects just one important consideration. When it comes to leveraging foundation models, there are many other considerations to be made, like the privacy of the input data, the volume of data that goes in as input, and more.

This section describes four key factors that you should take into consideration when designing infrastructure around a foundation model.

Scalability and Flexibility

When planning the data infrastructure for your use case, make sure to keep in mind two important factors: scalability and flexibility. With growing data volumes and constantly changing user requirements, these factors should be top-of-mind.

A data infrastructure that will work in tandem with the foundation model needs to accommodate increasingly complex datasets to support analytics. This is what I mean when I say "scalable."

It's also important for you to select a foundation model that can support varying data types, formats, and new technologies, were things to change in the near future. This makes it "flexible."

Note

In the challenge at the end of this chapter, you can get some practice selecting a foundation model.

Integrations

Many companies find it increasingly challenging to combine data from multiple sources to create a unified view. Oftentimes, the data is locked away in different silos and remains inaccessible. Other times, it's just way too complex to bring together. The foundation model you select would need data that's already in a refined format.

A "converse with your data" feature could require data from multiple sources, such as customer management systems (CRMs), social media channels, ticketing systems, and many others. If and only if you have an infrastructure that unites these datasets, would you be able to feed that data to a foundation model and ask questions.

Note

Visit the challenge at the end of this chapter to get some practice doing discovery around integration alternatives.

Security and Privacy

When it comes to use cases that leverage foundation models, one of the most important factors to consider is the principle of "trust." At its core, this principle requires you to ensure data integrity, confidentiality, and compliance with industry standards. As part of this process, you'll need to put systems in place that define the what, why, who, and how of data access.

Tip

The principle of trust is especially important when building with foundation models. You must take proactive measures to amp up your security and privacy methods. Consider using tokenization, encryption, or anonymization techniques to mask personal details before there's interaction with the foundation model. This interaction would typically happen via API endpoints.

The challenge at the end of this chapter will provide you with the chance to get some practice assessing security and privacy issues.

ROI

When planning to build data infrastructure for a potential use case, you'll need to develop a clear idea of the cost and resources that will go into this work.

Note

Remember the golden rule that I mentioned in Chapter 2: aim for use cases with high-ROI, minimal risks, and maximum efficiency.

To get a rough estimate of the ROI associated with a data infrastructure alternative, do the following:

1. List the expenses for the current state of your data infrastructure.
2. Estimate the cost that you'll incur if you were to modify this; i.e., the cost required to get you from the current state to the future state.
3. Identify areas that do not require significant changes or steps that you can automate.
4. Map out the short- and long-term benefits of investing in this and what ROI you can potentially derive.

It's possible that one kind of data infrastructure may not meet your diverse needs and requirements and fall short in some areas. Say, for example, you may want a combination of data warehouses and data lakes for your use case. Or, you may want to set up an infrastructure that uses both cloud and on-premise data storage solutions.

Challenge: Technical Assessment

Here's a small technical assessment exercise for you to work on.

Part 1: Assessing a Sample Dataset

Choose a customer database or a similar dataset. Ask your core team to note their challenges and potential solutions related to four key criteria:

- Quality
- Relevance
- Usage
- Privacy

Compare your findings with that of your team. Get together to identify areas that you believe need improvement and brainstorm to find the best way to address them!

Perform these steps for each of your potential use cases. This will provide a detailed understanding of the efficacy and efficiency of your current data inventory in the context of each use case. Use your findings to decide which use case is the most relevant to your organization's current state.

Part 2: Foundation Model Selection

For the use cases you've chosen, detail the following:

- Current data volumes and needs
- Current support for data sources, types, and formats
- Anticipated data volume and future growth

Go through the different foundation models that are available and choose ones that can address your needs at a later stage. After selecting a foundation model, prepare an estimate for the data infrastructure that you'll need. What additional technology and data resources might you need? What resources do you already have in place in your current state?

Part 3: Integrations

Based on the foundation model you chose, perform the following steps:

1. List the current integration capabilities.
2. Look for data silos.
3. List the sources that you may need to integrate with for your use case.

Part 4: Security and Privacy

Continue with the following steps:

1. Evaluate the security measures that are currently in place for the data.
2. Consider specific guidelines that you'll need to follow with respect to the different data you collect.

3. Assess compliance with industry regulations and data protection laws.
4. Identify potential vulnerabilities in security.

The factors that we've just looked at should provide a gentle footing upon which you can further build, but remember that these types of activities are not to be done in isolation. Chapter 11 looks at the importance of stakeholder engagement in planning out your data infrastructure and, in fact, the entire data strategy.

11

Stakeholder Engagement and Data Literacy

In a world of more data, the companies with more data-literate people are the ones that are going to win.

– Miro Kazakoff

Chapter 10 detailed the steps involved in conducting a data and technology assessment. As you'll recall, at the end of the chapter, I mentioned that these activities are not to be done in isolation. Why is that? Let's have a look.

Returning to the house analogy from Chapter 10 just as building a house involves architects, builders, and residents, developing a data strategy requires various stakeholders to be involved. You'd hire an architect to develop a design, builders who will turn that vision into reality, and finally, your family who will decide how they want their rooms to look! A great collaboration would be one that involves all the parties—where each will provide their input or suggestions based on their forte.

Developing a data strategy works in a similar manner. Data strategists play the role of builders in designing the data strategy. Then you have your team of data scientists, analysts, and other IT staff who will work in tandem to implement this data strategy. Finally, you have the business end users who, like residents, will tell you how satisfied they are with your data products or services. I think of it as a cycle of continuous feedback and improvement.

In this chapter, I'll uncover why stakeholders are so vital to the success of your data strategy and how you can best collaborate with them to fortify the chances of that success.

Note

From my experience, the companies that involve a wide variety of stakeholders in all significant phases of planning and implementing a data strategy are the ones that also tend to have the most positive data culture—which, in my opinion, is the linchpin of a successful data-driven business.

Defining, Segmenting, and Prioritizing Stakeholders

The development and execution of a data strategy is a multidimensional process that includes various functional areas and roles across an organization. It requires the identification and inclusion of key stakeholders at an early stage. Involving stakeholders in all important data strategy decisions sets a terrific precedent for any data-driven culture.

Note

With respect to a data project, a *stakeholder* refers to any individual, team, or department within an organization who has a direct or indirect interest in the data strategy and can either affect or be affected by the outcomes of this strategy.

Stakeholders include people who influence business decisions or use the results of data analysis and those who take part in the technical, practical, and legal aspects of developing and implementing the data strategy.

Stakeholders in a data strategy often include data scientists, business analysts, managers, IT professionals, decision-makers, and sometimes even clients or external partners. Because of the large number of stakeholders potentially involved, you need a focused and strategic approach to stakeholder management. I'll discussing several ways to categorize, prioritize, and manage stakeholder relationships at the end of this chapter.

The Importance of Stakeholder Management

Stakeholders and effective stakeholder management play a critical role in data strategy for various reasons.

Stakeholders Provide Important Perspective   There are different ways stakeholders interact with data on an everyday basis. You'll want to look at the combined and overlapping perspectives of stakeholders to develop unique insights into how you should go about developing and executing a data strategy. Table 11.1 provides an example of how stakeholder interests overlap in any given project.

Naturally, all of these perspectives should be considered by a data strategist when they're working to formulate comprehensive, effective recommendations.

The Significance of Alignment   Consulting stakeholders early in the process helps to ensure that the data strategy aligns with the organization's broader goals and objectives. Each stakeholder has unique knowledge to address their department's goals, pain points, needs, and potential solutions. Their insights can help align the data strategy with these needs and ensure that the data initiatives provide meaningful value to the organization.

For example, imagine that you're considering developing a data strategy for a customer data platform as one of your potential use cases. One of the primary tasks would be to identify the data sources that you'd want to use if you were to select this use case. At this stage, you'll want to involve:

- Business analysts for translating business requirements into technical specifications,
- Data scientists who will assist in data quality checks and prepare data for model building,

Table 11.1   An Example of Overlapping Stakeholder Interests

Role	Example Interest
Data scientist	The quality and accessibility of data
Business analyst	How data can answer specific business questions
Manager	How data insights can be used to guide teams
Executive	How data can drive strategic initiatives
End user	Providing feedback regarding their experience with tools, data input and output operations, and usability aspects

- Data engineers to set the data pipeline infrastructure for the customer data platform,

- Data governance personnel who will ensure the data is standard and meets company and industry guidelines,

- Marketing personnel for crafting appropriate marketing messaging to be consumed by users at various touch points and for assessing the effectiveness of the platform at large,

- End users, such as beta testers, who share feedback about their experiences using your platform.

There can be many other participants, such as the data security team, customer success teams, and leadership team whose input would be vital to building a strategy to support such a use case.

Warning

Failing to involve key stakeholders can cause you to define technical requirements that are overly ambitious or ambiguous. You may also miss out on discovering data quality issues in the earlier stages of the project and end up passing over privacy and ethical considerations surrounding the datasets you plan to use.

Facilitating Buy-In   Including stakeholders early on helps build a sense of ownership and generally facilitates better buy-in for the successful implementation of the data strategy. When stakeholders feel their input is valued and that they're part of the decision-making process, they're much more likely to support the strategy and contribute to its successful execution. By securing buy-in, you'll also be able to bring together multiple teams who will work toward a common goal and encourage a culture of collaboration and teamwork.

Identifying Potential Challenges   Each stakeholder has a unique perspective about the data they work on or with. Stakeholders oftentimes will be helpful in your efforts to identify potential hurdles in data collection, storage, analysis, and governance. They can offer practical insights into the proposed strategy and help you identify blind spots on potential challenges before those challenges have the chance to grow into significant problems. When multiple stakeholders participate in the data strategy formulation process, they're able to collaborate and work on issues that you might have overlooked had you been working in isolation.

Clarifying and Managing Your Project Stakeholders

When ideating around potential stakeholders for the use cases you're evaluating, consider all individuals and groups who will be affected by the data strategy. It may be tempting to focus only on the main business decision-makers and influencers since these are the individuals who are ultimately responsible for reaching business objectives.

Yet, it's also important to consider data professionals, IT professionals, and legal/compliance teams as primary stakeholders. People in these roles have direct influence over the development, execution, and viability of a data strategy. They contribute significantly to the formation and execution of data strategies, as a data strategy cannot be developed or implemented in isolation from the technical, practical, and legal considerations that these roles own. While it's true that these roles might not have direct business decision-making authority, their influence on the feasibility and success of a data strategy can't be overlooked.

As previously mentioned, you'll want to consult the following stakeholders when formulating your strategic ideas for a potential use case.

Executives   These are the decision-makers who usually set the top-level direction for the data strategy. They often require a good understanding of how the data strategy aligns with the organization's vision and objectives.

Business Unit Leaders   These stakeholders understand the needs and challenges of their specific departments. They provide insights into how data can be used to address these needs and improve operations.

External Stakeholders   Sometimes, it might be necessary to consult with external stakeholders like customers or partners, especially if the use case would impact them directly.

Data Professionals   This group includes data scientists, data engineers, and data analysts who handle data directly and provide valuable input on what tools and processes are required for efficient data operations. They understand the data landscape of the organization and can make key recommendations on how best to use data to achieve business goals. They might also highlight potential data issues that could adversely impact the effectiveness of the use cases you're considering.

IT Professionals   IT personnel play a crucial role in the implementation of the data strategy and manage the systems and infrastructure that store and process data. They provide insights into the organization's technical capabilities and limitations. IT professionals also manage the technical infrastructure that makes the implementation of a data strategy plan possible.

Legal and Compliance Teams   These teams can help you to ensure that your data strategy plan adheres to legal and regulatory requirements. This is critical, especially when the data you're dealing with is highly sensitive.

Consider the previous example of a customer data platform that contains personal details, financial information, behavioral data, and in some cases health information. Sound legal and compliance teams should be able to provide you with protocols, security measures, and data governance guidelines that safeguard the confidentiality of the datasets you'll be working with. This is crucial to avoid non-compliance penalties, which can include hefty fines and damage to the organization's reputation.

Stakeholder Management Methodologies

Stakeholder management becomes increasingly complex with a larger number of parties involved. A focused and strategic approach is required to handle stakeholder relationships in an effective manner. For example, in the context of a retail organization, I categorize stakeholders as:

High-interest, high-influence stakeholders—These stakeholders include business executives, managers, or clients who directly influence or are influenced by the outcomes of the data strategy. Identify these stakeholders early on in the project.

Tip
Try to keep the number of high-interest, high-influence stakeholders to no more than 10.

High-interest, lower-influence stakeholders—These stakeholders include data professionals, IT professionals, and legal teams. They are crucial for the execution of the data strategy but don't directly determine business strategy.

For example, in the context of a retail organization:

Business executives, managers, and clients are high-interest, high-influence stakeholders as they directly influence business strategy and are significantly impacted by the results of data strategy.

Data professionals, IT professionals, and legal teams might be considered high-interest, lower-influence stakeholders since they're crucial for the execution of the data strategy but don't directly determine business strategy.

Follow the methods I prescribe below to manage your stakeholder involvement and ensure that you're considering all perspectives when developing a data strategy.

Segmenting and Prioritizing Stakeholders   While the two aforementioned roles are "stakeholders," technically speaking, you wouldn't want to consult all of them on the same frequency or at the same level of detail. You should prioritize stakeholders based on their influence on and interest in your project. Provide more regular updates to high-influence, high-interest stakeholders, and with the others you'll need to consider how you'll reduce the frequency of communication.

Role-Based Representation   Instead of involving every individual, identify key representatives for each role. The representatives you consult with should have a good understanding of their team's perspective and be able to make decisions on their behalf.

For example:

- For data professionals, the Chief Data Officer (CDO) or a senior data scientist represents the team's interests. They also raise awareness around the capabilities and limitations of data handling, analysis, and interpretation.

- For IT professionals, the Chief Information Officer (CIO) or IT director provides insights into the organization's technical capabilities and constraints, assesses the feasibility of the data strategy from a technical perspective, and highlights any necessary changes to IT infrastructure.

- For the legal team, the Chief Legal Officer or a senior compliance manager should be able to help align your strategy with data protection regulations and other legal requirements to avoid potential legal issues down the line.

Working Groups   Establish smaller working groups for different aspects of the data strategy. These groups work on their specific tasks and bring their findings and recommendations to the larger group. This approach allows for detailed discussions without requiring everyone to be involved in every conversation.

You can establish working groups to focus on specific aspects of the data strategy on an as-needed basis. For example, a working group comprising representatives from the data and IT teams could focus on providing perspective on technical execution related to implementing new data management tools or updating IT infrastructure. Another working group with legal and data representatives could focus on providing data governance and compliance perspectives. This way you're allowing individuals with special skill sets to focus on the specific aspects of the data strategy where they have the domain expertise you need and lack.

Also consider the scope for cross-team collaboration. The overlap of perspectives between different working groups can be extremely valuable!

Efficient Communication Channels This may sound obvious, but be sure you're making effective use of communication channels like shared project management platforms, regular meetings, and clear reporting structures. This helps you manage communications effectively so that everyone stays informed without being bogged down with unnecessary details.

Regular meetings with the representatives of each group are helpful for sharing updates, discussing challenges, and making collective decisions. Use an online project management platform to document these updates and decisions and to facilitate ongoing communication between the teams. This keeps everyone informed and aligned without needing constant, time-consuming meetings.

Gathering Requirements and Conducting Stakeholder Interviews

When evaluating potential use cases, you'll need to allocate time for requirements gathering from and interviewing of stakeholders who are both high-interest and high-influence.

The Importance of Requirements Gathering

The purpose of requirements gathering activities is to support you in developing clarity around the needs, desires, and concerns of the people who will be most affected by the success of the data initiative. Come to find out, these same individuals also tend to have the most influence over the success of the project as well, so you want them to be in your favor.

Requirements gathering also helps you get a rough idea of what each use case would require in terms of resources, technology, skills, etc. This, in turn, helps you assess the feasibility and likely impact of each potential use case.

Overall, your understanding of stakeholder needs directly supports you in identifying which potential use case is a prime target for selection as a "Winning Use Case." For this reason, it's essential for you to conduct requirements gathering from, and interviews of, all high-interest, high-influence stakeholders.

Bonus resource

To help you with stakeholder communications, I'm providing you with my Data Jargon Dictionary for Executives & Key Stakeholders. This resource is available for you to download for free at www.data-mania.com/book.

How to Perform Requirements Gathering

Let the following seven steps guide you in your requirements gathering work.

Step 1: Identify Your Stakeholders   As mentioned earlier, high-interest, high-influence stakeholders typically include business executives, managers, or clients who directly influence or are influenced by the outcomes of the data strategy. Always identify these stakeholders early on in the project.

Tip

Use a stakeholder matrix to understand and visualize each stakeholder's interest in your use case and what sort of influence they have over the outcome. This will help you narrow down the stakeholders that you'll want to involve in your assessment and planning work.

Step 2: Identify and Request Additional Documentation   Next, identify the types of documents you need to request from stakeholders. This typically includes data governance policies, data catalogs, business process documentation, system architecture diagrams, data privacy and protection policies, and any regulatory compliance documents. Request, collect, and review this documentation from stakeholders before conducting the stakeholder interview.

Step 3: Prepare for the Interviews   Develop a set of key questions prior to the interviews that'll help you understand each stakeholder's needs, objectives, and concerns regarding the potential use cases. These questions should aim to uncover the business problems they want to solve, the data they consider most valuable, and the outcomes they hope to achieve.

Step 4: Conduct the Interviews Schedule one-on-one interviews with each stakeholder. These interviews should be structured but flexible, allowing for the exploration of new insights that may emerge during impromptu discussions. Listen actively, ask follow-up questions, and make sure you fully understand the stakeholder's perspective.

> **Tip**
>
> Always ask stakeholders about their pain points—don't just focus on what their perceived "data problems" might be. In addition to their ideas about data problems they're facing, you want to identify bigger, broader problems that—in their minds—might NOT be related to data at all. This approach exposes bigger organizational issues that you, as the data strategist, know could be solved by the right data-intensive use case.

Step 5: Document and Analyze the Results After each interview, document the responses while they're still fresh in your mind. Look for commonalities, differences, and unique insights across all stakeholder interviews. This analysis will help you understand the most pressing requirements and how each potential use case might meet these requirements.

Step 6: Validate and Prioritize the Requirements Share your findings with your stakeholders and validate that you correctly understand their requirements. You can do this through follow-up meetings or via written communication. Once validated, you can prioritize requirements based on factors such as business impact, feasibility, and alignment with the organization's strategic goals.

Step 7: Map the Requirements to Use Cases Finally, map the prioritized requirements to each of the three potential use cases. This will help you understand which use case(s) are most relevant to stakeholders' needs. Based on your stakeholder interviews, decide which use case seems most useful and necessary at this time.

Reviewing and Assessing Executive-Level and Company-Wide Data Literacy Needs

Each of the potential use cases that you chose will have its own nuances. For example, one use case might require you to collect data from different silos while another might require you to set up a hybrid infrastructure of existing data warehouses and data lakes for data storage needs. The third might need you to invest significant capital upfront to purchase and configure new infrastructure.

When you're speaking with high-interest, high-influence executive stakeholders, you need to speak their language. In many cases, this only becomes possible after you've assessed their data literacy levels and needs. Let's look at how to go about assessing executive-level data literacy in the most tactful manner possible.

The Importance of an Executive-Level Data Literacy Assessment

Your selection of use case should be informed by the findings you generate from a thorough review and assessment of executive-level data literacy. While this type of assessment is important for many reasons, the following four stand out to me the most.

Securing Executive Support Data literate executives are more effective decision-makers. They also tend to be more ardent supporters of novel data initiatives. Plainly put, an executive who understands the value and potential of data is far more likely to invest in your data strategy and provide the resources and backing that are necessary for its success.

Developing Strategic Alignment By assessing the data literacy level of your executive team, you can more closely align your chosen use case with their existing knowledge and comprehension. You need to make sure that your winning use case is both technically feasible and strategically aligned with the leadership's expectations. When you're clear on the data literacy levels of executives, you'll stand improved chances of securing executive buy-in.

Capacity-building Your assessment of executive-level data literacy supports you in identifying areas for improvement. In turn, these insights enable you to develop targeted training and capacity-building programs. We'll talk about the development of training programs in greater depth in Chapter 15, by the way. But for now, suffice it to say that any program that increases the data literacy of your executive team will improve the effectiveness of your data strategy overall.

Culture of Data-Driven Decision-Making Executives play a crucial role in creating a culture of data-driven decision-making. By developing a deep understanding of their level of data literacy, you can choose a use case that might help promote such a culture within your organization.

Tip

After you finally settle on a winning use case, it's a good idea to start off the implementation phase with a minimal-investment pilot program. In such a program, your team can build an affordable prototype to show to the executive team. This will require only a little investment and stands the chance of getting the team excited about the possibilities of the winning use case were they to invest further.

How to Conduct an Executive-Level Data Literacy Assessment

An assessment of executive-level data literacy requires a multi-step process. Approaching executives about their data literacy requires tact and diplomacy. You want to avoid making them feel that their competence is being questioned. One way to go about this would be to position the data literacy assessment as a strategic initiative for organizational growth and an opportunity for continuous learning. Let the following tips guide your approach.

1. Start by communicating the importance of data literacy as a strategic advantage for the organization. Make it clear that this isn't about questioning competence but instead is about empowering the executives to lead effectively in an increasingly data-driven business environment.

2. Underscore how the role of data in decision-making is evolving, with an increasing need for data-informed strategies. You could do this in a board meeting or a dedicated session and talk about the value of data in modern organizations. The key here is to make the case for the necessity and benefits of improving data literacy. You can also present interesting case studies that are relevant to your use case.

3. Propose a data literacy initiative as a proactive step toward building a data-driven organization. Emphasize that it's a learning opportunity for everyone in

the organization, not just the executives. This approach removes the focus from individual knowledge gaps and places it on organizational growth.

4. Instead of conducting an assessment, provide a self-assessment tool that allows executives to evaluate their own data literacy. This gives your executives the autonomy to identify areas where they'd like to improve through a less confrontational process.

5. Based on the self-assessments, offer customized learning opportunities such as executive workshops, expert-led seminars, or curated learning resources. This allows executives to learn at their own pace and focus on the areas that they feel are most relevant to their role.

6. As the data literacy initiative progresses, share insights and progress with the entire organization regularly. This helps reinforce the importance of data literacy and demonstrates that it's a priority for the organization.

7. Encourage an environment of continuous learning, where it's okay not to know everything, and people are esteemed when actively seeking knowledge development. This approach helps to normalize the learning process and removes the stigma associated with needing to improve certain skills.

The Importance of a Company-Wide Data Literacy Assessment

An assessment of company-wide data literacy needs is another crucial step before choosing a winning use case. There are several reasons why this is important.

Improved Data Utilization　A data initiative can succeed only if employees across the organization understand the value of data and how to use it. This requires a certain level of data literacy. By assessing company-wide data literacy needs, you can ensure that your chosen use case will be understood, utilized, and beneficial to as many employees as possible.

Training and Capacity Building　Assessing your company-wide data literacy helps you to identify areas where additional training is needed. This will inform the training plans that you build to support your data strategy. More on this in Chapter 15.

Change Management　When you fully grasp data literacy levels across the organization, you're better able to manage the change that's brought about by a data strategy you lead. When data literacy is low, employees resist these changes, which will inevitably hinder the success of the strategy. Identifying these challenges upfront allows you to address them head-on by including any change management plans within your data strategy plan. There's more on how to build a data strategy plan coming up in Chapters 16 and 17.

Democratization of Data When assessing company-wide data literacy, an often-overlooked consideration is the lack of access employees have to the data they need. A move toward data democratization makes sure that even the non-technical staff have basic access to data so that they can explore, query, analyze, and visualize. This goes a long way in encouraging data-driven decision-making and slowly building a culture of data literacy in the organization.

Tip

You can add role-based access control approaches to restrict access to sensitive data.

Improved Company-Wide Communications Last but not least, there are the communication improvements that result from your clear grasp of company-wide data literacy. When you're clear on the data literacy level of your organization, you're better able to tailor your communications regarding the data strategy, the chosen use case, and its benefits, such that the language you use is most aligned with the employees' understanding. This will result in greater adoption rates overall.

How to Conduct a Company-Wide Data Literacy Assessment

Conducting a thorough company-wide data literacy assessment ensures that your data strategy aligns with the skills and understanding of your workforce. But what are the best ways to go about doing this? The following is a detailed step-by-step process that you can use to guide your way.

Step 1: Define What Data Literacy Means Start by defining what data literacy means in the context of your organization. Naturally, these parameters would include an understanding of basic data concepts, the ability to interpret data visualizations, a comprehension of data collection and processing, and an appreciation for data's role in decision-making, but I encourage you to consider additional parameters you'd like to add to the list.

Step 2: Identify Key Data Concepts and Skills Identify the key data-related concepts and skills that are relevant across your organization. These will vary depending on your industry and the specific roles within your organization.

For example:

- A marketing professional might need to understand customer segmentation analysis, whereas,
- A product manager might need to interpret product usage data.

Step 3: Develop a Data Literacy Assessment Create an assessment mechanism, like a questionnaire, an online survey, or a series of workshops that can support you in measuring the overall knowledge of key data concepts and skills across your organization.

Tip

When preparing questionnaires, include practical, scenario-based questions that will test an employee's real-world understanding of data. Don't limit these questions to theory.

Step 4: Conduct the Assessment Administer the assessment to the relevant departments across your organization. Encourage participation by emphasizing the importance of data literacy and how it can benefit team members in their individual roles.

Tip

Your survey completion rate might be very low in some cases. Try offering incentives for participation, such as recognition or small rewards, to encourage people to participate.

Step 5: Analyze the Results Analyze the assessment results to benchmark the overall data literacy level of your organization. Identify specific areas for improvement. You'll probably find that data literacy is high in some departments but low in others. That's normal.

Step 6: Consolidate Your Ideas on Potential Data Literacy Improvements
Based on your analysis, document a list of ideas on ways to improve data literacy across your organization. This might involve facilitating in-house training sessions or providing resources for self-learning. The purpose is to address the specific gaps you identified in your analysis. You'll want to be aware of these issues and refer back to this list when selecting your winning use case in Chapter 14 and when developing training recommendations in Chapter 15.

Data Literacy Requirements for Interacting with Foundation Models

Data literacy becomes important when we talk about our interactions with foundation models like GPT-4 or Claude AI—especially the input and output of these models.

The following are some basic data literacy requirements that you can provide non-technical stakeholders to better support them in their use of foundation models.

Understand the input data—The data that you input to a foundation model needs to be of high quality, relevant, and accurate. This will help you generate more meaningful insights.

Delegate when needed—The data that you provide a foundation model needs to be free of errors and mustn't have outliers or missing values. If your data is error-prone, consider handing it off to a data analyst so they can transform it into a format that's suitable for your needs.

Consider data privacy and ethics—This is one of the most critical requirements when you're working with a foundation model. Take the time to get educated on different data protection acts and compliance requirements before you send your data for processing. We cover the basics of these coming up in Chapter 13.

Be careful about model bias—Foundation models can give output that is patently false—also called AI hallucinations. Make sure that you're aware of the limitations of the foundation model before you start.

(continued)

(continued)

Learn how to interpret data—Learn how to interpret visual data, tables, and stats—know what the data is trying to tell you. Ultimately, this ability is what makes you "data literate."

You can opt for training programs or sessions that will help stakeholders gain the necessary skills and technical acumen when working on a use case that's built atop a foundation model. We'll talk more about this in Chapter 15.

Now that you've seen how to manage stakeholders and assess data literacy, it's time to make a bold move into assessing the current state of your organization as a whole.

CHAPTER

12

Assessing Your Current
State Organization

You can't manage what you can't measure.

– Peter Drucker

In Chapter 11, we looked at the benefits of involving stakeholders within your data strategy planning activities—and how doing so fortifies your chances of successfully transforming your organization to a more data-driven one. In this chapter, we'll focus our attention on assessing the current state of your organization and its four pillars—process, organization, technology, and information. We'll also assess its data maturity, data skill sets, data resources, infrastructure, and ethics as they pertain to future state goals and the use cases you're considering to drive your organization toward those goals.

Producing a Basic Process, Organization, Technology, and Information Model That Reflects Your Current State Organization

As a data strategist, you should always use a Process, Organization, Technology, and Information (POTI) model as a fundamental tool for developing a comprehensive view of the current state of your organization. This will help identify the interconnectedness of the core elements—process, organization, technology, and information—and how they potentially impact your data strategy.

When developed systematically, a POTI model provides you with clear insights into your organization's current state. To help you get started with POTI models, we'll first have a look at why the POTI model is so important, and then we'll delve into the steps that are involved in building one.

The Importance of the POTI Model

While POTI models are often used prescriptively to describe the future state vision of processes, organizational roles, technology, and information systems, for our purposes we're using the POTI model as a diagnostic tool to assess a company's existing processes, organizational structure, technology stack, and information management capabilities.

The POTI model is defined as follows:

- **Process**—The process pillar encompasses the procedures and activities your organization undertakes to achieve its business objectives. This could include everything from customer relationship management to product development.

- **Organization**—The organization component relates to the people in your organization and how they are structured. It includes organizational hierarchies, roles, responsibilities, and the way teams and departments interact.

- **Technology**—The technology aspect of the POTI model pertains to the systems, software, hardware, and data management tools that your organization uses to execute its processes and achieve its objectives.

- **Information**—The information pillar represents the data that your organization generates, collects, processes, and uses in its operations, including how this data is structured, stored, secured, and analyzed. The core idea here is to strengthen the quality, reliability, and trustworthiness of the information within your organization.

When developing a data strategy, it's vital to understand how each of these is connected and interdependent. To help illustrate such interdependence, here are some examples:

- The design of the processes within your organization is such that they utilize the technology and information efficiently.
- You select the technology such that it supports all the processes running within your organization while also aligning with the organizational culture and capabilities.
- The information within the organization is such that it supports all of your processes and decision-making initiatives.
- The organization's culture (the people and their practices) is core in deciding effective ways of implementing various processes, how best to use the technology that's currently available, and how to share information such that it's accessible to those who need it.

I'm sure it makes sense now how this assessment is crucial to identifying gaps, inefficiencies, or opportunities that you can address through a data strategy.

Warning

A failure to take a systemic approach toward building a POTI model often results in surface-level, superficial insight into each of the core pillars. This tends to eventually result in unnecessary investments and the accumulation of needless risks. It may also jeopardize your chances of getting buy-in for your strategy.

The POTI Model Delivery Format

POTI models are generally documented in a POTI table similar to that shown in Table 12.1.

How to Build a POTI Model

You already mapped out the business objectives back in Chapter 9. These business objectives set the foundation for the POTI model as you want to ensure that all processes, organizational structures, technology, and information are aligned with these objectives. With your business objectives serving as the foundation, I suggest the following six steps when building a POTI model and using them to support a use case selection.

Table 12.1   An Example of a POTI Table

Program Area	Current State	Future State	Changes Requirements
Process Describe how this data initiative will impact the business's operations processes.	...	...	...
Organization Describe how this data initiative will impact the people and culture at your organization.	...	...	...
Technology Describe how this data initiative will impact technology across your organization.	...	...	...
Information Describe how this data initiative will impact the type of information that is served to people and to business systems across your organization.	...	...	...

Step 1: Identify Key Processes   Identify and map out all the key processes within your organization. This could include product development, sales and marketing processes, customer service, supply chain management, etc.

Focus on three important questions here:

1. How are these processes performed?
2. Who performs them?
3. What tools or technology do they use?

Your answers to these questions support your understanding of how these processes generate, use, or influence data and information within your organization.

> **Tip**
>
> Don't forget to use KPIs to evaluate how well your processes are working. For example, if you're focusing on process KPIs, you can focus on metrics such as product quality, compliance with safety regulations, and process efficiency.

Step 2: Outline Your Organizational Structure   Using the organizational chart you collected with your RFI in Chapter 9, outline your organizational structure. Detail teams, departments, roles, and responsibilities. You'll also need to understand who the decision-makers are and how decisions are made. This is a really important step in your organizational analysis as you want to make sure you have the full support of the high-influence stakeholders in your data-driven initiatives—not to forget that this will also improve your chances of getting a quicker executive buy-in.

Also consider how the organization uses data in its day-to-day functions, and who is responsible for data-related tasks.

Step 3: Catalog Your Organization's Technology   You already conducted a preliminary technology analysis back in Chapter 10. Now it's time to review that work and catalog the technology that your organization currently uses. This should, of course, include software, hardware, databases, analytics tools, and any other technologies that are integral to your operations. You'll also need to consider how these technologies interact with each other and with the processes and people within your organization.

> **Tip**
>
> In my experience, the technology analysis should focus on three important factors: modernity, support, and scalability. Time and again I've stressed the importance of having a technology stack that's future-proofed.

Step 4: Reassess Your Data Inventory   You already assessed your data inventory back in Chapter 10. Those findings are especially relevant here. Review those findings again and take a second pass to:

1. Identify the types of data your organization generates and uses.
2. Consider where this data comes from, how it's collected, how it's processed, where it's stored, and how it's used.
3. Consider data privacy and security, as well as data quality and governance processes.

> **Tip**
>
> When performing this step, you should pay extra attention to how usable your data is in terms of making decisions. Also, identify different data silos within your organization and consider ways to centralize the data to increase its usability.

Step 5: Define a POTI Model   Next, bring together your analyses to form a POTI model by doing the following:

1. Illustrate how processes, organization, technology, and information interact with each other.

2. Identify any gaps, weaknesses, or inefficiencies in your current state, and think about how these might impact your data strategy.

3. Since all gaps don't affect the overall strategy equally, prioritize them based on their impact and address those first.

4. Use the strength areas you identified in the POTI model to your advantage and see if they can add to your organization's capabilities.

To produce a POTI model deliverable, all you need to do is populate a table that's similar to the one shown in Table 12.1 and fill it with written descriptions of your organization's current state POTI.

Step 6: Consult with Your POTI Model When You Select a Winning Use Case   Now that you have a full understanding of your organization's POTI and have summarized your findings in a POTI model, consider which of your potential use cases makes the most sense against it. Keep that consideration in mind moving forward.

Assessing the Data Maturity of Your Organization

Regarding data maturity, the first thing you need to know is that a data maturity model and a data maturity assessment are NOT the same things. As a data strategist, you need to know the difference between them.

A *data maturity model* is a framework that outlines the stages of evolution in an organization's ability to leverage data for strategic, operational, and tactical goals. It provides a road map of progress, starting from ad-hoc processes and culminating in optimized data-driven practices.

A *data maturity assessment*, in contrast, is the process you undertake to identify exactly where your organization stands within the data maturity model. This requires you to consider things like data governance, quality, literacy, and the overall data culture of your organization. This assessment helps you pinpoint strengths, weaknesses, and areas for improvement in the organization's data-handling practices.

What Is a Data Maturity Assessment?

Before performing a data maturity assessment, you need to understand how a data maturity model works and the stages that comprise it. You'll use this model to identify your organization's current level of data management sophistication across multiple dimensions, so clarity here is key. Data maturity models typically comprise the following progressive stages:

1. **Initial**—This is where you rely on individual heroics for data tasks—with no improvement plan in place.
2. **Managed**—In this stage, you develop a plan to ensure consistent data practices and standards.
3. **Defined**—This is where you standardize the data practices and procedures across your entire organization.
4. **Quantitative**—Here you'll measure the effectiveness of the systems you've put in place through quantitative metrics and KPIs.
5. **Optimized**—This stage is where you'll leverage data strategically for continuous improvement and innovation across the organization.

Tip

Remember that the number of stages in your data maturity model can vary based on how complex your data processes are. There can be anywhere between three and six stages.

Tip

Consult the Capability Maturity Model Integration (CMMI) Institute's data management maturity model that outlines the best practices to follow when assessing your organization's current data state.

The Importance of Your Data Maturity Assessment

A data maturity assessment highlights the strengths and weaknesses in an organization's data capabilities, revealing areas that need improvement. It offers a clear road map for progress by showing what the next level of maturity looks like. It helps you answer questions like:

- Where does my organization stand with respect to data handling, management, and utilization?
- What are the gaps or areas that'll need improvement?
- What resources will go into addressing these gaps?

- Are there any additional training programs or workshops required to improve the organization's data culture and literacy levels?
- Is the data strategy aligned with business objectives at every stage?

Knowing where your organization stands in terms of data maturity allows you to set more realistic goals and to build a data strategy that is more realistic overall. Rather than attempting large leaps that may not be feasible, you'll want to aim for more incremental changes that move your organization closer to a more mature state.

Figure 12.1 summarizes each of the stages of a data maturity model.

How to Build a Data Maturity Model

Before conducting a data maturity assessment, you'll need a data maturity model that you can use as a tool.

If your organization already has a data maturity model, then you should just work with that and skip to the data maturity model development phase. In this case, go straight into data maturity assessment steps that are detailed in the next section. But, in the case that your organization does not have a data maturity model, you'll need to take on this significant undertaking so that you can use the

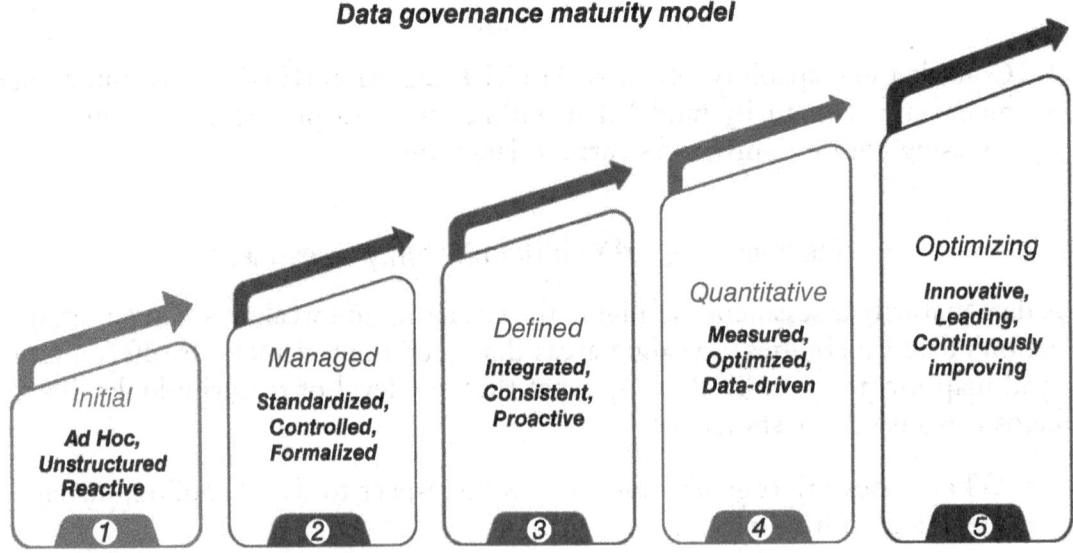

FIGURE 12.1 Stages of a data maturity model.

data maturity model as a resource when building out your organization's data strategy. This section details the steps for building a data maturity model.

Step 1: Define the Purpose   Before starting, clearly define why you're creating a data maturity model. Your firm grasp on this underlying purpose will guide your design of the model and ensure it effectively meets your organization's needs.

Step 2: Define the Stages   Data maturity models consist of several stages, representing the journey from initial, ad-hoc data handling to mature, optimized data utilization. We've discussed these stages in the previous section. The progression road map in the form of stages helps you evaluate your progress over time.

Step 3: Identify Key Considerations for the Model   Choose the considerations upon which the model will focus. Common areas include data quality, governance, architecture, literacy, culture, and analytics as they relate to your potential use cases.

For example, if one of your potential use cases is heavily reliant on the collection and integration of datasets from multiple sources, then a core consideration of your model could easily be "data integration and interoperability." If a potential use case would require personal information, then an important consideration might be "data privacy and security." You get the idea…

Step 4: Develop the Criteria for Each Stage and Consideration   For each aspect in each stage, determine the criteria that must be met to achieve that level of maturity. Developing these criteria provides a clear benchmark for what's expected at each stage and allows you to identify areas of improvement.

For example, if "data integration and interoperability" is the aspect you're focusing on, then the model stages might look like this:

1. **Initial**—Data is often stored in silos and excessive employee hours are spent manually combining datasets to get a unified view.

2. **Managed**—There are some basic data integration tools that are able to automate certain processes of data integration.

3. **Defined**—There's a focus on standardizing data integration procedures and practices—with an additional focus on real-time data integration and access.

4. **Quantitative**—There's a focus on evaluating or "measuring" the effectiveness of the procedures and practices that are put in place.

5. **Optimized**—An advanced data integration strategy is in place that helps bring data from multiple sources seamlessly.

Step 5: Create a Visual Representation   The visual representation here might be a graph, table, or diagram that clearly shows the stages, considerations, and the progression path. This visual will be helpful in your efforts to communicate the model to stakeholders. Effective communication like this goes a long way in cultivating stakeholder understanding and buy-in.

Step 6: Validate the Model   Present the model to a selection of stakeholders for feedback. Validation here helps to ensure that your model aligns with your organization's reality and has wider acceptance.

Tip

Aim to have interactive sessions where different stakeholders discuss the pros and cons of the data maturity model you've developed. Survey forms are a great way to collect feedback from attendees after the presentation.

Step 7: Refine and Finalize the Model   Based on the feedback, refine and finalize your data maturity model. This step ensures your model is as effective and useful as possible before it's implemented.

With your validated data maturity model in hand, you're ready to conduct a data maturity assessment. Let's look at how to go about doing that.

How to Conduct a Data Maturity Assessment

In the step-by-step process that follows, you'll find instructions on how to assess your organization's data maturity in order to identify how well the company currently aligns with its data maturity aspirations.

Step 1: Familiarize Yourself with the Data Maturity Model   Before you begin the assessment, familiarize yourself with the data maturity model. While models will vary, your knowledge of what each stage comprises will provide you the clear understanding you need to accurately evaluate your organization's current position.

Step 2: Overview Model Considerations   If your data maturity model was properly formed, then its considerations should be clear. Take a glance over those considerations and make sure you've got them in mind as you move into the next step.

Step 3: Develop an Assessment Tool   Now it's time to develop an assessment tool. This can often be a survey or questionnaire that asks detailed questions about each of the key areas identified. Developing this tool allows you to systematically gather the information you need for the assessment.

Examples of questions one might include in such an assessment include the following:

- What is your opinion on the current state of data governance within our organization?

- What steps can we take to make sure the data we use is reliable, trustworthy, and accurate?

- What steps are we taking to ensure that our data is safe from external threats? What systems do we currently have in place?

- Is our data helping us make informed business decisions? If not, why not?

- What is the relationship between the organization's employees and its data? Are people using data to improve their decisions?

Step 4: Distribute the Assessment   Send the assessment tool to key stakeholders and other relevant personnel across your organization, such as data stewards, IT professionals, and business executives. These people are in the best position to provide accurate information that's relevant to the current state of data maturity in your organization.

Step 5: Analyze the Results   Once you've collected the responses, analyze them to determine your organization's current stage of data maturity. This might involve calculating an average score for each key area that you've based your questions on or identifying the lowest maturity level across all areas. Analyzing the results gives you a clear picture of your organization's current data maturity.

Segregate the responses into buckets based on the key considerations they address, such as governance, quality, and literacy. Analyze them in a systematic manner to find out if there are any patterns or ambiguities in the responses. Once you have done this, present these findings to your important stakeholders to get their opinions.

Step 6: Identify Gaps   Based on your analysis, identify any gaps between your organization's current stage of data maturity and the next stage. These gaps represent areas where your organization needs to improve its data management practices.

Step 7: Use Your Findings to Inform Your Choice of a Winning Use Case   At this point, you will have a firm understanding of your organization's data maturity. Summarize your data maturity assessment findings so that you can refer back to it when you're selecting your winning use case.

Conducting a Data Skills Survey and Audit

After you've built a data maturity model and conducted the first round of data maturity assessments, you'll have a good idea of where your organization stands with regard to data practices and infrastructure that are currently in place. That's amazing!

You will, however, also need to get a clear view of your workforce's data competencies. Next, I recommend you conduct a data skills survey and audit that'll help you dig deeper into areas that are lacking—especially in relation to the potential use cases you're considering.

The Importance of a Data Skills Survey and Audit

While the two are related, a data skills gap audit serves a purpose that's quite distinct from the company-wide data literacy assessment discussed in Chapter 11, especially in the context of planning a data strategy.

I'll explain using the house analogy that we referenced in the previous chapters. Conducting a data literacy assessment is sort of like ensuring that each resident of the house has basic maintenance skills. That is, each person knows how to do basic maintenance tasks like changing a lightbulb, fixing a leaky faucet, or resetting a tripped breaker. In the same way, you want all the employees in your organization to at least have a basic understanding of data and how they can use it to improve their everyday business decision-making. Some basic data literacy skills would be reflected in their understanding of simple stats, their ability to interpret a chart, or their ability to ask prescient data-related questions.

On the other hand, in reference to our house analogy, a data skills gap audit leans more toward identifying specific maintenance needs or upgrades of which the house is in immediate need—maybe something like a re-plumbing job or an electrical system overhaul. These requirements fall under the responsibility of a specialist, not a generalist. Similarly, a data skills gap audit involves evaluating the skill level of your data analysts, scientists, or engineers. Are they well-equipped to use a certain tool? Can they build a CI/CD pipeline around a foundation model? Are they aware of the latest ML or DL techniques in the market? You need to audit this so you can identify your team's ability to execute each of the potential use cases.

Let's speak in textbook terms now, shall we? A data skills gap audit focuses on evaluating the specific technical competencies and abilities within the organization and identifying where there might be deficiencies in executing particular tasks or utilizing certain tools and technologies. It seeks to pinpoint areas where training or hiring might be necessary to fulfill the technical requirements of a given data strategy. This kind of audit is essential for ensuring that the team has the practical know-how to carry out specific data-related tasks, such as data analysis, modeling, or visualization. You should aim to conduct a data skills audit for specific advanced data skills and roles at least every six months to keep up with the industry changes.

In contrast, the data-literacy assessment we discussed earlier is more concerned with assessing the broader understanding of data across the organization. It examines how well employees, often at a wide variety of levels, comprehend data concepts, terminology, and the role data plays in decision-making and achieving business goals. This type of assessment goes beyond technical skills, exploring the ability to interpret, communicate, and make informed decisions based on data. Conducting this assessment will go a long way in building a data-driven culture in your organization and empower your employees to make decisions that are more informed and backed by data.

In this section, we're focusing on conducting a data skills survey and audit as it's needed to inform your selection of a winning use case. In addition to evaluating the data-related skills and competencies of the individuals within an organization, you also need to identify who within the organization can effectively work with data, what their current skill levels are, and where there might be skill gaps that need addressing. Remember that this is a fundamental step in building a data strategy around a use case.

Getting a clear understanding of the data capabilities of the organization can also help guide you in deciding:

- Which potential use cases are most readily feasible and
- What support might you need from external partners or consultants?

Now that you know the value of a data skills audit, let's look at how to perform one.

How to Conduct a Data Skills Survey and Audit

To conduct a data skills survey and audit for use in informing use case selection, I recommend the following six-step approach.

Step 1: Define the Required Data Skills Looking at your three potential use cases, write a list that identifies the range of skills that will be required for each of those use cases.

This could include technical skills like SQL, Python, or R for data manipulation and analysis, data visualization tools like Tableau or PowerBI, data engineering skills for managing data infrastructure, and softer skills like critical thinking and communication for interpreting and presenting data.

Tip

It's also a good idea to look up what technologies are trending and relevant to your potential use cases. Consider whether incorporating these would be helpful. For example, you may come across a data integration tool that can ease the process of data exchange and integration. Or you might find a data visualization tool that can seamlessly incorporate real-time data and convert it into visual diagrams to create an interactive dashboard. If you discover such technologies, go ahead and add those to your skill requirements list as well.

Step 2: Build an Existing Skills Inventory Develop a comprehensive list of all existing data-related skills within the organization. This should include information on each employee's level of proficiency in each skill. The inventory should include both technical competencies as well as strategic, analytic, and communication skills as they relate to data.

Step 3: Develop a Data Skills Survey   Incorporating both your list of required data skills from step 1 and the existing skills inventory from step 2, create an employee survey. The survey should be designed to assess employees' confidence and proficiency in these data skills. It might also seek to understand their interest in further training or development. You can structure your questions this way:

- How would you rate your proficiency in the following skills?
- How frequently do you use the following tools?
- Which areas do you need additional training in?
- What are the daily challenges you face as they relate to the data you work with?
- Are there any new technologies you're interested in learning?

Step 4: Administer the Survey   Distribute the survey to all relevant employees. Be sure to include an introduction blurb that details the purpose of the survey and how the information will be used. My advice is to present this survey as a means of identifying possibilities for advancement—not as a tool to monitor employees' performance.

Step 5: Analyze the Results   Once the survey responses are collected, analyze the data to identify trends, skill gaps, and areas of strength. This analysis will give you an idea of your organization's current state of data competency.

Step 6: Document and Plan   Document the findings from your audit and use this information to inform your selection of a winning use case and also to plan future state requirements. These requirements could include training and development programs to address skill gaps or the recruitment of new talent.

Now that you know how to do a data skills audit in general, let's look at how you should approach evaluating skill set needs when your potential use case involves a foundation model.

Evaluating Skill Set Needs for Managing and Fine-tuning Foundation Models

Even if you're not developing an LLM from scratch, working with foundation models is its own beast. For that reason, we should look at these advanced skill set requirements separately.

Warning

Working with foundation models is a constantly evolving space, and it's challenging, even for teams with considerable experience in data science and engineering. Due to supply and demand in early 2024, it's currently very difficult to source personnel with development experience in foundation models. One way to address this supply and demand issue is for you to upskill your existing development team. I suggest you consider ways to go about doing that.

From my experience, companies have just started to get their hands dirty by fiddling with different foundation models to see how they can leverage them for their use cases. The space is poised for exponential growth over the next decade, and if you're looking to work with foundation models now, you'll want to make sure you do things right from the beginning.

Note

Before digging into skill set requirements for working with foundation models, let me remind you that you can refer to Chapter 2 for the basic definition of fine-tuning and how it works. You can also refer back to Chapter 10, where we looked at several factors you need to consider when ideating around data infrastructure requirements to support a potential use case that sits atop a foundation model.

When people approach me asking what kind of skill sets their teams need to be successful in working with foundation models, they're generally referring to the skills that are required to select a foundation model, build a data infrastructure pipeline, and maintain the product or service. As I see it, there are four core pillars that'll remain evergreen, even if you happen to change your foundation model.

Those pillars are technical expertise, domain-related knowledge, data governance and ethics, and cross-team collaboration. Let's look at each in more detail.

Technical Expertise

With respect to the technical expertise that's required to work with foundation models, your team needs to be familiar with exactly how LLMs work—the architecture, training techniques, and deployment methods. Team members should also have knowledge of how they can set up the data infrastructure so the data that the foundation model ingests is of high quality, relevant, and up-to-date. At some point, you'll also want to automate these steps by using a continuous integration and continuous delivery (CI/CD) pipeline that can:

- Automatically take in new datasets (along with data augmentation techniques to increase training dataset size),
- Update model parameters,
- Test model performance based on predefined metrics, and
- Deploy changes to the production environment.

Personnel should also be acquainted with different types of fine-tuning techniques like:

- Traditional techniques, such as feature-based fine-tuning where you unfreeze some or all layers of the foundation model based on your requirements and the resources at your disposal.
- Newer techniques, such as low-ranking adaptation (LoRA) or Quantized LoRA that only focus on updating layers that are important to the model's performance. Another popular emerging technique is the Parameter Efficient Fine Tuning (PEFT) method, which works by updating a small fraction of the model's parameters important to the specific task at hand.

Domain-Related Knowledge

You can bring in domain-related subject matter experts to better customize the foundation model. A part of their job involves guiding the development team on the data collection, cleaning, and transformation steps to make sure the input data to the foundation model is of good quality and relevance.

Data Security, Governance, and Ethics

Since generative AI is a relatively new field, there's a lot of confusion and uncertainty around how data should be handled. There are growing concerns around compliance with data privacy laws and regulations, especially for sensitive information.

> **Warning**
>
> Often a company's personnel will feed sensitive information into a foundation model, and the model leaks that information in its output elsewhere (as a response to another prompt online). That's obviously a huge security risk. The solution for mitigating this risk is to deploy foundation models locally using "Local AI" software like Jan AI or Ollama.

There's also the problem of bias and misinformation along with the model hallucination issues mentioned in Chapter 11. These issues need to be addressed and can be reduced to some extent with the help of RAG, as discussed in Chapter 2.

In my experience, it's a good idea to have an AI ethics specialist or a data protection officer (DPO) provide focus on and clarity around AI fairness issues.

Cross-Team Collaboration

To select a foundation model and build a data infrastructure for your winning use case, you'll need multiple teams working in tandem. As I mentioned in Chapter 11, you'll also need the constant involvement of high-interest, high-influence stakeholders who are capable of making sound decisions with regard to the organizational implications, benefits, and limitations of what you're building.

Conducting and Producing a Data Resources Audit

Conducting a data resources audit is a great way of making the best of the data assets you have, getting a clear picture of their current state, and charting out the steps you'll need to take to address any gaps. As part of this activity, you'll mainly be evaluating four important components—data sources, storage systems, data management practices, and related technologies. Let's look at the importance of this undertaking and the sequence of steps that you'll need to follow to perform this activity successfully.

The Importance of a Data Resource Audit

A data resource audit is an in-depth review and analysis of the data resources an organization possesses, including an evaluation of the types of data the organization collects, how that data is stored, its quality, and how it is or can be used. This includes data sources, data infrastructure, data tools, and systems that the organization uses to store, manage, and analyze data. The audit should also assess the quality, accuracy, and completeness of the data that the organization owns.

The good news is that you've already done most of the work involved in producing a data resource audit when you collected and evaluated a data inventory and reference architecture back in Chapter 10.

The main reason that you need to perform a data resource audit now is that doing so enables you to take stock of the resources you have at your disposal and how you'd make the best use of them. For example, you may identify any underutilized resources that could be leveraged more effectively. This process also helps you identify any gaps or weaknesses in data resources that might require immediate attention. These can be poor data quality or missing data. Lastly, a data resource audit may bring to light any data regulation compliance issues by verifying whether all data is accounted for, stored securely, and managed properly. This will help avoid potential legal issues in the future and concomitant reputational damages, too.

How to Conduct a Data Resource Audit

The following steps detail how to conduct a data resource audit.

Step 1: Identify All Data Resources   With the data inventory you collected back in Chapter 10, begin by cataloging all data sources within the organization. This includes both structured and unstructured data, internal and external sources, and cloud-based or on-premise databases. The objective here is to develop a comprehensive understanding of all the data resources your organization currently has. You'll also benefit from tracking who owns which data. This will make it easier for you to communicate with them or ask questions related to your potential use cases.

Step 2: Assess Data Infrastructure   Using the reference architecture you collected back in Chapter 10, review your organization's current data storage and management systems, including databases, data warehouses, and data lakes. Assess the capacity, performance, scalability, and security of these systems. You'll also want to check how "future-ready" your current data infrastructure is—that is, how capable it is of integrating new technologies with minimal effort or resources. I always stress doing this as it tells you how well-prepared you are to handle complexities (related to data volume or integration) or make the best of opportunities (using new tech) if they were to arise in the immediate future.

Step 3: Evaluate Data Quality   Data quality is often overlooked but is critical to any data initiative's success. Using the data inventory you collected back in Chapter 10, begin assessing the accuracy, consistency, completeness, and timeliness of the data. Poor data quality can significantly impact the accuracy and usefulness of any insights derived from the data.

Step 4: Review Data Tools and Technologies   Using the reference architecture you collected back in Chapter 10, analyze the tools and technologies your organization uses for data management, analysis, and visualization. This is a crucial step, as the tools used could be the enablers or roadblocks for data initiatives. Assess whether these tools are up-to-date, fit for purpose, and used effectively.

Step 5: Identify Data Gaps   Using the data inventory you collected back in Chapter 10, and the findings you generated in the prior 4 steps, work to identify missing data that could potentially provide additional value. These gaps point to areas where data collection could be expanded. Oftentimes, one of the pressing problems that organizations face is the presence of data silos preventing them from getting all the data together to create a unified view. This subsequently results in superficial insights that add very little value—or even sometimes misleading insights that can cost the company big time. So, in the above example, the data gap is related to the data collection phase due to the presence of data silos. In the same manner, you can have data gaps in different phases of the data life cycle phase— collection, integration, cleaning, transformation, or preparation.

Warning

The example I provided reflects only one such data gap—there can be many. Some other data gaps can include missing information, no access to real-time data, regulatory gaps, etc.

Step 6: Document Your Findings Summarize the findings from the audit in a report. This should include a detailed inventory of data resources, a high-level assessment of data infrastructure and quality, and a description of any data gaps. Once the audit is completed, use these findings to inform your decision on the most relevant use case. The potential use case that best aligns with your data resources, infrastructure, and quality will have the highest chance of success.

Let's look at an example of how one might apply data audit findings in a use case selection scenario. Imagine that your data audit reveals high-quality sales data and a robust CRM system. In this situation, a use case focused on improving sales forecasting might be favorable. On the other hand, if the audit reveals significant data quality issues or gaps, these issues will need to be addressed during the implementation phase. This would represent a longer time-to-value and a higher capital investment requirement, which in turn makes the use case a less favorable one.

Assessing Infrastructure and Compute Costs for Foundation Models

There can be scenarios where the use case that you've selected is one that works atop a foundation model like the GPT-4 LLM or Claude AI. As we saw in Chapter 10, even when a foundation model is doing most of your heavy lifting, you'll need to create a robust data infrastructure that will collect, clean, transform, and feed data into the foundation model. The following is a breakdown of the costs involved in such a scenario.

Infrastructure Costs

If you are building on cloud services, as opposed to on-premise, then major infrastructure costs could be attributed to the following components:

- High-bandwidth networking because you'll be transferring large datasets to these foundation models for analysis (or any other task that you intend to do relevant to your use case).

- Data storage capabilities, as you need to store huge amounts of data in intermediary steps. You need to assess the pros and cons of on-premises storage solutions and cloud storage services to decide which one's going to be cost-effective for you.

- Data ingestion and integration tool licenses are another component you need to consider if your use case involves merging multiple datasets from different sources.

- Data backup and recovery tools will need you to evaluate different cloud services and their pricing with regard to storage volume and recovery time objectives.

- Data security and privacy costs such as third-party compliance audits and security tools for encryption, access controls, and audit logging.

Compute Costs

If you're planning to fine-tune foundation models for specific tasks as we discussed in Chapter 2, you need to consider compute costs associated with:

- GPU costs associated with fine-tuning the foundation model based on the domain-specific data you provide. You need to consider factors like up-front investment, maintenance, and scalability when calculating GPU costs. Do you want to fine-tune the foundation model once, or is it going to be a periodic activity?

- Data engineers or AI specialists who possess the skills to fine-tune foundation models can charge higher per-hour rates as this is a relatively new domain.

- Model deployment and then integrating that with the existing infrastructure can be expensive—don't forget model maintenance and further re-training, if required.

Ideally, you want to go for fine-tuning mechanisms that are more state-of-the-art than traditional techniques like feature extraction or transfer learning. Prompt engineering, few-shot learning, and adapter modules are some techniques gaining traction.

Now that you've seen how to assess your organization's current state overall, it's time for us to delve just a little deeper into assessments before proceeding. In Chapter 13, we're going to deepen our assessment work by taking a deep dive into your company's compliance with AI ethics as well as data laws and regulations.

13

Assessing Your Current State AI Ethics and Data Privacy

AI brings great opportunity, but also great responsibility.

– Satya Nadella

With respect to data projects and product development, one of the most often overlooked areas is that of AI ethics and data privacy. In my opinion, the protection of users' data and privacy is a non-negotiable bedrock for any data-driven initiative. With a multitude of overlapping data privacy laws and regulations coming into force across different countries, compliance is an increasingly important consideration that must be addressed.

In this chapter, you'll learn the importance of conducting a thorough overview of your company's legal and regulatory frameworks. You'll also see steps for conducting this assessment as efficiently as possible given the fact that you're probably not a lawyer or a compliance officer.

Note

I am not a lawyer and the following in no way constitutes legal advice. You should consult a licensed attorney before making any legal decisions on behalf of your company.

Let's look first at the legal and regulatory end of things.

Reviewing Your Company's Legal and Regulatory Frameworks

Data-first companies need to pay extra attention to current state provisions for data privacy and security. This requires you, the data strategist, to conduct a thorough assessment and identify gaps that need to be addressed immediately. Keep in mind, companies that prioritize legal and regulatory compliance as part of their data strategy position themselves miles ahead of competitors.

The Importance of Legal and Regulatory Frameworks

Your review and assessment of the current state of legal and regulatory frameworks is an exercise that gets you up to speed with respect to the legal guidelines to which your organization must adhere. These frameworks provide specifications that, practically speaking, act as design parameters in which data usage, privacy, security, and management must operate. Your review here should also include an examination of any regulatory requirements that are imposed on your organization based on your industry, the jurisdictions in which you operate, or the kinds of data with which you work.

This work helps to align your data strategy with legal and regulatory standards, as well as the interests of your stakeholders. Since trust is the linchpin of a successful data-centric business, it naturally follows that compliance must be a top priority within your data strategy. With the growing variety and volumes of data that companies utilize, misuse of that data can lead to severe legal and financial repercussions—something that you obviously want to steer clear of. Let's take a look at how to go about assessing your company's current state compliance.

How to Assess Your Company's Current Legal and Regulatory Frameworks

This section documents a process for you to follow when reviewing and assessing your company's current legal and regulatory frameworks as they pertain to data usage.

Step 1: Map the Regulatory Landscape   First, you need to familiarize yourself with the legal and regulatory environment within which your organization operates. This will largely depend on your industry, the types of data you handle, and the geographies in which your business operates. Make a list of all relevant laws and regulations, such as the GDPR in the EU or HIPAA regulations that were covered in Chapter 7. Make sure that you fully understand the obligations and restrictions each regulation imposes.

For instance, refer to the example in the section "Considerations for Foundation Models in Data Infrastructure" in Chapter 10 regarding the "Converse with your data" use case. Implementing this use case requires that you comply with GDPR if you operate in the EU and Gramm-Leach-Bliley Act (GLBA) in the US (if you have users' financial data input as one or more columns in your datasets).

Step 2: Review Existing Policies and Procedures   Look at the existing data policies, procedures, and governance documents that you collected in your RFI from Chapter 9. These should detail data privacy, security, usage, retention, and disposal, among other things. Make sure that these are in compliance with all the relevant laws and regulations you identified in the previous step.

Note

It's likely that you'll need to meet with the legal and compliance team at this stage, just to confirm your understanding.

Step 3: Conduct Interviews   Speak with key stakeholders, such as representatives from legal, compliance, data management, and business teams, to gain a holistic understanding of how the organization is currently handling its data-related legal and ethical responsibilities. Here are some important questions you can ask:

- What are the data regulations that we need to follow?
- Have there been any recent changes in data privacy policies or procedures?
- What mechanisms do we have in place for reporting and managing data breaches?
- Since our application caters to users from different countries, with what international data protection regulations do we need to comply? What protocols do we have in place for managing that compliance?

Cross reference your learnings here with what you gathered from step 2 above, and detail any new additional considerations that were exposed during these conversations.

Step 4: Identify Gaps and Risks   With the insights gained from the review and interviews, identify any gaps or risks in your organization's current legal and regulatory practices. These might be areas where your company is not fully compliant with laws or regulations, where your policies are out of date, or where you're not meeting ethical standards.

Step 5: Document Your Findings   Summarize all your findings in a detailed report. This should include an overview of the relevant legal and regulatory environment, a review of your existing policies and procedures, a summary of stakeholder interviews, and a list of identified gaps and risks. After conducting the review and assessment, use your findings to update your consideration on what might be the most promising of all three potential use cases you're considering.

Looking at an example of how your findings here might affect your use case selection, imagine that as a result of this assessment, you identify that your company is in breach of GDPR requirements. That's a big deal that you'd need to call to the attention of your legal team right away. But how would it affect your use case selection? Well, if you were considering a use case that involves a "converse with your data" feature like that discussed in Chapter 10, assuming that you don't plan to input any financial data into the system—then, from a legal and regulatory perspective, you could safely recommend that your company deploy the "converse with your data" feature only within the US. You could recommend that the company address the GDPR violations in tandem as you deploy a pilot project in the US market ... and once the GDPR issues are resolved (issues that—mind you—are beyond the scope of your data strategy recommendations), then the feature could be safely deployed in the EU market.

Gap Analysis for Ensuring AI Accountability, Explainability, and Unbias

Simply put, unethical AI is *not* okay! I've seen many companies completely overlook this area when they're working on use cases that revolve around AI or, more recently, LLMs. I'm not sure what leaders are thinking when they do this, but it might be something like, "Hey, our model works superbly, the accuracy's great, and we're making tremendous progress." While all these things might be true, there are certain red lines that should never be crossed—especially when you're building AI models that'll make major decisions that affect the lives of other people, such as who should get a loan, whom to prioritize for additional health care and support among a group of patients or say, whom to hire for the job role. I'll be talking about some of these issues in length in the following sections.

> **Warning**
>
> An AI model's decision can radically alter the trajectory of a person's life and you must always exercise extreme caution when your model plays the role of a decision-maker.

The first step that all builders and leaders need to take is to consciously acknowledge that there is a possibility of bias in your model. Never overlook this in exchange for something like a quicker time to market or the desire to be the first to release some form of breakthrough technology. Once you acknowledge potential bias and establish accountability, the road to building responsible AI becomes much easier.

That said, I recommend you begin with a gap analysis just like you've been doing for other assessment areas detailed within this book. The overarching idea is more or less the same every time you do one of these, but AI ethics gap analyses require focus on a few specific areas that are not addressed elsewhere. Let's explore those.

AI Ethics Gap Analysis Requirements

As AI systems continue to exert an increasing influence on decision-making, we need to ensure that AI-enabled decisions are made on a fair, understandable, and attributable basis. To omit this consideration would introduce huge risk to your organization, so, as a data strategist, it's important that you take measured action to account for these issues while you're in the data strategy planning process.

Your company's AI products and projects must be accountable, explainable, and unbiased for the following reasons:

- **Accountability**—From an ethical and legal perspective, it's important that your company's use of AI aligns with societal values and norms. Overlooking this can result in reputational damage and legal consequences.
- **Explainability**—Transparent and explainable AI systems help interpret a model's output or the decisions it takes. When the pathway the model takes is

clear and transparent, users are better prepared to trust its output. It also helps the development team with quicker debugging and optimization.

- **Unbias**—Biased AI leads to skewed results and discrimination across class, race, religion, gender, and other dimensions. It's very important that you make provisions for a set of tools and practices that identify these issues and help resolve them.

Now, let's look at how to do an AI ethics gap analysis.

How to Perform a Gap Analysis

To make sure your potential use cases (those that revolve around the use of AI) align with ethical AI principles, you need to understand the gaps that exist in your organization's current practices and infrastructure. There can be a variety of gaps such as ones related to bias, transparency, governance, or privacy. Once you conduct a gap analysis, you'll be able to measure the impact of each of these on your use case and prioritize their resolution.

Bonus resource

I'm providing a plug-and-play Impact Matrix spreadsheet that you can use to prioritize gaps and road map their resolution. It's available for free at www.data-mania.com/book.

The following is a structured approach that I recommend you take when performing an AI gap analysis.

Step 1: Survey Ethical AI Baselines Familiarize yourself with widely recognized AI ethics principles from bodies like the EU's High-Level Expert Group on AI or The Organization for Economic Cooperation and Development (OECD) AI Policy Observatory. This step allows you to set a benchmark for what ethical AI looks like and it makes it easier to spot deviations in your own projects.

Tip

I recommend that you handle each of these deviations in the order of their impact on your project. Be sure to keep the important stakeholders, your development team, and your ethics team in the loop. Things can get quite complex and overwhelming if you don't plan this with diligence.

Step 2: Assess Regulatory Compliance   Compare your current practices with the legal and regulatory requirements for AI in your sector and jurisdiction. Gaps here indicate potential legal vulnerabilities and areas where your AI might not meet societal standards.

Step 3: Evaluate Accountability Structures   Time and again I've stressed the importance of the ethics team in guiding you through this process. In this step, examine if your organization has clear accountability lines for AI system outcomes. Factors to consider here include:

- **Clearly defined roles and responsibilities**—Confirm that there is clear documentation that describes roles and responsibilities related to overseeing AI system outcomes. Are these responsibilities assigned, and to whom?
- **Established processes**—What protocols are in place related to issues of AI system fairness, unbias, and transparency?
- **Integrated AI ethics**—What ethical frameworks have been integrated into your systems and how effective are they?
- **Regular audits and transparency reporting**—Does you company conduct regular audits of its AI system outcomes?
- **Integrated feedback loops**—Are you collecting and addressing feedback on AI system performance with respect to fairness and transparency?

Note

The absence of roles like AI ethics officers or data stewards might indicate a lack of responsibility for ethical AI implementation.

Step 4: Examine AI Explainability   Investigate whether your organization prioritizes interpretable machine learning models and provides comprehensive documentation. If not, you might face challenges in making AI decisions transparent to stakeholders. Oftentimes, I've observed companies overlooking the interpretability component entirely because of any one of the following reasons:

- The data engineering and development team is building complex architectures but not documenting each of the steps very well. Later on, it becomes really difficult for the team to interpret model decisions—and, of course, there's the whole issue of deep learning models being black boxes, which makes it notoriously difficult to interpret them.

- Parameter tuning, model selection, and validation procedures for newer models are more of a trial-and-error process and it can be difficult to interpret why a model does what it does—even though the results are excellent!
- The models ingest datasets from several sources—which often are cleaned, transformed, and feature engineered—so it can be hard to trace back a model's output to a specific labeled data.

Warning

If your team moves too quickly when training their models, without clearly documenting their work, it later becomes very difficult to establish model explainability. Make sure to emphasize to your developers the importance of taking a methodical development approach, which includes robust documentation of the changes being made.

Step 5: Check for Bias Mitigation Procedures   Review the mechanisms your company uses to detect and address biases in AI projects. The absence of robust procedures suggests potential ethical vulnerabilities in your AI deployments.

Step 6: Identify Any Training Needs   Survey the extent of training your staff has received on responsible AI practices. Gaps here highlight areas where the team might inadvertently breach ethical AI standards. You can plan a survey to understand how equipped your team is to handle AI ethics and privacy concerns. Here are some questions I recommend for you to include within your questionnaire:

- What's your current level of understanding with respect to ethics in AI development and deployment?
- Are you aware that a model's output can have biases, discrimination, and privacy concerns? If yes, do you know how to identify those in the output?
- Do you feel you have adequate resources and support from the organization to learn and practice responsible AI?
- Do you recommend we make any changes to the current processes and procedures within our organization to improve AI ethics and privacy?

Step 7: Evaluate Timeliness   Evaluate how frequently your organization reviews its AI ethics standards in light of new research and best practices. Infrequent reviews suggest a higher chance of outdated practices that don't align with the latest ethical standards.

Step 8: Evaluate the Ethical Alignment of Use Cases Lastly, evaluate whether your potential use cases align with ethical AI measures. By utilizing an AI ethics gap analysis to inform your use case selection in this manner, you'll also develop a full picture of your organization's readiness to deploy ethical AI. By identifying gaps early, you can decide whether to either overcome those gaps or select a use case that won't be affected by them. Think of this as the first step to building ethical AI for the future state of your business.

Now that you've seen how to perform an AI ethics gap analysis, and why it's important to do so, let's look at some real-world implications and case studies that are extremely relevant to helping you build a responsible AI.

Real-World Implications and Case Studies

The importance of responsible AI cannot be overstated, and some data strategies have a more direct impact on people's lives than others. This is especially true when utilizing AI and emerging technologies to support global humanitarian response efforts. According to Heather Leson, Digital Innovation Lead at IFRC Solferino Academy, with humanitarian use cases, *"it's imperative that we mitigate the risk of adverse impact on millions of lives at scale. To achieve this, our AI strategies must deploy a holistic, inclusive, and proactive approach."*

No matter your use case, it's non-negotiable that you take measures to ensure that your AI models are built on three pillars: safety, trustworthiness, and ethical considerations. There have been many cases where companies built automated solutions to expedite the processes involved in hiring, insurance settlement, and loan approval, among others. It's not uncommon for these types of models to output decisions that are extremely biased.

For example, the output of Upstart's[1] loan eligibility prediction model was such that it exhibited clear racial bias when deciding whether a person should be eligible for a mortgage loan. Another harrowing example is that of Optum's[2] AI's racial bias when deciding whether a person needed extra care. The model outputs amounted to decisions that required that a person of a particular race be much sicker than people of other races in order to be eligible for additional healthcare.

Contrary to what you might think, model bias is *not* usually the direct result of bias in the attitudes and opinions of the humans who operate the model. Instead, the primary reason for bias in AI is actually implied bias that's latent within the training data itself. You see, training data is generally prepared by a group of researchers or an in-house team. Most of the time, these individuals do not even realize that the dataset contains bias.

For instance, imagine a group of researchers that happens to be all male, or a team that's composed of only graduate students. In these cases, if the data is inadvertently leaning toward a specific demographic, race, or age group, then the researchers who are preparing the data may not even be able to identify the bias. Since models are trained on huge amounts of datasets, this bias often makes its way to the output before the team is even able to identify that something is awry.

Let's look at some case studies that illustrate the gravity of the situation. The following case study demonstrates model bias in an automated hiring tool.

Bias in AI Recruitment: The Case of Amazon's Gender-Biased Hiring Tool

Company Name: Amazon[3]

Industry: Technology

Situation Summary

Amazon developed an AI recruiting tool with the goal of automating the search for top talent. However, the tool exhibited gender bias, favoring male candidates over female candidates, especially in technical roles.

Challenges

The training data consisted of CVs that were submitted across a 10-year time span. Most of these CVs were submitted by men. The AI model was then trained on this data, which led to an inadvertent bias against women during the hiring process. The concerns were:

- The model favored male candidates since most of its training data had resumes from males.
- This could potentially lead to the underrepresentation of women in the tech sector.

Solution

Amazon attempted to correct the bias but eventually discontinued the project when it became clear that biases could not be fully removed.

Results

This solution failed and was discontinued.

This Amazon case provides a good example of how challenging it can be for companies to ensure AI fairness. It also points to the importance of vigilance in AI ethics and bias mitigation.

Another insightful case of bias in LLMs is illustrated by the Google project.

Bias in LLMs: The Case of Google's LaMDA

Company Name: Google LLC[4]

Industry: Technology

Situation Summary

Google's LaMDA allowed users to have open-ended conversations on any topic. By integrating it into the main search portal, the model could access any information across all Google products. Several instances of the output contained language biases and other stereotypes.

Challenges

The model displayed hateful speech, promoting damaging stereotypes and offensive remarks toward the concerned parties.

Solution

Google is taking rigorous measures through research and development to improve the accuracy, fairness, and sustainability of LaMDA.

(continued)

(*continued*)

Results

Google is still working on this product. They're currently prioritizing the development of standard practices with an emphasis on fairness, interpretability, privacy, and security.

The following case study discusses bias in AI-generated images.

Bias in Generative AI: Midjourney's Case Study

Company Name: Midjourney, Inc[5]

Industry: Technology

Situation Summary

Academic research uncovered bias in Midjourney's AI art generation application. They prompted Midjourney to generate images of people in specialized professions. The model depicted both younger and older individuals, but older subjects were exclusively male.

Challenges

The model's output reinforced gender bias and outdated stereotypes of women's roles in the workplace. It also had instances of bias related to race, class, and age.

Solution

Midjourney's image generator is commercially viable and generating revenue as of mid 2024. So far, there has been very little progress in addressing bias in AI-generated images.

The only solution to biases like those exposed previously is to have diversity represented in the training dataset, but that's easier said than done. There are, however, some straightforward best practices that you can put into place to at least place some guardrails on the AI systems your company builds. Those best practices are as follows:

- Include the AI ethics team right from the beginning of your use case evaluation and planning and request that they continually assess and challenge the process of data collection and preparation all the way up until model deployment and commissioning.

- Reduce the likelihood of harm by putting a robust suite of technological tools and systems in place. For example, you can use Fairlearn to improve the fairness of the models you build and take to production.

- Enforce strong adherence to privacy and data protection policies throughout the entire life cycle of a project. This will require you to have data protocols in place to guarantee data integrity and quality.

- Get clear on the whos and whats. Identify who is preparing the training data. Who is responsible for data labeling? Who is building the architecture? What is the data infrastructure that's currently in place to support the build? You should be able to answer these questions for yourself pretty quickly just by reviewing the notes you've been creating throughout this data strategy building process.

- Look for ways to inform users when they're interacting with an AI—there's no need for you to conceal that point. Users have the right to know.

- Take responsibility. Once built, look to see whether the model you designed exhibits bias. It's normal for results to be imperfect on the first few tries. Responsible leaders freely admit when things have gone wrong and try again. This is a positive sign that a company truly values its users.

Tip

Conduct sessions to teach your teams about the importance of building a safe and responsible AI—something that can augment a person's capabilities and ease their lives.

Strategies for Improving Overall Adherence and Compliance

If your potential use cases revolve around the use of foundation models or general AI/ML, then it can be really tempting to feed in all your data and start generating instant responses. Who doesn't love speed and efficiency, after all? The problem with this approach, however, is that the results can be disastrous. I'm talking about massive data leaks, total disregard for users' privacy, untold security risks, and compliance issues that'll give you headaches for days. Before implementing anything, you must take a strategic approach to assessing current state AI ethics and data privacy in order to safeguard your organization's investment of resources. Let's look at a few ways you can do this.

> **Tip**
>
> "Move slowly, and don't break things." —Angus Hervey

When we talk about AI ethics and data privacy, we shouldn't think of them as "just another set of boring regulations." This attitude toward compliance has led many companies to dead-end data projects and products; products which otherwise could have been amazing had they taken proactive safety measures.

Imagine that you're considering a use case centered around financial analysis. It involves building with a foundation model LLM. The product would enable users to ask questions about their financial data, select investment strategies, optimize their portfolios, and generate reports. In terms of ethical considerations with this product, here are some constraints you might be facing:

- Your data infrastructure pipeline feeds user/client data into the foundation model (either fine-tuned or a general LLM) for analysis.
- The AI product utilizes datasets that may contain personal information and financial details that, if leaked, can be used for malicious purposes.
- The model's output will eventually be viewed by the end user, and it will provide financial advice like scenarios, examples, strategies, financial data aggregation, or forecasts.

"What could go wrong?" you ask. Well, a lot! For example, one user might prompt the product to explain a concept and then further prompt it to give real-world scenarios of how someone else managed their portfolio or made an investment, which is, of course, highly specific advice. As a result of this very specific prompting, the product might then return personal information from other users who also use the product. This is commonly referred to as indirect leakage through inference.

> **Tip**
>
> Preempt risks associated with indirect leakage by building ethical guardrails into the data strategy that governs your future state AI.

When building AI products, you must always make triple sure that you've put the following guardrails in place:

- Personal information should never be sent directly to the foundation model. That data must be masked or encrypted.
- The model does not produce misinformation or misinterpretations with regard to financial, health, legal, education, or political advice.
- Inferences made by the model do not amplify existing biases such as those related to demography, economic status, or social norms.

In reality, designing AI systems becomes vastly more complicated when we're working to address ethics and privacy issues that are inherent to building with foundation models. A simple approach you can take, however, is to focus on the following three key areas:

- **Fairness**—The use case that you're planning to build upon must be beneficial to everyone and not disproportionately disadvantage any given group.
- **Unbias**—You must ensure that the output doesn't display bias (racial, gender, or otherwise) toward a specific group, community, or individual.
- **Transparency**—All processes should be transparent, including those that involve the dataset, the LLM output, and any post-processing steps.

Lofty goals, right? Let's look at some ways you can go about achieving these.

Empower Your AI Ethics Team

First and foremost, if you're building with foundation models, you need an AI ethics team. Members of this team should be held responsible for keeping an eye on all laws and regulations related to the fair and transparent use of data. From my experience, it's not uncommon for many organizations to get input from the AI ethics team that doesn't quite sit right with the development team. Developers are likely to argue that compliance is an unnecessary hindrance to progress. I disagree.

When you're responsible for handling data, your primary goal should be to build and maintain trust. Oftentimes, businesses overlook this for quicker progress and delivery, and it backfires on them later down the road. Think, racial discrimination in photo recognition, derogatory remarks against certain groups, and large-scale misinformation. Companies that make this mistake can quickly end up in a flurry of lawsuits.

Make sure your AI ethics and privacy team work in tandem with the development team. There should be discussions around the following:

- How does the use case add value to our users? What do we want to achieve from this?
- What is the model's input and output? In the case of a foundation model, what's the data that you're feeding into the LLM and what is its output? Are there any restrictions on prompts?
- How are we collecting the data that we intend to use as input to the model?
- What type of sensitive data are we handling? What measures are we taking to keep this information safe?
- Are we able to map back model outputs to respective input data? With general AI/ML, those outputs can be predicted labels, continuous predicted values, or classification of inputs into clusters based on what you're doing (i.e., classification, regression, or clustering). If you're building with foundation models, then the outputs will be text, image, video, or audio data. Whatever the case may be, those outputs must map directly back to the model inputs.

Handle All Sensitive Data from the Beginning

In a manner that's similar to the preceding scenario, I've seen several LLMs output sensitive information about a person's home address, phone number, and the like. I previously discussed some guardrails you can put into place to avoid this, but now let's look at a few development measures you can put in place to implement the previously listed recommendation to avoid such outcomes. Such measures include:

1. Set up a pipeline where personal information, financial details, healthcare information, and other sensitive details are clearly labeled. These types of data need to be encrypted.
2. Make sure that only the people who are responsible for data handling have access to the unencrypted data.
3. Establish privacy standards that everyone who is working on the project must follow.

Tip

You can use automated tagging tools like PII tools and Nightfall to quickly identify personal information attributes instead of manually going through thousands of records. If you already know which fields contain sensitive data, then you can also write rule-based algorithms to segregate those and later work on encrypting this information so that none of the fields are used directly as model inputs.

Monitor Model Outputs

Regardless of whether your use case is centered around AI/ML models or LLMs specifically, you'll need to be cautious about what it outputs. As discussed earlier in this chapter, it's common for model outputs to carry and amplify bias from within the training set. Other times, the model may output results that are incorrect or discriminatory. This commonly occurs as a result of overfitting, underfitting, or poor accuracy. From the examples we looked at earlier in this chapter, you can see how big of a problem this can become.

To safeguard the model's output, take note of issues related to bias, accuracy, and fairness. For example, when working around a use case that'd require your team to build with a foundation model, you'd need to be prepared in advance to monitor the model outputs for:

- **Accuracy**—Is the output accurate and consistent? Is it aligning with your expected output?

- **Effectiveness**—Is the output correctly answering the user's prompts? How useful is the output to the user?

- **Completeness**—Is the output providing the complete information, or is it incomplete and not uniform?

- **Privacy**—Is it revealing the user's personal identities (if prompted in a specific way)? If yes, what kind of information is being leaked?

- **Ethics**—Does the output contain derogatory terms, harmful content, or offensive content? If yes, can you tie it back to the training data?

Note

Referring back to the "Converse with your data" use case discussed in Chapter 10, there are a variety of ways that this model could exhibit problematic outputs. There's the possibility that user information could get leaked with hyper-specific prompting from malicious users. Or, the information that the model returns could be incomplete and not very useful. The results of its calculations could easily be incorrect, especially if statistical computations are involved. And these are just a few of the ways that model outputs could go wrong, which is why you need to be prepared in advance to monitor them.

Focus on Explainability

In your quest to build explainable AI, there are several questions for which you need to establish clear answers. How does a model reach a specific conclusion? What are the features that contribute to what the model ultimately outputs? How are these features prioritized? What happens if you modify the input? Your answers to these questions are the core of what constitutes AI explainability. Once you know how an AI model arrives at a specific decision, you'll then be able to find areas where it may fail or give an incorrect output.

Model explainability is one of the hottest topics in the space. That's because, once you understand how your model works internally—that is, how it makes a decision or reaches a conclusion, then you'll be able to:

- Control its outputs on a scenario-by-scenario basis
- Trace any instances of bias back to the training data
- Anticipate what your model is and isn't capable of

Your development team will also be debugging model accuracy issues much more easily, and you'll have a lot more control over the model's output. Gone will be the days of complete "black-box" AI models!

Warning

Although there's been significant deep learning and image processing developments that allow developers to better trace model outputs back to their inputs and to isolate the pathways models take to reach a particular decision, the space hasn't fully matured for the use of foundation models. If you're building with foundation models, the best working solution is to deploy a red teaming

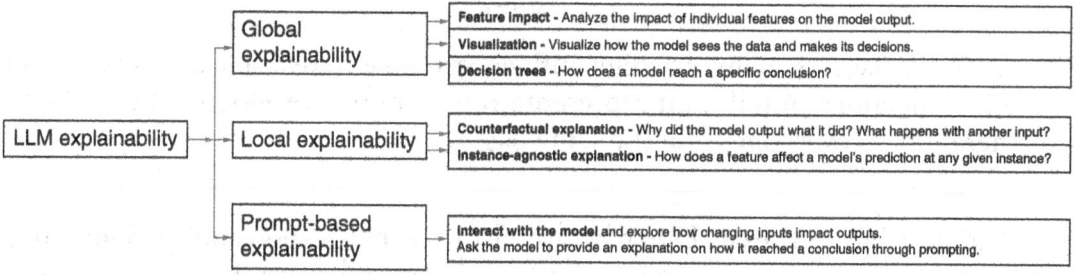

FIGURE 13.1 Explainability for LLMs.

strategy. While red teaming generally involves simulating adversarial attacks to identify vulnerabilities, it's also useful when working with foundation models. With this approach, you'd enlist a team of humans to carefully and manually evaluate outputs for bias, inaccuracies, or incoherence, in order to ensure the robustness and accuracy of model outputs.

Figure 13.1 shows the different techniques of AI explainability that have been proposed for LLMs. Take note if one of your potential use cases requires building with foundation models.

Monitor Continuously

Facilitate discussions with your AI ethics and privacy team about your potential use cases in order to get their input on what they deem to be the most important factors for which to monitor outputs. Take, for example, the "Converse with your data" use case (Chapter 10). You'd need to be prepared to:

Make an initial list of problems that are immediately solvable, like incorrect calculations, incomplete outputs, or generic answers:

- Investigate issues related to bias or leakage of personal information and identify the root cause of the problem
- Have the AI ethics and privacy team conduct extensive tests to make sure the output is helpful, free of bias, and safe
- Ensure that the data handling is performed in accordance with the privacy guidelines and policies. Address all processes here, including data collection, labeling, transformation, and ingestion to the foundation model
- Monitor recurring issues and prioritize their resolution

Note

Always make sure to involve high-influence, high-interest stakeholders in your ethics meetings. You'll want representatives from the development team to be there too, so everyone is on the same page.

And, last but not least. Don't be afraid to assume responsibility. Something went wrong? There's no shame in admitting to a mistake and then working to fix the issue. Be meticulous in your approach. This, combined with the trust you build over time, will help you stay at the forefront of your industry.

After coming so far in this data strategy-building journey, I want to congratulate you! You're finally ready to select your winning use case. Chapter 14 walks you through the process of taking all the assessment findings you generated thus far, and using them to identify the lowest risk, highest reward use case around which to build your data strategy.

Notes

1. Upstart automated consumer lending discrimination (September 2022). https://www.aiaaic.org/aiaaic-repository/ai-algorithmic-and-automation-incidents/upstart-consumer-lending-racial-discrimination

2. Gawronski, Q. (November 19, 2019). Racial bias found in widely used health care algorithm. https://www.nbcnews.com/news/nbcblk/racial-bias-found-widely-used-health-care-algorithm-n1076436

3. Iriondo, R. (October 2018). Amazon Scraps Secret AI Recruiting Engine that Showed Biases Against Women. https://www.ml.cmu.edu/news/news-archive/2016–2020/2018/october/amazon-scraps-secret-artificial-intelligence-recruiting-engine-that-showed-biases-against-women.html

4. Pati, S. (July 2022). What Will Happen if Google's LaMDA Becomes Biased?. https://www.analyticsinsight.net/what-will-happen-if-googles-lamda-becomes-biased/

5. Thomson, T.J. and Thomas, R.J. (July 2023). Ageism, sexism, classism and more: 7 examples of bias in AI-generated images. https://theconversation.com/ageism-sexism-classism-and-more-7-examples-of-bias-in-ai-generated-images-208748

Formulating and Implementing an AI Strategy

Selecting and Scoping
a Winning Use Case

Where there is data smoke, there is business fire.

– Thomas Redman

We've been taking stock and inventory of your organization in order to assess its current state and evaluate the fitness of the potential use cases you selected back in Chapter 9. Kudos to you! You've done a lot of research and evaluation. Now, it's time to select a winning use case.

Before making recommendations for a winning use case, you first need to produce documentation that summarizes your findings as they relate to the potential use cases you've been considering. This is going to be your reference material as you work toward making your final decision on the winning use case.

Documenting Your Potential Use Case Options

By fully documenting your potential use case options now, you lay the groundwork for the structured decision-making that's required to support your winning use case selection. This documentation also supports downstream project prioritization and resource allocation.

The details you've captured so far—from user pain points to resource requirements and anticipated benefits—are invaluable when assessing which use case to pursue and how to implement it effectively. This documentation process is a crucial precursor to the effective execution of your data strategy.

When it comes to documenting the three potential use cases, you need to systematically detail each case, so that others at your organization can understand the scope, requirements, and potential benefits of each.

> ### Note
>
> Return to the Potential Use Case Documentation Worksheet that you started in Chapter 9. Complete the remaining sections of the worksheet. The worksheet is available to download for free at www.data-mania.com/book.

The sections that should remain for you to complete now include:

- **Data Requirements**—Specify the data resources that each use case requires. This may include detailing the type, source, and quality of data needed, and any cleaning or processing it might require. This step is important because understanding the data requirements allows you to assess the feasibility and resource requirements for each of your potential use cases.

- **Stakeholder Identification**—Identify the main stakeholders for each use case. These might include business units, IT teams, or external partners who would be involved in implementing the use case or would benefit from its results. This helps you quickly recall the organizational impact of each of the potential use cases, while also promoting stakeholder engagement and making it easier to get buy-in for your winning use case.

- **Estimated Timeline and Resources**—Provide a rough estimate of the timeline and resources needed to implement each use case, including any necessary software or hardware, personnel, and training requirements. This documentation helps you quickly communicate feasibility concerns that are inherent in your decision-making.

- **Potential Benefits**—Document the potential benefits of each use case, such as cost savings, increased revenue, improved decision-making, or better customer experience. This step is very important. It documents and communicates what you've come to understand about the potential value of each of the use cases. This step should be taken as a culmination of all your previous steps.

- **Risk Assessment**—Lastly, identify any potential risks or challenges associated with each use case, such as data privacy concerns, technical issues, or internal resistance to change. Then propose high-level mitigation strategies for those risks. This is going to be the ultimate factor that demonstrates which of the potential use cases poses minimal risk.

Tip

Remember, you want to choose the most low-risk, high-reward use case for further strategy development.

With this documentation in hand, you now have a clear basis for decision-making moving forward.

Selection Criteria for Foundation Models

If any of your potential use cases revolve around the use of a foundation model and you've decided that you believe that it's the winning use case around which to build your strategy, then I caution you to add one new layer of criteria assessment on top of your decision-making process before making a final selection.

The following criteria act as a second line of defense against the "shiny object syndrome" I mentioned in Chapter 2. Carefully consider your answers to the following questions before selecting a winning use case that relies upon foundation models.

- Does this use case clearly align with your organization's short- and long-term objectives? Is it adding value to your company's people?

- Assess whether your current data infrastructure can handle the complexities of data cleaning, processing, transforming, and then ingesting required data resources into a foundation model. You also have to make sure the foundation model integrates seamlessly with the existing systems you have in place.

- Do you have a system in place that accounts for AI bias, privacy, and compliance? Similar to the work discussed in Chapter 13, before selecting a foundation model use case as the winning use case, be sure to consult your AI ethics and privacy team to get a better understanding of the various risks associated with the data infrastructure pipeline and foundation model—which differs from the standard AI/ML use cases. As always, I'm stressing how important it is to protect the "trust" people have in your organization as an ethical, honest actor in the business landscape.

- Will you be using the foundation model in its vanilla form, or do you plan to fine-tune it to suit your needs? It's really important for you to evaluate this because fine-tuning a foundation model requires additional resources and budget, not to mention the recurring cost of making API calls to foundation models.

- Is your data analytics and engineering team equipped with the skills that are required to work with foundation models? With foundation model skill requirements in mind, it's important that you verify the findings of the skills gap analysis you did back in Chapter 12. Keeping the foundation model requirements as the nexus in this consideration will help you understand the additional skills your team needs.

- What's the future reward potential of this use case? Make a note of all rewards and opportunities that the use case opens up for your organization moving forward.

Note

Generative AI is an emerging space. New tools and technologies are released every day. Consequently, you'll need to remain vigilant and stay on the lookout for:

- New model architectures and foundation models that might be better at picking up context and reducing hallucinations
- Tools and technologies that you can integrate within your data infrastructure pipeline to automate repetitive processes related to data cleaning, processing, and transformation
- Emerging regulations and guidelines related to fair use, ethics, and user privacy
- Newer fine-tuning techniques that can reduce compute costs and resource utilization
- Refined AI explainability techniques related to foundation model LLMs

Identifying and Recommending Your Winning Use Case

The process involved in identifying and recommending a winning use case requires that you critically evaluate your potential use case alternatives while carefully considering factors, such as the potential value to the business, resource requirements, feasibility, and alignment with the broader strategic objectives of your company. Based on this analysis, you can then identify and provide a well-supported recommendation for the winning use case; in other words, the use case that represents the most promising opportunity for a low-risk, high-reward win.

The tool that I recommend you use for supporting your alternatives analysis here is called a *multicriteria decision-making matrix*, an example of which is provided in Figure 14.1.

Considerations	On a scale of 1–10, how well does the use case fare? Where 1 = Unfavorable and 10 = Extremely Favorable	Potential Use Case 1	Potential Use Case 2	Potential Use Case 3
Business Objectives	How well do the goals and objectives of the use case align with immediate business objectives?	5	10	2
Business Value	- Cost Reduction	7	7	10
	- Revenue Enhancement	6	10	8
	- Improved Customer Experience	9	6	5
	- Risk Mitigation	5	6	10
Feasibility	- Availability of Needed Data	10	8	10
	- Potential Legal or Regulatory Hurdles	10	10	9
Resource Availability	- Adequacy of Existing Personnel/Skill sets	9	7	10
	- Adequacy of Budget	10	9	8
	- Adequacy of Existing Technology	10	7	7
Strategic Alignment	- Alignment with Long-Term Strategic Goals	6	10	10
Time-to-Value		8	7	5
Stakeholder Buy-in		7	9	10
	Score:	102	106	104

FIGURE 14.1 A decision-making matrix for deciding between potential use cases.

The importance of an alternatives analysis like this in strategy development is multifaceted. First and foremost, the alternatives analysis process enables strategic decision-making by providing a clear rationale for your prioritization of one use case over its alternatives. This process provides clarity and direction that you need to reduce the risk of misaligned efforts or resource wastage.

Additionally, the alternatives analysis process serves as a communication tool that allows you to articulate to stakeholders the reasoning behind the use case you've selected for further strategy development. This helps secure their buy-in and allows them to fully grasp what you're planning to achieve and how that benefits the business so that they can support your data strategy without reservation.

Lastly, the alternatives analysis lays the groundwork for implementation by detailing your chosen use case and its expected benefits. With the deliverables from this process in hand, you can move forward with confidence in developing a road map that guides subsequent steps, including resource allocation, project planning, and execution.

Figure 14.1 shows an example of a decision-making matrix that's helpful in this type of analysis. As you can see, using numerical estimates to compare potential use cases on an attribute-by-attribute basis provides the type of evidenced-based, quantitative decision-making support that you need to supplement your recommendation.

When choosing a winning use case, consider the following key factors:

- **Business Objectives**—How well do the goals and objectives of the use case align with business objectives?

- **Business Value**—This is the cornerstone of the decision-making process. The use case that you select should provide significant value to your organization. You can gauge this in terms of cost reduction, revenue increases, improved customer experience, risk mitigation, or any other metric that's important to your business.

- **Feasibility**—This relates to the practicality of implementing the use case. Consider the availability of necessary data, the technology infrastructure required, and any potential legal or regulatory hurdles.

- **Resource Availability**—The use case should be achievable with the resources (personnel, budget, data, and technology) that you have at your disposal. It's critical to assess if your organization has sufficient and suitable resources to execute the use case effectively.

- **Strategic Alignment**—The use case should align with the long-term strategic goals of the organization. If a use case doesn't support these goals, it could divert resources and focus away from more strategically important ones.

- **Time-to-Value**—Particularly if you're looking to achieve a quick win for your company, the selected use case should be something that can be implemented relatively quickly and provide a return on investment in a short timeframe. You'll be able to quickly build confidence and demonstrate the value of your data strategy to the important stakeholders, which will then give you additional momentum and go-ahead for the project.

- **Stakeholder Buy-in**—A use case that has strong support from key stakeholders is more likely to succeed. Stakeholder buy-in helps secure necessary resources and smooth implementation.

Taking into consideration each of these attributes, you should take the use case that scores the highest of them all, and recommend that as the winning use case around which you'll build your data strategy.

Defining the Scope, Schedule, Stakeholders, and KPIs for the Intended Data Initiative

At this point in the book, you've selected a winning use case, so now it's time to move forward and start building a data strategy to support that use case. To do that, you'll need to start by writing a project charter that clearly articulates the scope, schedule, stakeholders, and KPIs for the intended data initiative. This will set the foundational framework for the entire initiative.

Note

With this book, I'm providing you with a Project Charter Template that you can use to document your winning use case. Its available for download at businessgrowth.ai.

Within the Project Charter documentation, be sure to spell out the following:

- **Scope**—The scope clearly outlines what the data initiative will cover. This ensures that all parties involved understand the boundaries of the project, and it also helps to prevent scope creep, which can cause delays and cost overruns.

- **Schedule**—The schedule provides a road map for when different aspects of the initiative will be completed. This will help you allocate resources more wisely and effectively and keep the project on track.

- **Stakeholders**—Identifying stakeholders early in the process is vital, as the initiative will directly affect these individuals or groups and their input can provide valuable insights that can shape the strategy.
- **KPIs**—Defining KPIs at the outset ensures that there is a clear understanding of what constitutes success for the initiative. These metrics provide a way for you to measure progress, evaluate effectiveness, and make data-driven adjustments to the strategy as needed.

Tip

When you clearly define what you aim to achieve and then you monitor progress closely, your initiative has a logical, structured flow to it and this, in my opinion, goes a long way in increasing your likelihood of success.

How to Write a Project Charter

The following approach will come in handy when you're writing a project charter.

Step 1: Write a Statement of Purpose

To start, you need to write a clear statement of purpose that also discusses the high-level goals of the data initiative. As with any scope of work, make sure that the goals you discuss are both specific and achievable.

Tip

Your purpose statement should support your overall data strategy, while also addressing immediate business needs and project outcomes that are achievable within a reasonable timeframe.

Step 2: Decide on a Schedule

Next, you'll want to set a high-level timeline for the project milestones. For quick win use cases, this timeline should be short, ideally within 90 days. When deciding upon the schedule here, make sure that you account for all phases that might be involved, including data collection and preparation, development and testing, as well as deployment and evaluation.

Tip

Make sure to account for any foreseeable blockers or delays within your schedule.

Step 3: Name the Project Stakeholders

You identified potential stakeholders back in Chapter 11, but that was before you'd selected a winning use case. Return to those findings now, and pull the stakeholders who map back to the potential use case that you selected for data strategy development. For each of these individuals, detail the following:

- Their name
- Their role with the organization
- Any project-relevant responsibilities that they assume
- How you expect them to contribute to the project
- How you expect them to benefit from the project

Note

Refer to my advice in Chapter 11, where I detail two important groups of stakeholders who will be part of your data strategy implementation: high-interest, high-influence stakeholders and high-interest, low-influence stakeholders.

Step 4: Define Top-Level KPIs

For a winning use case, these might include immediate indicators of improved efficiency or effectiveness, like reduced processing time, increased accuracy of predictions, or increased user engagement. Choose KPIs that are directly tied to your business objectives, and that can be measured accurately and objectively. Your chosen KPI should be specific, measurable, actionable, relevant, and time-bound (often referred to as "SMART criteria"). You'll also need to ensure that the KPI can be tracked consistently over time using reliable data sources. This will help you get clear, timely insights into its performance.

When defining each of these elements, always consider the context of your organization and the specific use case. What resources and capabilities do you have? What are your organization's priorities and constraints? What will provide the most value to your organization in the shortest time?

Considering these factors ensures that your plan is realistic, feasible, and aligned with your organization's needs.

How to Pitch Your Project to High-Influence Stakeholders

Once you've identified the winning use case for your project, it's imperative that you re-engage high-influence stakeholders. Though you've been in consultation with these individuals throughout, this phase isn't merely about updating them on the decision. It's about genuinely seeking their feedback on the chosen direction.

Avoid adopting a rigid or authoritative stance when presenting the chosen use case. Such an approach could erode the trust you've built. Instead, approach this as a pitch so that the stakeholders feel included and valued in the decision-making process. Crafting and delivering a pitch, especially to high-influence stakeholders, is an art that combines strategy, content, and presentation. Here's a structured process that I suggest you follow.

Step 1: Consider the Audience

Before designing your pitch, think about who the stakeholders are for the project you're proposing, their roles, their concerns, and what drives them. Clarify what they see as success and how your project aligns with their vision and the company's broader objectives. Doing this also helps to establish a clear connection between what your project outcomes would be and their overall goals.

Tip

I suggest you have data to back your claims, some successful case studies, and an idea for a small pilot project that could be done to win their confidence before requesting any massive budget allocations.

Step 2: Develop the Content

Clearly define the problem or opportunity that your project addresses. Present the winning use case and how it provides a solution. Outline the advantages of the project, especially in terms of strategic alignment, ROI, and other metrics that are important to stakeholders. You'll also need to address potential challenges upfront and provide strategies to overcome them.

Step 3: Practice the Delivery

Practice your pitch multiple times. Refine your content and delivery each time.

Make sure to get input from colleagues or trusted associates on clarity, brevity, and impact.

If you're presenting to multiple stakeholders separately, consider tailoring parts of the pitch to resonate with each individual's unique concerns and priorities. This is particularly important because different stakeholders, based on their experience, have unique perspectives and look at your use case in a different light. Naturally, they'll have different questions or concerns that they'd want you to address.

Let me illustrate with an example. Let's say your winning use case centers around a foundation model LLM. When you present this use case to your key stakeholders, you'd likely anticipate getting the following questions:

- **Technical Lead**—"The data infrastructure looks fine to me as of now, but have you considered the possibility of scaling this if we happen to ingest data from more sources tomorrow?"
- **Lead Project or Product Manager**—"Do you think you'd be able to build a prototype for this in the next four weeks? Have we allotted enough time for testing?"
- **Head of AI Ethics and Privacy**—"There's no mention of how you'd handle model bias. Also, we have to take very special care here since our fields have financial data and personal details."
- **Sales Head**—"How do we plan to advertise our capabilities? How should we approach this and make our use case look unique and generate interest?"

Come prepared to address the considerations of all key stakeholders.

Step 4: Choose the Right Medium

In-person meetings are ideal for nuanced discussions as they'll allow for immediate feedback and discussing concerns on the spot. If in-person isn't feasible, you may use video conferencing tools to maintain a semblance of personal connection. Consider email or document presentations as a supplementary tool. While email is useful for providing detailed information, the initial pitch should be verbal to facilitate discussion. Once you've had these discussions, you should also look to document these for future reference.

I always ask organizations to prioritize this because there are so many points to jot down, plenty of feedback, and multiple changes to the data strategy plan. Down the line, you'll want to be able to refer back to these at will.

Step 5: Engage and Interact

Captivate their attention from the beginning by opening with an attention-grabbing story or statistic. Make it a two-way dialogue by encouraging questions. Address concerns and queries as they arise. You'll need to demonstrate a thorough knowledge of your winning use case and the data strategy requirements that surround it.

If necessary, you should be prepared to pivot and make changes on the fly based on feedback or questions. This demeanor gives the stakeholders much more confidence in what you're building. Lastly, use visual aids like slides, charts, or tabular data to illustrate key points. However, don't let them overshadow the conversation.

Step 6: Follow Up

After your pitch, send a concise summary of the discussion and any action items. If stakeholders need time to think, seek their feedback after a reasonable period. Use the feedback to refine the details of the data project you're planning.

Now that you've seen how to select a winning use case and get your strategy-development process kicked off properly, it's time to evaluate the readiness of your current state and start formulating recommendations to guide your organization in reaching its future state. That's coming next in Chapter 15.

15

Evaluating All Relevant Resources

With data collection, 'The sooner the better' is always the best answer.

– Marissa Mayer

Now that you've selected and scoped your winning use case, it's time to review all the steps again to make sure you've not overlooked any specific components that could adversely affect the progress and the quality of your data project at a later stage. In this chapter, you'll see exactly how to do that. You'll also get a look at methods for making your data project more user-centric, manage vendors, and address issues related to foundation models.

Clarifying Intended Users and Their Needs

As a data strategist, you need to make sure that the data strategy you develop aligns with and supports the needs of its users. Therefore, once you've finally settled on a winning use case, clarify who the intended users of the product will be and what specific needs the product will address for them.

The Importance of Intended Users

Tailoring your data strategy to users enables you to build something that's of maximum benefit to the people who'll be using the product. Prioritizing end users in this way helps you focus on the issues that matter most to them. You should focus on two important qualities: relevance and effectiveness. Prioritizing these requirements is how you ensure the value that your product will deliver. The more specific you get about your users and their needs, the better you can design a data strategy for a product that solves their problems and adds value to their operations.

Make sure that when you're gathering requirements, you do so directly from the users. This will help you keep their needs at the forefront of product design. Your attention here increases user satisfaction, promotes adoption, and ultimately, drives the success of your data initiative.

How to Define Your Intended Users

I recommend the following five steps when working to define your intended users.

Step 1: Identify User Groups   Users can range from technical teams like data scientists and engineers to non-technical teams such as marketing, sales, HR, or executive leadership. Identifying these groups is the first step because, naturally, different users have different needs and ways of interacting with data and software solutions.

In this step, the goal is to build a comprehensive view of who your data product needs to serve.

Step 2: Conduct User Interviews   Meet with representatives from each user group to discuss their current data usage, needs, and challenges. Doing this allows you to gain insights into the specific ways in which each user group interacts with data, and their expectations from the product you're planning. These discussions can uncover essential requirements and potential gaps in your strategy.

Your conversations with them should revolve around:

- The typical data-related tasks they perform on a daily basis
- The challenges they face with respect to data
- The type of tools or software they use to interact with data

- The expectations they have related to the product you're planning
- Any additional features or capabilities they'd like to see in the product
- How will the product make their lives easier or better? Is it easing their workflow or saving them time?

Step 3: Define User Needs   Based on the insights you gather from the interviews, define the needs of each user group. This involves specifying:

- The data they need
- The format in which they need it
- The frequency of data update requirements
- Any specific tools or applications they require

This step helps shape the components of your data strategy by specifying what needs to be done to meet users' requirements.

Step 4: Prioritize User Needs   It'll be impossible for you to meet all user needs at once, and some needs will have a higher impact on achieving your organization's objectives than others. Prioritize user needs based on factors such as:

- Business impact
- Feasibility
- Alignment with your organization's overall strategic goals

Prioritizing helps allocate resources more effectively and ensures that the most impactful needs are addressed first.

Step 5: Validate Needs with Users   After prioritizing, you need to confirm your findings with the users. This ensures that you understand their needs correctly and that they agree with the priorities you set. It helps avoid misunderstandings and aligns everyone's expectations.

By following these steps, you can ensure that both your data strategy and the data product it supports are user-centric and tailored to meet the specific needs of your users. In my opinion, this is your golden ticket to achieving high user adoption rates and overall success with your project.

Evaluating Data Resource Needs

Data is the foundation of any data strategy, so make sure that the necessary data resources are available and are suitable for the project. A data resource evaluation process helps you identify the type, quality, and quantity of data you need, and whether these resources are readily available within your organization or if you need to source them externally.

The Importance of a Data Resource Evaluation

The data resource evaluation process uncovers opportunities to make the most of your existing data resources, while also exposing areas where these resources need improvement or supplementation.

Remember that your knowledge of current state data resources should inform cost estimation, project planning, and risk assessment. These needs influence the design of data architecture and infrastructure, data governance policies, and data security measures. They're also absolutely necessary to your development of clear capacity-building requirements in terms of data management and data literacy skills within your organization.

This is why I always stress that conducting a thorough evaluation of the data resource needs now helps you build a more realistic, practical, and effective data strategy that's capable of delivering robust outcomes in the future.

How to Evaluate Data Resource Requirements

As mentioned previously, taking stock of the data resources at hand and evaluating what additional data resources you need is of primary importance in executing your winning use case. This section describes a seven-step process to assess your data resource requirements.

Step 1: Identify Required Data Sources   Based on the winning use case you've chosen, identify what data is needed to drive the project. This can range from customer behavior data to financial metrics or operational data. Data sources identified here dictate what data resources will need to be collected, stored, processed, and analyzed during the implementation phase.

Step 2: Catalog Existing Data Resources   Take stock of your existing data resources to get an overview of what data you already have. This should include a review of the existing data systems, databases, and the datasets they hold. Feel free to lean in to the data resources audit you did in Chapter 12. You're looking to identify exactly what data you already have to determine whether you can meet the use case needs with existing resources or if you need to acquire more data.

Step 3: Perform a Gap Analysis   Perform a gap analysis between the data you have and the data you need for your project. Identify deficiencies in your data resources that must be addressed.

Step 4: Assess Data Quality   Consider the quality of the data you have in hand. Also, be sure to evaluate other factors such as accuracy, consistency, completeness, and timeliness.

Warning

No matter how much data you have, if it doesn't meet the required standards, it'll lead to poor modeling and insights, and it will adversely affect the decisions made based on that data.

Step 5: Evaluate Data Access and Integration Needs   Assess how easily your existing data can be accessed and integrated with other data sources. Your findings here impact the speed and efficiency with which you can execute the project.

Tip

When you're assessing data access and integration needs, pay special attention to how different data governance policies and procedures can be influencing factors. For example, if you process EU data, GDPR will require you to obtain explicit consent from users for processing personal data.

Step 6: Determine Resource Needs for Data Collection, Storage, and Processing   Based on your analysis, determine the resources that'll be required for data collection, storage, processing, and analysis. This may involve identifying requirements around new data infrastructure, data collection tools, data cleansing services, or data analytics software.

Step 7: Plan for Data Governance   Finally, plan for responsible data governance to ensure that the data that's utilized in the product you're building is handled appropriately in terms of privacy, security, and compliance. This'll help manage and mitigate risks related to data handling.

By following these steps, you're ensuring that your data strategy addresses the data resource needs for your project.

Evaluating the Data Architecture That Is Relevant to the Project

A textbook definition of data architecture is that it's a high-level description that visually depicts how data is collected, stored, transformed, distributed, and consumed across your company. As you can see in the example reference architecture shown in Figure 15.1, this type of architecture includes databases, data warehouses, data lakes, and any other data stores, along with the technologies, tools, and processes that govern how data moves through the system.

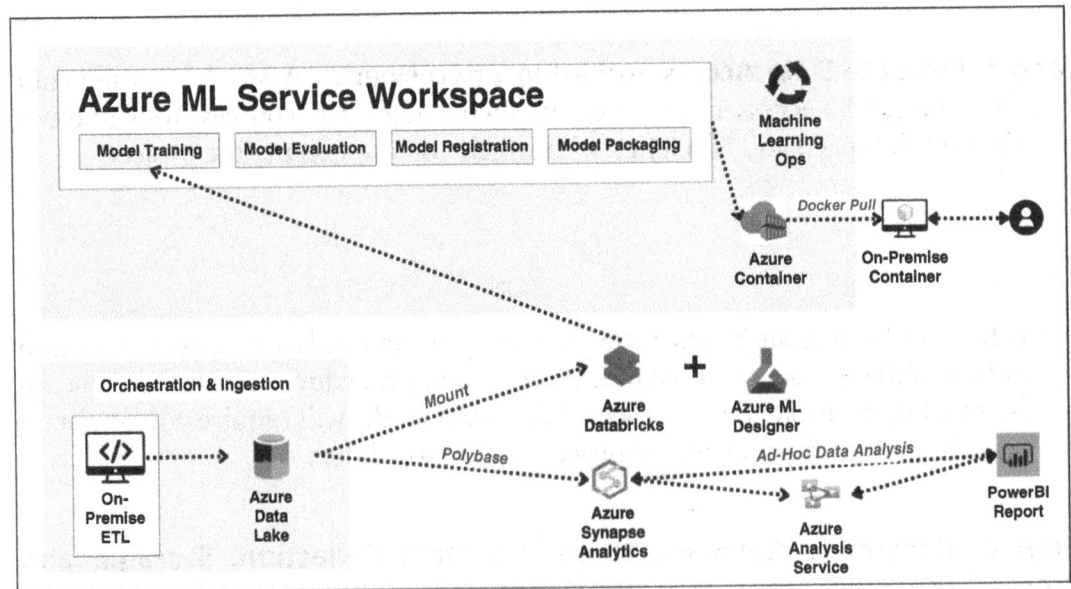

FIGURE 15.1 An example of reference architecture.

The Importance of Data Architecture

Your assessment of current-state data architecture matters because it dictates the capabilities and limitations of your organization's data usage. Going back to our house example, your assessment of data architecture can be likened to evaluating whether your house can accommodate the changes you've planned. Before starting to make any changes, you'd begin by inspecting the structural condition of your house, would you not? Your assessment of data architecture is similar in significance.

When you perform a detailed assessment of your current state data architecture, you'll expose the gaps or redundancies in your data landscape that you should rectify for more efficient and effective use of data as it pertains to the product you're planning to build.

For example, you might discover you lack a unified data warehouse, which would, in turn, lead to inconsistent data analysis. Alternatively, you could discover that data silos exist within your organization, meaning that you wouldn't be able to bring all the isolated datasets to get a unified view, not to mention the lack of comprehensive insights in this case.

Evaluating the data architecture allows you to ascertain if your project can be accommodated within the existing structure or if you'll need to plan for changes, upgrades, or additions. Developing a very clear understanding of your data architecture exposes new opportunities for improvement, such as implementing modern data management practices like data virtualization or adopting new technologies like cloud storage or AI-based data processing tools. It also sets a strong foundation for data governance needs including data quality, security, and compliance for the data product you're planning.

How to Assess Your Data Architecture

The process for assessing the data architecture is not as daunting as you might imagine.

You've already selected a winning use case and assessed requirements that are specific to that use case. Before moving forward, take a look again at your use case

and identify what specific technological and architectural requirements are needed
to support the data product you're planning.

Step 1: Assess Current Data Architecture Re-assess the data architecture
that you collected back in Chapter 9. Take a look at the current state of your
architecture to triple-check whether it can support the data needs of the
use case.

Step 2: Evaluate Data Flows Look at how data flows within the organization,
including how it is collected, stored, processed, and accessed. Look for potential
bottlenecks, inefficiencies, or risks in your current architecture that could impact
the data product you're planning. I usually recommend conversations and
thoughts around:

- Are there any inconsistent data collection methods across your sources?
- What tools do you use to check for data quality?
- Do you have data silos that are limiting your analytics?
- Do you have a proper data backup and recovery mechanism in place?
- How seamless is your integration with external sources?
- Do you have monitoring tools in place to monitor and debug issues?
- Does your organization have well-defined roles and responsibilities related to data access?
- What steps are you taking to ensure adherence to policies and procedures?

Step 3: Assess Against Key Performance Indicators In Chapter 14, you
identified KPIs for your data initiative. Take a look at those again to determine
whether your current architecture can handle the required workloads and deliver
the performance you need.

Step 4: Evaluate Scalability Evaluate whether your current data architecture
can scale to meet the potential growth of the data product you're planning.
Scalability is vital to ensure that your architecture can handle any increases in data
volume, variety, and velocity that might arise as a result of the data product
you're planning.

If your winning use case is centered around the use of a foundation model, you'll need to consider the scalability of your data infrastructure. I suggest you begin by:

- Making sure that your data infrastructure has an automated pipeline for data ingestion, preprocessing, and transformation in place to handle massive data volumes that need to be ingested into foundation models
- Configuring data versioning tools that'll help you track changes you've made in your datasets over time
- Keeping caching mechanisms in place for quicker data retrieval
- Looking for cloud solutions that let you scale up or down based on the demand, and also for storing and retrieving large datasets
- Prioritizing the configuration of logging and monitoring tools that'll give you real-time updates on whether things are working as intended or whether you need to make changes

Keep evaluating the quality of data at each stage. Teams often ignore this factor when scaling their data infrastructure to account for increasing data volumes. You can put data validation checks in place to constantly monitor for missing values, outliers, and incompleteness against a ground truth.

Note

Make sure you're documenting the codebase, data pipelines, and infrastructure during periods of rapid scaling. If and when things break, you'll be able to refer back to these to resolve any issues.

Step 5: Review Data Security and Compliance   Take a second pass at the security and compliance requirements that you collected in Chapter 9. Against these, closely examine the reference architecture to make sure it adheres to the necessary data privacy laws and maintains a high level of data security. If it doesn't, you'll need to address it in your data strategy plan.

Step 6: Perform a Gap Analysis   Identify gaps between the current state of your data architecture and the requirements of the data product you're building. This exposes areas of your architecture that need improvement or change.

Tip

Avoid overestimating what you have and underestimating what you might need. A thorough gap analysis will help you get a better idea of this.

Step 7: Develop a Road Map for Updating Your Data Architecture   Based on your gap analysis, develop a road map for updating your data architecture such that it'll satisfy the needs of your data initiative. This could involve implementing new technologies, reconfiguring existing systems, or even doing a complete overhaul of your architecture in rare cases.

Addressing Data Skills and Literacy Gaps

Now, let's look at how to go about identifying and addressing data skills and literacy gaps that could hinder the success of the data product you're planning.

As discussed in Chapters 11 and 12, you must conduct a data skills and literacy gap analysis to uncover opportunities and expose training needs when developing a data strategy. This process involves assessing the current skillsets and data literacy levels within your organization and identifying where gaps exist between the current state and the desired future state.

Note

The significance of this step was covered in-depth in Chapter 11 (on data literacy assessment) and in Chapter 12 (on data skills gap analysis). In those prior chapters, you already conducted both data literacy and data skill gap analysis. You used your findings from those analyses to inform your selection of use cases when you selected a winning use case in Chapter 14.

Now it's time to take the gaps you've identified and build a plan for addressing them. The following is a process for you to follow when conducting a data skill gap analysis.

You've already selected a winning use case and assessed requirements that are specific to that use case. Before proceeding, take a look again at your use case and identify what specific data literacy or data skill requirements are needed to support the data product you're planning.

Step 1: Validate Your Assessment Findings

Review the findings you generated in Chapter 11 and Chapter 12. Take a look at the current state of data literacy and data skills across your organization to validate whether they're sufficient to support the needs of the winning use case. Usually, they won't be sufficient, and you should proceed to step 3.

Step 2: Map Skills to Organizational Roles

For every role that's relevant to this project, identify what data literacy or data skills are critical. Be sure to assess both the data professionals and also the business users who'll either use the data product or make decisions based on it.

Step 3: Identify Skill Gaps

With the skill requirements of your use case in mind and the skills mapped back to roles, identify gaps that will detract from the success of the data initiative you're planning. These could be in terms of depth (i.e., not enough expertise) or breadth (i.e., not enough people with a certain skill).

Step 4: Prioritize Skill Gaps

Not all skill gaps are of equal importance. Prioritize the gaps based on their impact on:

- The use case
- The strategic importance of the skills
- The feasibility of filling these gaps

Step 5: Address Skill Gaps

Define strategies for closing each gap:

- **Training and upskilling**—Consider training and upskilling to build skills that can be developed among the existing workforce. Consider internal training, workshops, or external courses. I'll discuss this further in Chapter 17.

- **Hiring**—For skills that are critically needed immediately and can't be developed in-house within a short timeframe, you'll need to consider hiring alternatives. I discuss this further in Chapter 17.
- **Collaboration and partnerships**—Sometimes it's possible to collaborate with other organizations or academic institutions that possess skills you need.

Round out this process by documenting your findings, and you'll be in a strong position to drive forward into the next step of the data strategy building process.

Developing Training Plans

Devising and implementing training plans improves the data skills and literacy of existing staff, while also maximizing their potential to contribute to the success of your data initiatives. This helps turn your organization's most valuable resource—its people—into a driving force for the success of your data strategy.

> **Note**
>
> Data-driven decision-making requires proper technology and processes, but equally so, it requires individuals who are skilled and confident in their ability to understand, interpret, and act on data insights.

Providing training opportunities to your team members is an amazing way to increase employee satisfaction and engagement. I mean, who doesn't feel more valued when their employer steps up and invests in their professional development?

The upskilling of existing team members can be a more cost-effective and efficient solution compared to hiring new staff, as it eliminates the costs and time associated with recruitment, onboarding, and acclimatization. Your existing employees already understand your business, its context, and its culture, so they're well prepared to make the best use of data in alignment with your strategic goals.

The following is a process you can use to develop training plans that optimize existing human resources.

Step 1: Define Training Objectives

Back in Chapter 12, you looked at your winning use case, and against it, you identified and prioritized skill gaps. Skill gaps in hand, now it's time to use those to define clear training objectives.

In alignment with Chapter 14, the goals you set here should be specific, measurable, achievable, relevant, and time-bound (SMART). This helps to focus the training effort and sets a clear direction for what the training needs to achieve.

Step 2: Explore Training Formats

Next, explore the various training format options that are currently available within your organization. These could be online courses, on-the-job training, workshops, seminars, etc. It's important to choose training formats that not only cover the necessary content but also fit with your team's learning styles and the organization's budget and time constraints.

Step 3: Compile a Training Plan

With skill gaps identified and prioritized, and your training options assessed, it's time for you to produce a detailed and comprehensive training plan to support your data strategy. You'll need to make sure that your training plan aligns with your data strategy recommendations and that they cater to both immediate and long-term needs.

Tip

The training plan should include what trainings are to be undertaken, by whom, when, and the expected outcomes. Having a detailed plan like this ensures that everyone knows what they need to do, and it helps to keep the training on track.

Table 15.1 details what you need to include within your training plan.

By including a comprehensive training plan like this within your data strategy, you ensure that skill development is a central component to the success of that strategy. Taking this proactive approach significantly increases the chances of successful strategy execution while also encouraging a culture of continuous learning within the organization.

Formulating Hiring Recommendations

As you move to implement your winning use case, you'll likely identify new roles that need to be filled, or existing roles that need to be expanded, to ensure the success of your data strategy. To make hiring recommendations, you'll rely upon the

Table 15.1   Training Plan Inclusions

Feature	Description
Skill-wise breakdown	List the specific skills that you have identified as lacking or underrepresented.
Training formats	For each skill gap, determine the most appropriate training format, be it in-house workshops, online courses, external seminars, or hands-on project-based learning.
Timeline and phases	Depending on the urgency and importance of each skill, assign a timeline for completion. For complex skills, consider phased training where foundational knowledge is built first, followed by advanced topics. A detailed flowchart like the one shown in Figure 15.2 can be helpful in these cases.
Responsibilities	Assign responsibility for overseeing and implementing each training segment. Responsible parties could be a departmental manager, an HR representative, or an external consultant.
Budget allocation	Estimate the costs associated with each training modality. This might include fees for external trainers, subscription costs for online platforms, or resources for in-house training programs.
Feedback mechanisms	Come up with a method to collect feedback on the training programs. This can help in refining the programs in real time and ensuring they remain relevant and effective.
Integration points	Make sure to underscore how each training initiative maps back to the broader data strategy recommendations. This will emphasize why the training is important in the context of successful data strategy execution.
Success metrics	For each training initiative, set clear success metrics. These could be in terms of participants trained, feedback scores, or more tangible outcomes such as the number of projects completed using the newly acquired skills.

comprehensive understanding that you've already developed as you undertake the measures prescribed within this book, particularly those that relate to data skills, knowledge, and experience required for your data initiative to be successful.

The truth is that data-intensive projects are almost always complex and multi-dimensional. They usually involve a range of tasks, such as data collection, management, analysis, and interpretation, as well as the development and maintenance of data infrastructures and systems. These tasks often require specialized skills that are not currently present within your team.

Identifying these gaps in expertise and addressing them through strategic hiring can ensure that your team has the capabilities to execute your data strategy effectively. Here is a process you can use to formulate your hiring recommendations.

As always, you want to start by reviewing your winning use case. Since you've already assessed skill gaps that are specific to that use case, you want to now take

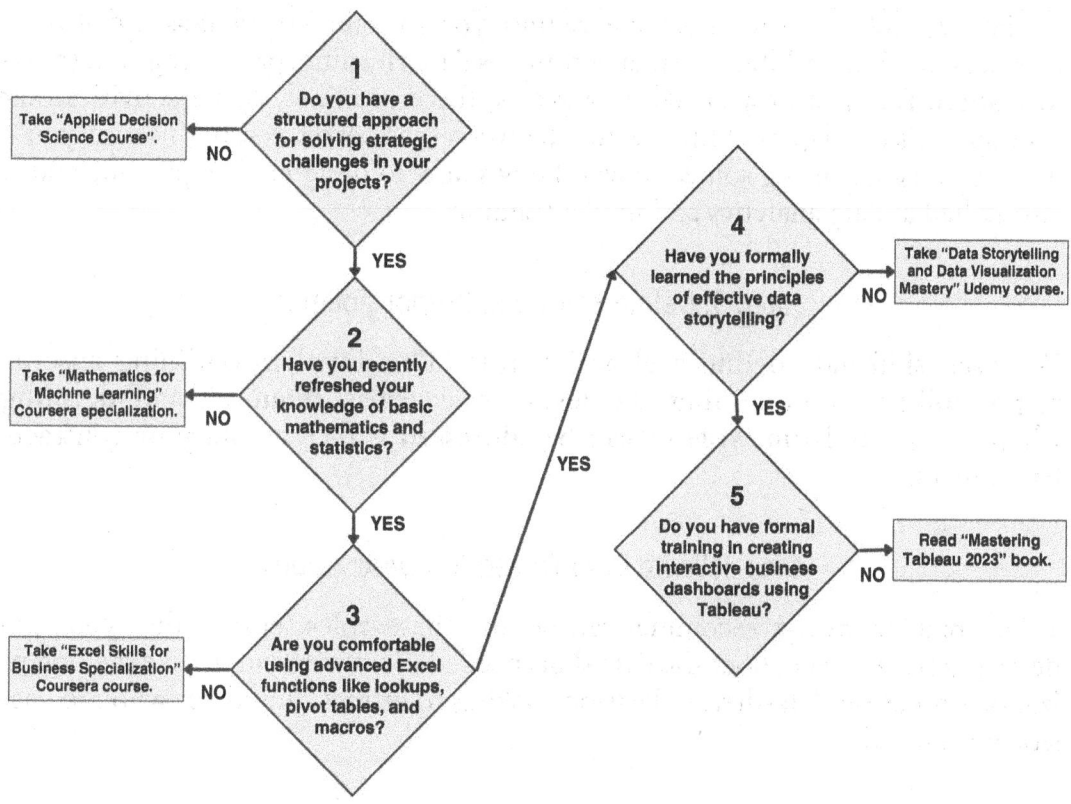

FIGURE 15.2 A training flowchart.

another look at those skill gaps and the training plans you just made to pinpoint what remaining skills need to be filled with strategic new hires.

Step 1: Classify Skills Into Immediate and Long-Term Needs

While certain skills are immediately crucial for the use case, others might be necessary for the long-term vision and sustainability of your data strategy. Categorize them accordingly so that you can prioritize hiring for critical immediate needs while keeping an eye on the future.

Step 2: Consider Hybrid Roles

For certain roles, consider a hybrid approach where you hire for a mix of skills rather than a very niche expertise. This ensures adaptability as your data strategy evolves.

For example, your use case may require you to train ML models and also set up a data pipeline architecture that automates data cleaning, processing, and transformation. But as a project like this grows, there are likely to be activities that overlap. This overlap can blur the lines between these two roles. In this case, you'd want to consider hiring someone who knows how to design a data pipeline and is also skilled at data analytics and model training.

Step 3: Define Roles and Responsibilities

For each skill gap, define a clear job role. This involves outlining specific responsibilities, determining the level of expertise required, and deciding whether it's a full-time role or can be addressed with temporary or contract-based hiring.

Step 4: Write Data-Driven Job Descriptions

When making hiring recommendations for these roles, ensure that your job descriptions are clear about the data skills needed. Be sure to emphasize the organization's focus on data-driven decision-making to attract candidates who are passionate about data.

Tip

With respect to tools and software skill needs, don't be overly specific with your requirements. It's often possible to find strong candidates who have strong problem-solving skills and experience in similar, but maybe not exactly the same, projects. These individuals are generally quick to pick up new tools or technologies.

Step 5: Foster Collaboration Between HR and Data Teams

To ensure that your hiring plan addresses the specific needs of your data initiative, take measures to foster a collaborative relationship between HR and data teams. This collaboration ensures that HR understands the nuances of the roles required and can tailor recruitment strategies accordingly, while the data teams can handle the requirements related to the technical and strategic skills they're hoping to see in a candidate. Regular joint meetings, shared documentation, and open channels of communication are important for building any knowledge gaps and streamlining the hiring process.

Step 6: Compile Hiring Plan Recommendations Within the Data Strategy Plan

As the culmination of your efforts in this segment, you'll want to compile and integrate your hiring plan recommendations within the overarching data strategy plan you'll build in Chapter 17. Doing so ensures that your data strategy is supported by tools, systems, processes, and the right human capital.

Begin by summarizing the identified skill gaps, the roles and responsibilities defined, and the hiring priorities (both immediate and long-term). Then, provide clear rationales for each hiring decision and its alignment with the use case and broader data strategy objectives. This helps stakeholders understand and appreciate the importance of the human component so that they're more willing to support and invest in your hiring recommendations.

By following the preceding steps, you'll be strategically positioned to bring in the right talent that complements your existing team and provides a strong foundation upon which you'll build your data product.

Assessing Vendor Relationships and Recommending a Plan for Vendor Management

Because vendor relationships directly impact the availability, quality, cost, and effectiveness of a company's data and data products, it's important that you assess those relationships and make plans to manage them. As you build a data strategy to support your winning use case, evaluate existing vendor relationships so that you can make sure they align with and support your strategic goals.

Data vendors provide an array of services and tools that are integral to the execution of your data strategy plan. These could range from data storage and management solutions to advanced data analytics and AI tools. The capabilities, reliability, and cost-effectiveness of these services could significantly impact the success of your data strategy.

Effective vendor management requires that you assess the value delivered by vendors in order to ensure that their offerings align with the evolving data needs of your company. This could include evaluating:

- The quality of their services
- The competitive advantage their products offer
- Their ability to fulfill their contractual obligations
- Their adherence to data privacy and security standards

Building strong collaborative relationships with vendors also opens opportunities for:

- Preferential pricing
- Enhanced support
- Access to the latest tools and innovations in the data space

Assessing vendor relationships is essential when looking to expose potential risks associated with:

- Vendor lock-in
- Data ownership disputes
- Non-compliance with regulatory requirements

This type of assessment allows for the early identification and mitigation of such risks and ensures the sustainability and legal compliance of your data strategy.

The following is a process you can use to assess vendor relationships and how well current vendors are able to support your use case needs.

Step 1: Identify the Vendors

Instead of diving into all vendors serving your organization, you want to pinpoint those specifically related to the winning use case. These vendors may provide essential data, tools, or services for the successful implementation of this use case.

This narrowed focus helps you address vendors who are pivotal to your project without encroaching on areas that might cause unnecessary tensions or turf wars. When identifying and narrowing down vendors, you'll want to consider the following factors:

- How closely do their tools align with your winning use case?
- How smooth and easy is it to integrate their tools into your current system? Will it require minor changes or do you have to make significant ones?
- Can their solutions grow or scale with your data project?
- How good are their after-sales support and customer services? What's included and what's not?
- What's the cost-to-benefit ratio for each of the vendors?

Step 2: Evaluate Vendor Relationships

For the vendors identified in Step 1, assess the current status of your collaboration. Consider other factors such as product or service quality, agreement terms, responsiveness, and any past issues or successes.

Step 3: Set Clear Relationship Objectives

From your evaluation, draft specific objectives for each vendor relationship as they align with the needs and goals of your winning use case. Examples of such objectives could be improved data quality, cost optimization, or strengthened collaboration efforts.

Step 4: Define a Vendor Management Plan

With your objectives in hand, define a vendor management plan specifically tailored for each vendor, respectively. This plan should outline actionable steps on an as-needed basis, for example revising contracts, introducing new communication channels, or setting up regular check-ins.

Step 5: Engage and Align with Vendors

Initiate constructive conversations with these vendors. Explain the purpose of your data strategy and winning use case. Communicate your intentions of having a productive and long-term relationship with the vendor. Collaboratively, discuss objectives and the management plan, so that you can confirm that all parties are aligned and committed to the success of the data strategy.

Addressing Ethical and Societal Implications of Foundation Models

Chapter 13 included several case studies related to bias and non-transparency in foundation models and their real-world implications on society at large—the consequences being so acute that it can perpetuate and amplify already existing biases. If your winning use case is centered around foundation models, you need to be very cautious at each step of your implementation, especially if your data strategy involves working with financial or healthcare data. Though there are no rules or laws currently set in stone, I recommend the following steps to address the ethical and societal implications of building with foundation models.

Step 1: Consult Your Ethics Team

As you move closer to implementing your winning use case, you need your ethics team to plan out various activities such as ethics audits and assessments for your data project. They'll also be looking into recent laws and policies related to your winning use case—and go through case studies that discuss its challenges and complexities. You need to triple-check that there are no existing lawsuits, data privacy violations, or intellectual property infringements surrounding similar use cases.

Step 2: Address Bias and Data Privacy Issues

As part of this activity, you need to start setting up procedures that help mitigate issues related to bias and data privacy. Here are some tips:

- Implement a pipeline that systematically tags personal identifiers, financial records, healthcare data, and other sensitive information.
- Make sure you have dedicated personnel or a team—depending on the complexity of the use case—who will manage this sensitive data.
- Look up advanced encryption methods that'll help you mask personal identifiers before data is sent to foundation models.

To address bias:

- Try to ensure fairness in the data collection stage itself—such that the data you're using is representative of all the groups it encompasses or is centered around.

- Use techniques such as adversarial debiasing to reduce bias during model training (if you're fine-tuning).

- Use methods like equalized odds in the post-processing stage to adjust your model output.

Step 3: Prioritize Model Transparency and Explainability

If you refer back to Chapter 13, Figure 13.1, you'll see how you can use various techniques to better explain a model's output or the decisions it makes. The techniques include global explainability, local explainability, and prompt-based explainability.

You can also look into:

- **Local Interpretable Model-agnostic Explanations (LIME)**—LIME works by perturbing the input data and subsequently observing the changes this perturbation makes to the model's output. This helps you to identify which features have the most significant impact on the model's predictions so that you can develop a better understanding of and trust in the model's output decisions.

- **SHapley Additive exPlanations (SHAP)**—SHAP calculates the average marginal contribution of each feature across all possible combinations of features. This measurement is helpful in developing an explainable understanding of the importance of each individual feature and how that feature affects the model's output predictions.

Note

When it comes to building with foundation models, explainability is still a relatively new field; there's plenty of ongoing research about making AI models more transparent and interpretable. You need to make sure you stay updated with the latest research in the field.

Note

You need to prioritize model explainability and transparency within your organization. This will require you to instill a culture within your data engineering team that appreciates and understands the importance of building fair, transparent, and safe AI.

Step 4: Involve Stakeholders from Different Departments

Make sure your data engineering team is in continuous discussion with your ethics team. This is really important to strike a balance when making expeditious progress. Of course, you want things built quickly, but time must be spent addressing ethical AI considerations so you should avoid rushing into releasing a product.

Step 5: Monitor Continuously

You need to constantly monitor the output of your model to make sure it's not propagating any form of bias or misinformation. You should look for anomalies or outlier cases in your output by using natural language processing techniques that can indicate the presence of negative sentiment or biases in the model output.

Monitoring and Maintenance Challenges When Building with Foundation Models

It can be rather challenging to monitor the output from foundation models while also maintaining your data infrastructure. This section looks at a few of those challenges, based on working with different use cases.

Monitoring Challenges

There are several challenges related to monitoring that you'll have to consider.

Data Drift   Oftentimes, foundation model outputs tend to deteriorate over time. This usually happens because the foundation model is trained on specific data but then the data that you receive over a period will have changed significantly. This is prevalent in the finance and healthcare sectors. So, the model output becomes more and more irrelevant over time.

The only way to address this problem is to constantly monitor your model's output against a benchmark and evaluate the extent to which it differs from what it's supposed to output. Then, you'll need to retrain the model periodically for the new data that's coming in—which in this case, would be fine-tuning your foundation model (which you already fine-tuned at the beginning) on new datasets. Instead of retraining it entirely, you can fine-tune it on smaller but more recent datasets in an incremental fashion.

Bias and Data Privacy   As previously mentioned, issues related to bias and privacy are of primary importance when considering the implementation of your winning use case. But there are some challenges related to monitoring for bias and data privacy of which you should be aware:

- Biases across different dimensions of groups, race, gender, age, socioeconomic status, and geographic location can be subtle and hard to identify using algorithms.

- The presence of negative tones, derogatory remarks, slurs, etc. The model's output can be hard to track, especially if your output has different tones, dialects, contexts, etc.

- Unintended and unexpected model behavior can be complex to resolve.

- The reason for the appearance of private and sensitive information in the output can be hard to trace because there's no clear way to understand why the foundation model outputs personal information. Maybe it's piecing data together that it saw during the training process, who knows?

AI Transparency and Interpretability   One of the more pressing problems of today's AI space is that of transparency and interpretability. Though I've already mentioned some popular techniques that are being used, it can be notoriously difficult to trace back the model output to its input. Here's why:

- The complex architecture and the inherent nature of LLM models, the "black boxes" that they are, make it very difficult to interpret results.

- The lack of a "standard" technique that you can use to interpret a foundation model's response or decision is another problem. Although general AI/ML models have some level of interpretability, LLMs don't have any concrete techniques.

- There is always a trade-off between a model's interpretability and its accuracy. Using complex architectures and lesser tried-and-true techniques may yield good results, but you'll lose out on interpretability.

Maintenance Challenges

Maintenance requirements are a major consideration when developing data strategy. One big hurdle here is that maintenance requirements related to foundation models and the data infrastructure you've designed tend to become cumbersome at later stages. This is especially true when you need to:

- Adjust for growing data volumes and complexities in formats, sources, and integration

- Clearly label massive amounts of data for fine-tuning

- Focus on the interpretability of your model's output based on user feedback—related to the issues they observe—which can again differ based on perspective, context, and sentiment

- Modify the data pipeline (in some cases) based on new data that comes to account for data drift problems

- Spend more resources and budget for additional tools, storage, and processing to account for an increase in data volume and usage

- Modify or even overhaul your entire system (in the worst-case scenario) when there are new laws and policies with which you need to comply

Advanced Risk Mitigation and Management in Data Projects

You're already aware of various data-related issues related to conducting a data inventory analysis (refer to Chapter 10) or performing a data maturity assessment (refer to Chapter 12). This section discusses strategies to help you address those issues and bolster the success of your data strategy.

Using AI to Predict Future Risks

You can use AI and predictive analytics to identify patterns of data-related issues even before they occur. For example, say you have large volumes of confidential data (finance and personal information), which is highly susceptible to breaches and external attacks. In such a scenario, taking a reactive approach is out of the question. You'd just end up compromising data, losing money, and jeopardizing trust.

Instead, you can take a proactive approach. Identify data-security-related risks using predictive analytics. It would typically involve training a model on historical security incident data to detect the likelihood of a breach occurring with the current data.

Another example is the use of AI to detect data quality issues. You'd have to train a model on a labeled dataset with known data quality issues. Here, the model would learn specific patterns that signify data quality problems (such as missing information, outliers, erroneous values, etc.) and then run the inference on the datasets you bring in from different sources. This technique can also be applied to a small component of a larger data pipeline, such as the data cleaning phase, the validation phase, and other phases in the data life cycle.

Building Standard Frameworks

As part of this step, you need to build a framework that clearly defines roles, responsibilities, and data standards within the organization. Here are some components you can standardize:

- **Clearly define who's responsible for what**—Who handles which aspect of the data life cycle process within an organization? Who has access to which data?

- **Assess the procedures in place to check for data quality and resolve any issues**—To what extent are these processes automated? Can the pipeline, if automated, handle large volumes of data?

- **Test the endpoints of the data life cycle**—How is data stored, retrieved, and archived for future reference?

- **List all the policies and guidelines to which you must adhere**—How is the team keeping track of all the changes in the policies? Are there periodic audits being conducted?

- **Examine your current security measures carefully to ensure data privacy**—Are the data security measures proactive or reactive? What is the response time to a data breach?

Involving Stakeholders in Your Discussions

Chapter 11 discussed the importance of involving various stakeholders as part of your use case. Stakeholder involvement is vital to risk mitigation, as each one of them can provide unique perspectives about unforeseen risks and potential solutions. The following is a list of considerations you can expect to gather from different types of stakeholders:

- IT professionals can point out technical and security risks, including those related to vulnerabilities in the application.

- Data science and engineering teams can identify data-related risks, such as issues with quality, bias, and interpretability.

- The ethics team or data officers can pinpoint compliance and data privacy issues and suggest procedures that you need to follow to avoid non-compliance scenarios.

- The project management team can bring to light any issues related to resource allocation, finances, timelines, etc.

- End users can provide feedback on usability, functionality, and any issues they observe with respect to model output (if your use case is centered around AI).

Implementing Advanced Data Lineage and Provenance Systems

When you're working with hundreds of datasets that you've collected from multiple sources, you'll need a way to track its history, transformations that were made, its movements, and what purpose it serves.

You can think of your data here as if it were a parcel that you're waiting to receive in the mail. If the parcel is valuable, you want to be able to track each and every step of the shipment delivery process. Excellent logistics companies like DHL and FedEx are able to provide you with that level of detail. Data lineage tools offer analogous tracking, but these tools report on characteristics related to your data resources, instead of parcels. They shed light on the journey and transformation of data between endpoints.

Data provenance systems function in a similar manner, but they have a deeper focus on the history, authenticity, and integrity of data. Examples of such considerations include:

- Who created the data?

- Who has made what changes to it?

- Who's been using it?

- What is the original source of the data?

Ideally, you want an automated data lineage tool that can track repos, ETL processes, and other platforms to discover and document the flow of data across systems and processes. I also recommend using visualization tools so you can clearly see complex data flows and transformations. In parallel, you can also focus on metadata creation that clearly details the data's origin, format, updates, and numerous relationships.

Tip

For creating metadata, I suggest using automated tools that can quickly go through the content of the data and create the needed metadata. This is especially important when you have massive volumes of data and infeasible to create metadata on a manual basis.

By following the preceding recommendations:

- You're making sure you have a complete history of the datasets you use—this helps you improve data integrity and quality.
- You'll be able to quickly track issues with data such as inconsistencies, corruptions, incompleteness, etc.—just like you'd be able to tell if your package is stuck at a hub!
- You'll be able to eliminate data security risks related to unauthorized access and modification.
- You'll be in a good position during your external data audits as a result of the systems you put into place to track *everything* about your data.

Tip

When using automated tools for creating metadata, you want to bring in an expert to validate the correctness of the metadata.

Building Robust Data Storage and Backup Systems

When building a data infrastructure for your winning use case, you need to allocate some time for also setting up data storage and backup systems.

Note

I cannot overemphasize the importance of data storage and backup systems! Organizations end up disrupting their entire operations life cycle when they lose data due to technological failures or data breaches.

One way to set up data resource redundancy is to shift your data to the cloud. This method is generally safer and more flexible, which is favorable because it can accommodate changes in your needs. Oftentimes, however, it's a good idea to consider alternatives or hybrid approaches to double-protect your data. For example:

- **Air-gapping**—This is a great technique that works by storing an offline copy of your data that's totally separate from any kind of insecure networks, platforms, or production environments.

- **Geography-based storage**—With this method, you'd store data physically in different geographic locations, so that you have backups in case of any natural disasters.

- **Continuous data protection**—With this method, you're able to capture every single update made to your data (or periodically). This way, you can always restore to an earlier checkpoint or version if something goes wrong.

I've only listed a couple of methods, but you can explore many more depending on the requirements you identify for your winning use case.

Tip

If you're going for cloud solutions, you should choose ones that provide multi-region storage options.

Now that we've double and triple-checked everything, we'll move on to Chapter 16, the penultimate chapter of our book, where you'll learn to build a data strategy plan for your winning use case.

16

Data Strategy Recommendations for Reaching Future State Goals

The skill of data storytelling is removing the noise and focusing people's attention on the key insights.

— Brent Dykes

We are in the final pillar of the STAR Framework, where you'll be recommending a strategy for reaching future state goals. To deliver your recommendations, you need to produce a technical strategic plan in writing.

This strategic plan will guide you on how technology can support and meet the strategic objectives of an organization. It goes beyond a standard strategy plan that addresses business goals, objectives, and priorities by delving deeper into the specific technological solutions, infrastructures, and tools required to meet those overarching goals.

Exploring the Anatomy of a Technical Strategic Plan

A technical strategic plan has three main components: the Foundational Overview section, the Technical Vision section, and the Implementation and Management section.

The Foundational Overview Section   The Foundational Overview section provides background information that sets the stage for your data strategy recommendations. I'll be sharing more details about what you should include in each component, but for now just know that your Foundational Overview section should include the following four subsections:

- Executive Summary (including the vision statement)
- Introduction and Technology Background (including an organizational chart)
- Business Units and Intended User
- Current State Analysis

Including these elements at the start of your plan is helpful in presenting a crystal-clear picture of your organization's current approach to data operations as well as the core areas you're planning to focus on throughout your data strategy.

The Technical Vision Section   In the Technical Vision section of your plan, you'll produce your data strategy recommendations. The Technical Vision section includes the following elements:

- Alternatives Analysis
- Future State Description
- Recommended Strategy/Solution
- Reference Architecture
- Best Management Practices

The Implementation and Management Section Finally, there's the Implementation and Management section of the plan, which is discussed in great detail in Chapter 17. In this section, you'll provide concrete details to support the execution of your data strategy. This section should include the following:

- Road Map and Milestones
- Compliance
- Resource Allocation and Budget
- Stakeholder and Departmental Alignment
- Training and Hiring Recommendations
- Risk Management and Contingencies
- Continuous Improvements
- Conclusion and Appendices

Now that you know how a technical strategic plan is structured and what's included in each part, let's take a look at the requirements involved in writing the Foundational Overview and Technical Vision sections of your plan.

Deep Diving into the Foundational Overview

Let's look in detail at the steps you need to take to lay a strong foundation for your data strategy plan.

Crafting a Compelling Executive Summary

All strategic plans start with an executive summary. An executive summary outlines the plan's goals, strategies, and expected results. It's typically just one or two pages. This part of the plan allows stakeholders to quickly grasp the essence of the plan overall. It should help decision-makers conceptualize the vision you're proposing and the steps that are required to achieve that vision.

The goal of an executive summary is to capture the interest of its readers, so it should be written in a compelling manner that's not overly full of technical jargon. Within the executive summary, you'll want to include the following core components:

- **Mission**—A brief description of the organization's mission
- **Vision statement**—The vision for the data strategy plan along with a description of the high-level recommendations for achieving that vision
- **Primary tech challenges**—The obstacles the organization is facing with its data-intensive goals
- **Current approach**—Main current strategies being used to address those challenges

Bonus resource

The reference sheet and recommendations for writing an effective vision statement are available for you to download for free at www.data-mania.com/book.

The main thing you need to keep in mind is this: Your executive summary should inspire and inform. It should provide a lucid snapshot of the future by showcasing the potential of the winning use case. But always remember that the vision you're setting must resonate with the overall organizational objectives.

Warning

Throughout the years I've spent working in an executive level capacity, I've seen many talented technical teams that focus far too much on technological capabilities and far too little on how technology supports the business in reaching its objectives. This malalignment of focus overly complicates implementation requirements while also tending to put the organization's business objectives in the backseat. By taking a strategic approach to your data initiatives, you help ensure that your tech team doesn't fall into this trap.

Delivering Context with an Introduction and Technology Background Section

The Introduction and Technology Background section should help stakeholders familiarize themselves with the current technologies and see how the proposed data initiative aligns with existing infrastructure and trends. This section delivers basic technology context for all readers, but it is especially important for those who might not be deeply familiar with the technology or domain in question.

This section should include the following:

- **A brief overview**—A concise statement about what the strategic plan covers
- **Statement of importance**—A description of why technology is vital to the organization
- **A general technology background**—For readers who are less familiar with the topic, this section provides a primer on the key technologies, methodologies, or practices that the plan will address
- **A general organizational background**—This includes an executive organizational chart to inform readers about the company's current technical organizational structure; i.e., the various roles and departments relevant to the technology strategy
- **Plan objectives**—Includes a clear statement of goals for the strategic plan

Tip

Your plan objectives should be the same as the business objectives of your winning use case.

This section provides a high-level view of the organization's current state without delving into any of the technology specifics. It's also especially important to provide an executive organizational chart at the beginning of a data strategy plan, so let's cover this in greater detail.

The organizational chart provides needed clarity on the hierarchical structure, roles, and responsibilities that are relevant to the plan's execution. Clarity here helps stakeholders understand decision-making pathways and collaboration touch points regarding the strategic process.

The executive org chart passes along key information about who is doing what, how decisions are being made, and how information is flowing across the

Table 16.1 Key Characteristics of an Effective Organizational Chart

Characteristic	Description
Relevance to use case	Only include departments, teams, or roles directly connected to or impacted by the winning use case. This keeps the org chart concise and relevant to the context.
Key decision-makers	Identify and mark the primary stakeholders and decision-makers associated with the use case. Use color codes, icons, or annotations to underscore importance.
Inter-departmental relationships	Use connecting lines or arrows to indicate specific collaborations or dependencies between departments for the winning use case.
Responsibility indicators	Next to the roles or teams on the org chart, briefly mention their primary responsibilities or roles as they relate to the winning use case. This helps readers quickly understand their involvement.
Visual clarity	Make sure the org chart is easily readable. Use clear fonts, consistent color schemes, and a hierarchical design that's easy to follow. Remember, executives and stakeholders should be able to understand this chart at a glance.
A legend	If you use any symbols, color codes, or annotations, then provide a concise legend or key that explains them. This makes it easier to interpret the chart.

organization. Your organizational chart needs certain key characteristics for maximum effectiveness, which I detail in Table 16.1.

You want to keep these characteristics in mind when producing an executive organizational chart for inclusion within the Introduction and Technology Background section of your data strategy plan. Now let's turn to your description of business units and intended users that are also to be included within the Foundational Overview section of your plan.

Describing Business Units and Intended Users

After outlining the current technical context, you need to identify who will use the proposed data solution and how. Turn back to the work you did in the assessment phase. Recall that you already clarified the intended users and their needs back in Chapter 15, so most of the work here is already done. All you need to do now is document your findings within your data strategy plan.

Keep in mind that we are still in the Foundational Overview portion of the plan, so you shouldn't unveil the winning use case just yet! Instead, you want to focus on who the users will be from a more high-level perspective by discussing their roles, pain points, and most urgent needs—*needs which, "coincidentally," will be addressed by the winning use case that you present in the recommended strategy/solution portion of the plan.*

Note

Regarding the length of this section, one to two pages is often suitable for smaller organizations or more narrowly focused data initiatives, whereas three–five pages is typical for medium to large organizations with multiple business units or diverse user groups.

Table 16.2 details a few things to include in the Business Units and Intended Users section.

Table 16.2   What to Include in the Business Units and Intended Users Section

Characteristic	Description
User dependencies	Describe any dependencies these users might have on other departments or tools. This can include data sources they rely on or other teams they collaborate with for insights.
Training and upskilling	Assess the current proficiency level of these users with respect to data tools and technologies. State the additional training needs that you've uncovered in your skill gap analysis back in Chapter 15.
Strategic alignment	Emphasize the importance of these business units in the overall organizational strategy. Highlight how data plays a role in their strategic objectives and the potential impact of improved data-driven decision-making.
Roles and responsibilities	Start by outlining the roles of these intended users, their daily tasks, the types of decisions they make, and the challenges they face.
Future engagement	Discuss how you envision their engagement evolving once the data product is in place. When you're discussing this, you'll want to center the conversation around the potential for greater productivity, collaboration, and decision-making through this engagement. Make sure you tie it back to the winning use case.
Feedback and expectations	Bring in any notable past feedback or expectations you collected from users. This ensures that the plan acknowledges their needs and preferences. The feedback and expectations you detail here should be relevant to your winning use case.
Current data interactions	Briefly touch upon how these users currently engage with data. This includes the tools they use, the frequency of data interactions, and any existing pain points in their data journey.

By painting a comprehensive picture of the business units and intended users, you're setting the stage for a data strategy that's laser-focused on real-world user needs and preferences. Doing so helps you build trust and win the confidence of stakeholders.

Performing a Current State Analysis

The Current State Analysis section serves as the foundation upon which future improvements and strategic decisions are made. In the Current State Analysis portion of the plan, you'll describe your organization's current state as you've documented it throughout your taking stock and assessment work within the STAR Framework.

Within the Current State Analysis section of the plan, you want to be sure to detail:

- An inventory of existing systems, technologies, and platforms as well as your analysis of their effectiveness, scalability, and integration capabilities. You developed this in Chapter 15.

- A description of the current state data teams' roles and responsibilities to describe the existing organizational structure, clarify how data responsibilities are distributed, and highlight potential overlaps or gaps.

- A description of the current state data security processes you gathered and evaluated in Chapter 12.

- A description of current state data skillsets and literacy that you assessed in Chapter 15.

Although you want to go into detail here about your organization's current state, you also need to try to keep this portion of the plan as brief as you can.

Note

Typically, a Current State Analysis section of the technical strategic plan might account for 15–25% of the total plan length.

Be thorough in this section while also keeping in mind that the entire plan should be balanced with forward-looking strategies and actionable recommendations.

Bonus resource

Download tips and checklists at www.data-mania.com/book for:

- Producing an inventory of existing systems, technologies, and platforms
- Detailing your analysis of their effectiveness, scalability, and integration capabilities
- Describing your current state data teams' roles & responsibilities
- Describing the current data security processes
- Describing current state data skillsets and literacy

Defining Your Technical Vision

Now that you've seen what goes into building a powerful foundation section for your plan, let's explore the nuances involved in crafting a technical vision that effectively communicates your evidence-based data strategy recommendations.

Analyzing Alternatives

After documenting the current state, but before you present a recommended course of action, you need to include your alternatives analysis within the plan. The Alternatives Analysis section showcases the thoroughness of the planning process you've executed. It shows that you evaluated multiple viable solutions and took adequate caution when selecting and recommending the most optimal approach. It also indicates your intent and action to both safeguard the organization's investment and align your recommendations with its strategic goals. Your due diligence will be evident from the work you present in this section, and this goes a long way in helping stakeholders understand why certain decisions were made.

Note

Typically, the Alternatives Analysis section should consume only 5–15% of the total content of your data strategy plan depending on the scope, complexity, and criticality of the decision at hand. An extensive alternatives analysis could be beneficial for stakeholders who require a deep understanding of all available options before making a decision. For audiences who prefer high-level overviews, a more concise section might be appropriate.

Within the Alternatives Analysis section, explore all feasible alternatives solutions that you've considered throughout the process of building this data strategy. In other words, you want to take the time to describe the three potential use cases that you identified in Chapter 9.

Tip

I always recommend tables or charts that you can use to show a side-by-side comparison of the recommended course of action and the alternatives analysis against different evaluation criteria. This helps stakeholders get a quick glimpse and delve deeper, if necessary. You can see what I mean in Figure 16.1.

Considerations	On a scale of 1–10, how well does the use case fare? Where 1 = Unfavorable and 10 = Extremely Favorable	Potential Use Case 1	Potential Use Case 2	Potential Use Case 3
Business Objectives	How well do the goals and objectives of the use case align with immediate business objectives?	5	10	2
Business Value	- Cost Reduction	7	7	10
	- Revenue Enhancement	6	10	8
	- Improved Customer Experience	9	6	5
	- Risk Mitigation	5	6	10
Feasibility	- Availability of Needed Data	10	8	10
	- Potential Legal or Regulatory Hurdles	10	10	9
Resource Availability	- Adequacy of Existing Personnel/Skillsets	9	7	10
	- Adequacy of Budget	10	9	8
	- Adequacy of Existing Technology	10	7	7
Strategic Alignment	- Alignment with Long-Term Strategic Goals	6	10	10
Time-to-Value		8	7	5
Stakeholder Buy-in		7	9	10
	Score:	102	106	104

FIGURE 16.1 A comparison of alternatives based on a quantitative criteria analysis.

While an alternatives analysis demonstrates due diligence, be sure to leave ample space in the plan for coverage of the chosen direction, implementation strategy, risks, and other mission-critical topics.

Drawing upon the use case documentation you created in Chapter 14, for each alternative use case, write a narrative that details the pros and cons, potential risks, costs, benefits, and any other relevant metrics. Show comparisons of the alternatives on a consistent set of criteria, perhaps even borrowing directly from the evaluation you prepared in Chapter 14, an example of which is shown again in Figure 16.1. Draw from the quantitative and qualitative decision-making methods you used when evaluating the potential use case alternatives. To create an alternatives analysis for your data strategy plan, revisit the work you did in Chapter 14. Repurpose your analysis from that section to build out a robust alternatives analysis for your data strategy plan.

Bonus resource

Tips for writing a compelling alternatives analysis narrative are available for you to download for free at www.data-mania.com/book.

Writing a Technical Vision Statement

A technical vision statement is a statement that describes the overarching goal or aspiration for the data strategy plan. This statement should depict the aspirational technological future of the organization and describe the desired future state of the organization's technology landscape.

This is distinct from the vision statement you created earlier in this chapter when you wrote the executive summary. The technical vision statement addresses where the organization aims to be, technologically, in the future; whereas the vision statement within the executive summary provides a more holistic view of the organization's overall future direction, of which technology is just one part.

Note

A technical vision statement should typically be concise, ideally ranging from one to three sentences.

The Technical Vision Statement section anchors the entire data strategy plan and should be presented as a standalone section, despite its brevity. This brevity ensures that it's easily remembered and communicated, yet powerful enough to capture the overarching direction and ambition of the technical aspects of the data initiative.

Note

Your technical vision statement should be clear and easily understandable by both technical and non-technical stakeholders. Avoid using jargon or overly complex language. This statement should inspire and motivate your team.

A great technical vision statement serves as a guidepost while also inspiring and uniting your team in pursuit of a common purpose.

Challenge: Technical Vision Statements

Let's test your critical thinking when it comes to writing technical vision statements. Here's an example of an effective technical vision statement:

"Our technology vision is focused on transforming raw data into actionable insights. By leveraging advanced analytics, machine learning, and data visualization, we want to empower decision-makers across the organization with the tools they need to make informed, data-driven choices in real time."

Consider this statement and try to identify what about it makes it effective?

Once you formulated your ideas, check the challenge solution for the answer that I left for you at businessgrowth.ai.

Bonus resource

Tips and guidelines for writing a well-defined technical vision statement are available to download for free at www.data-mania.com/book.

Recommending Strategies and Solutions

Data strategy recommendations are generally placed in the Recommended Strategy/Solution section within a data strategy plan. In this section, you provide a detailed strategy to fully utilize the data initiative you're planning in a way that translates the broad objectives into practical steps.

This section is where you'll do the grand unveiling of your selection of the winning use case and your recommendations for implementing it. It naturally flows from the alternatives analysis and technical vision statement. The Alternatives Analysis section informs your selection of the winning use case, after all. So now you need to detail your proposed solution here in the Recommended Strategy/Solution section of the plan.

This approach ensures that the strategic plan aligns with the strengths you've identified while also addressing the weaknesses and limitations you've exposed within the alternatives analysis. At this stage, your final recommended solution will have been developed with meticulous strategic planning and analysis, so you can rest assured that it will drive your organization toward its growth objectives.

Note

As a general guideline, the Recommended Strategy/Solution section typically occupies around 20% to 30% of the entire plan.

The recommendations you make within this section should include, but not be limited to, your recommendations for a winning use case. You need to recapitulate the details of the winning use case and why you've selected this use case as the optimal path forward for your organization. In support of this use case, you should also recommend needed changes to facilitate its implementation.

These recommendations should address the following:

- Legal, ethical AI, data governance, and data management change requirements
- People changes with respect to positioning, business units, training needs, and hiring needs
- Organizational data culture improvements

Let's look at an example of a recommendation for a winning use case. After examining what makes this example effective, I provide you with some tips that you can use to write your own recommendations within this section of your plan.

An Example of a Recommendation for a Winning Use Case

"Recommendation: Implement a cloud-based data warehousing solution (e.g., AWS Redshift) to centralize data storage and facilitate real-time analytics. This recommendation is in line with improving data accessibility and cross-functional collaboration. By leveraging cloud scalability and cost-efficiency, we anticipate a 20% reduction in data retrieval times and a 15% decrease in infrastructure costs within the first year. To mitigate potential data security concerns, we will implement encryption protocols and regular security audits. Key success metrics include a 30% increase in query performance and a 25% reduction in manual data integration efforts. The implementation plan involves a phased migration of data, beginning with pilot departments, and full deployment within six months. This solution is designed to accommodate future data growth and technological advancements."

This recommendation statement is effective because it provides:

- **Clear solution identification**—The recommendation specifies a concrete solution—implementing *a cloud-based data warehousing solution, AWS Redshift*—which is readily comprehensible to both technical and non-technical stakeholders. This level of clarity ensures that everyone understands the proposed change.

- **Alignment with goals**—The recommendation explicitly states how the proposed solution aligns with a higher-level goal to *improve data accessibility and cross-functional collaboration*. This shows a clear link between the solution and the organization's strategic objectives.

- **Quantifiable benefits**—The recommendation provides quantifiable benefits of the proposed solution, *such as a 20% reduction in data retrieval times and a 15% decrease in infrastructure costs within the first year.* These specific metrics help monitor and assess the success of the implementation.

- **Leveraging cloud advantages**—The recommendation shows a strategic understanding of cloud technology by highlighting its scalability and cost-effectiveness. These features directly address the organization's needs while showing the potential benefits.

- **Risk mitigation**—The inclusion of encryption protocols and regular security audits to mitigate potential data security concerns shows a proactive approach to address potential risks related to the recommended solution.

- **Defined success metrics**—The recommendation outlines key success metrics—*a 30% increase in query performance and a 25% reduction in manual data integration efforts*. These provide clear criteria for evaluating the effectiveness of the proposed solution.

- **Implementation plan**—The inclusion of an implementation plan, involving a phased migration of data starting with pilot departments and full deployment within a specified timeframe (six months). This showcases a practical approach to executing the recommended solution.

- **Future-proof design**—By mentioning that the solution is designed to accommodate *future data growth and technological advancements*, the recommendation demonstrates forward-thinking and an awareness of the solution's longevity.

- **Overall coherence**—The recommendation is well-structured and cohesive, presenting each aspect—solution, alignment with goals, benefits, risk mitigation, success metrics, implementation plan, and adaptability—in a logical sequence.

Since you've been following along with this book in a linear fashion, you've already done all of the assessment and evaluation work required to formulate your strategic recommendations. Now that we are in the plan-building phase, all that's left for you to do here is document and summarize those recommendations. Here are some of my top tips for writing effective recommendations.

- Ensure that your recommendations are detailed and specific. Each recommendation should directly align with the overarching goals and objectives outlined in the data strategy plan.

- Provide a strong rationale for each recommendation. Explain how and why the proposed strategy is the most suitable choice. Consider factors like cost-effectiveness, ability to scale, alignment with existing systems, and potential for long-term growth. Highlight the benefits the organization stands to gain from implementing the recommendations.

- From a high-level perspective, address potential risks or challenges associated with the recommended strategy. Avoid getting into too much detail here because you'll provide a detailed risk management and contingency plan in Chapter 17.

In this section, your job is to focus on your proposed recommendations and provide high-level guidance clarifying the plan of action for stakeholders. Try to keep your details concise because your implementation plan is not limited to this section.

Bonus resource

A checklist for writing effective recommendations for the Recommended Strategy/Solution section of your data strategy plan is available for you to download for free at www.data-mania.com/book.

Designing a Reference Architecture: System Design and Supporting Technologies

The Reference Architecture section combines your strategic vision with the underlying technology backbone required to make it achievable. This section presents tools and processes, but, more importantly, it illustrates how they work together to realize strategic objectives.

What to Include in a Reference Architecture   While reference architecture looks simple, it can be tricky to get right. Let's look at the components you need to include.

System Interactions.   System interactions define how different technological components "speak" to each other. When you're laying this out, you need to focus on core components, such as functionality, scalability, flexibility, and interoperability of these systems. For example:

- Functionality implies how "functional" each system or component is to enable easy exchange of data and commands between one another.
- Scalability refers to how easy it is to scale the components without disrupting the way they "speak" to one another.
- Flexibility measures how easy it is for you to remove or replace existing sub components in each of the components without disrupting any of the interactions.
- Interoperability is a measure of how easily different technologies can cooperate without causing breakdowns or having compatibility issues.

> **Note**
>
> When planning and detailing these interactions, think about redundancy—what if one system fails? Also, consider speed and efficiency—how do these interactions affect latency or throughput?

Data Flows.　The life cycle of data is a story of its own. A well-defined data flow ensures that data is harnessed, processed, and utilized effectively without loss, duplication, or corruption.

> **Note**
>
> When planning and detailing these: pay attention to data transformation points, potential areas for data leakage, and where data might get stalled or bottlenecked. Make sure to have encryption and other security measures incorporated at necessary touchpoints.

Technologies and Tools.　Technologies and tools are going to be at the heart of your reference architecture and your overall data strategy. Here are some components you need to pay attention to:

Platform and Software.　Platform and software are the foundational blocks of your data strategy. Finding the right ones can help achieve scalability, performance, and alignment with organizational needs.

> **Note**
>
> When planning and detailing these, think about long-term support that'll be required for the platforms or software you choose, and how the tools you choose integrate with other tools in your stack.

Interfaces.　Interfaces act as bridges and enable seamless communication between disparate systems or platforms.

Note

When planning and detailing these, consider potential security vulnerabilities. Ensure interfaces are robust, can handle errors, and can accept varied data formats. It's also a good practice to follow the principle of least privileges, where you give a minimum level of access permissions to individuals so they can complete their tasks without hindrance—but nothing more.

Third-party Integrations.   Third-party tools can supercharge capabilities, be it visualization, analytics, or cloud solutions.

Note

When planning and detailing these, always consider the long-term viability and support of third-party tools. Get clear on their data handling practices and ensure they align with your organization's data ethics and compliance guidelines. You also need to make sure these third-party solutions have good customer support. Oftentimes, a lot of solutions have great functionalities but fail to provide timely support for the issues raised.

Network Topology.   The network defines the highways on which your data travels. Its design affects speed, reliability, and security.

Note

Prepare for failovers to protect against potential network attacks. Know the potential choke points and design for scalability.

Defining reference architecture requires finding a balance between current state analysis and future state requirements. Choices should be based on today's problems while also keeping in mind scalability, future integrations, and evolving business needs.

How to Draft a Reference Architecture   The Reference Architecture section should provide clear visual representations detailing how different technical components fit and work together to achieve the desired outcomes.

You want to make sure that within the reference architecture you:

- Use diagrams, flowcharts, and other visual tools to depict the various elements of the architecture.

- Ensure that the diagrams are clear and well-labeled. Use standardized symbols or icons to represent different components. Tools like Lucidchart, Visio, or draw.io can be instrumental here.

- Create visuals that quickly convey the main components, their interactions, and data flows. This helps stakeholders understand the architecture's essence at a glance.

Figure 15.1 in Chapter 15 provides an example of reference architecture done right, so feel free to use that as a template when drafting yours.

Tip

You should also write a narrative for this section to explain why the suggested reference architecture is appropriate for the proposed initiative and how it aligns with the technical vision. This will help both technical and non-technical stakeholders understand the significance and structure of the proposed architecture.

Documenting Best Management Practices for the Data Initiative

Before diving into the detailed implementation road map, it's important for you to outline the best practices that'll be useful in guiding the entire initiative. These serve as a road map by outlining the optimal ways to execute tasks, processes, and procedures based on accumulated experience and industry standards.

Just like every industry and sub-sector harbors distinct best practices encapsulating and describing the most effective ways of conducting work, companies and their divisions also frequently define their own best practices. They optimize their approach by drawing from past experiences to guide future achievements. That's the only logical way of leading an organization, but best practices are especially relevant within a data strategy plan because of the outcomes they support. I've detailed a few of those outcomes for you below.

- **Efficiency and productivity**—Using proven techniques, organizations can streamline their operations, reduce errors, and increase productivity. This saves time and avoids potential setbacks.

- **Risk mitigation**—Mistakes in data projects can be costly, both financially and reputationally. Best practices help prevent data breaches, misuse, and other risks.
- **Building stakeholder confidence**—Best practices demonstrate that the organization adheres to industry standards, which in turn helps build trust among stakeholders—including customers, partners, and regulatory bodies.

Although we've looked at best practices with respect to technical and procedural measures, they also safeguard against human elements that may jeopardize the success of an initiative. It's the human factor, after all, that most often determines the success or failure of a data initiative.

Leaders and stakeholders are the key "human elements" that are indispensable to the success of a data initiative. While you may have the entire technical and procedural measures laid out perfectly, it's the direction, support, and active participation of business leaders that cements success for a data solution.

An Example of an Effective Best Practice

Best Practice: Data Quality Assurance before Analysis

Description

Before beginning any data analysis or modeling, take measures to ensure the quality and integrity of the underlying data sources. This involves cleaning the data, handling missing values, and ensuring data consistency.

Steps

Data auditing—This requires you to go through the datasets to identify anomalies, inconsistencies, or unusual data points. This step also requires you to trace back the sources of these datasets to make sure they're credible.

Data cleaning—This step involves correcting any inconsistencies and data inaccuracies. As part of this activity, the primary focus points are removing duplicate entries, correcting mislabeled categories, or rectifying inaccuracies.

Handling missing values—This step requires you to decide on an approach for missing data—either removing those entries or imputing those values. You can also explore predictive modeling techniques to fill in for the missing data.

Validation—Once you complete data cleaning and pre-processing, you need to use statistical tests or data visualization techniques to validate its quality.

Documentation—Remember that this is the most important step in this series of activities. Make sure to compile a log detailing all changes made to the data, the reasons for those changes, and the methodologies you used. Oftentimes, teams ignore this step and struggle later on to replicate the algorithms or make changes to them because they're unaware of how they reached those solutions in the first place.

Rationale

Poor-quality data sources lead to misleading or inaccurate analysis results, which can then cause decision-makers to make misinformed, flawed business decisions. By paying attention to ensuring data quality right from the beginning, you can improve the accuracy and reliability of analytical outcomes for better-informed decisions.

Impact

Following this best practice can reduce the risks associated with data-driven decision-making. It can also increase trust in data reports and models and help get more consistent and successful outcomes in data initiatives.

Before telling you how to document your own best practices, let me first emphasize that the best practices you recommend should be clearly relevant to and supportive of the data initiative you're planning.

Warning

You'll review a lot of information here, so you want to make sure that you don't go on any unnecessary tangents but instead stay focused only on documenting best practices directly relevant to the data initiative you're planning.

Step 1: Review Existing Documentation   Begin by thoroughly reviewing any existing documentation related to data management, analytics, technology stacks, people issues, and data governance within the organization. This includes internal guidelines, previous project post-mortems, and any data-related policies. If you followed along with this book from the beginning, then you have collected or generated most of this documentation in Chapter 10. Pay close attention to the personal insights you gathered from stakeholders in stakeholder interviews you did when you worked through Chapter 11. Personal insights add context to the written documentation and often reveal undocumented practices.

Step 2: Catalog Findings   As you review, catalog specific practices, both successful and unsuccessful. Make a list of what has historically worked and what has posed challenges. Describe the "why" behind each practice.

Step 3: Consult External Standards   Compare the internal practices you've documented with industry standards and best practices. Sources like industry white papers, benchmarking studies, and guidelines from professional organizations can be valuable resources here.

Step 4: Analyze Patterns   Look for patterns and trends in your documentation. Which practices consistently lead to positive outcomes? Which ones frequently cause problems or inefficiencies?

Step 5: Prioritize Practices   Not all best practices will have the same impact. Prioritize them and choose to feature five or so of the most impactful practices, based on their potential benefit, relevance to your organization's specific challenges, and the feasibility of implementation.

Step 6: Document and Categorize   In the Best Practices section of your data strategy plan, create well-organized documentation, like the example provided earlier. For each practice, briefly describe its purpose, the problem it addresses, and any related procedures or tools.

Remember that the goal of compiling these best practices is to drive positive change and improvements within the organization's data strategy.

Now that we've gone through how you can most effectively communicate your data initiative through a solid technical strategy plan and looked at powerful ways for you to document the best practices for your data initiative, you're all set up to develop a data strategy plan in the most sequential, methodical manner possible. In Chapter 17, we'll go through the step-by-step process that's required to complete your data strategy plan of action—i.e., writing the Implementation and Management section—using all the knowledge you gathered throughout the pages of this book.

17

Finalizing Your Strategic Plan

Data is something we create, but it's also something we imagine.

– Kate Crawford

With the Foundational Overview and Technical Vision sections of your data strategy complete, it's time now to move into the Implementation and Management section. This section is where you map out all the high-level requirements to guide the execution of your data strategy. Once you have this section complete, you simply consolidate all your findings and recommendations into a single tangible data strategy deliverable. The goal of this chapter is to show you how to do that.

Creating an Implementation Road Map

A technology implementation road map offers a tangible, step-by-step guide to seamlessly transitioning from the current technological state to the envisioned future. This road map is helpful to you in maintaining alignment with strategic objectives while also providing your stakeholders a clear understanding of project timelines and milestones.

Ideally, this road map should include details, such as task sequences, any dependencies, resource allocations, and potential risks or barriers. Your road map should provide a visual representation of the major milestones, dependencies, and timelines for the data initiative you're planning.

Here's a brief process you can use for writing an implementation road map:

1. **Identify key delivery milestones**—Based on the recommendations you've made in the data strategy plan, identify its key steps or stages. These delivery milestones may include data audits, infrastructure upgrades, new technologies, governance changes, training programs, etc.

2. **Determine the sequence of milestones**—You may need to complete some steps before you can begin with others. This creates dependencies. Identifying and planning for these will help you avoid roadblocks later in the implementation.

3. **Assign responsibilities**—For accountability purposes, assign responsibility for each milestone to a designated team or individual.

4. **Establish a timeline**—Set a target completion date for each milestone. Be realistic and expect delays. I always suggest setting a buffer time duration that's at least 15–20% of your total project duration.

5. **Communication and updates**—Make sure to share the implementation road map with all stakeholders, and keep them updated regularly as the project progresses.

Since you're building a comprehensive strategic plan that's primarily intended for business stakeholders, you want to maintain a high-level perspective within this road map. Including a visual road map graphic like the one shown in Figure 17.1 is a great way to facilitate improved communication while making sure you don't go into too much detail here.

Beyond these basics, you should be prepared to let the executional team members handle the nitty-gritty details that are required for them to satisfy their responsibilities.

Bonus resource

You can get an editable copy of the road map shown in Figure 17.1 for free at www.data-mania.com/book.

Tip

Once you secure approval for your initiative, you can build a more detailed Gantt chart for better internal project management purposes, or you can delegate that to a project manager. Remember, as the data strategist, you're working in a leadership capacity, not a management capacity.

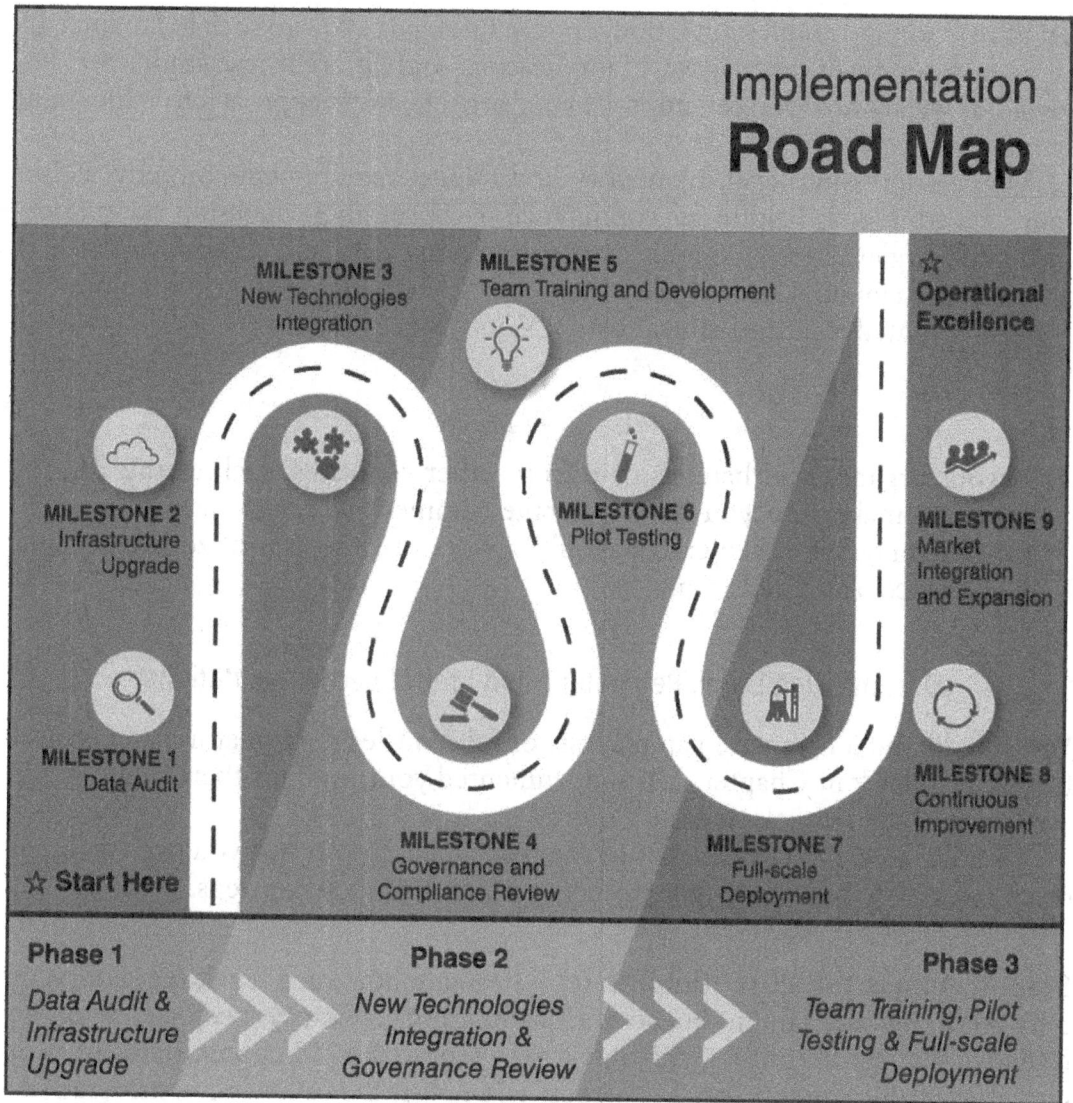

FIGURE 17.1 Adding a graphic to your implementation road map.

Compliance Requirements

After laying out the strategic course of action and your recommendations for its implementation, you need to get to work writing a Compliance Section of the plan to address relevant legal, regulatory, and ethical frameworks. By doing so, you're making sure that your data initiative operates in a compliant and ethical manner.

If you're working around foundation models, I'd suggest you go back to Chapter 13 for a quick review of the real-world implications and different case studies we discussed, as well as how you can improve your organization's approach to ethical and compliance requirements.

While addressing legal, regulatory and ethical requirements directly within your data strategy is helpful for compliance purposes, their inclusion also underscores the organization's commitment to handling data and AI innovation in a responsible manner. This, in turn, safeguards stakeholder trust while helping to prevent potential legal and ethical issues. Win-win!

Tip

If your organization handles data from other countries, such as the EU for example, make sure you have a detailed framework ready that follows the GDPR guidelines. Remember, you'll always need to prioritize privacy and compliance over innovation.

Documenting Legal, Regulatory, and Ethical Recommendations

You already did a complete gap analysis of relevant legal, regulatory, and ethical frameworks back in Chapter 7. You documented your findings there and considered them when you selected the winning use case.

In order to complete this part of the plan-building process, you need to build on the work you've already done by completing the following steps.

Step 1: Assess the Potential Impact   Evaluate how each legal, regulatory, or ethical consideration might impact the data initiative. Identify specific parts of the initiative that could conflict with an existing requirement. Highlight any areas of potential conflict or concern. I'd suggest you revisit the following considerations whenever you're doing this assessment:

- How well does your data initiative comply with existing data protection laws and regulations that the chief data officer (CDO) or the compliance team has recommended?

- Does your data initiative respect privacy and compliance above and beyond the rules and regulations ascribed?

- Do you have a system in place that'll continuously monitor and update privacy and compliance laws?

Step 2: Recommend Actions for Compliance   For each framework and potential impact you identify, you need to provide clear, actionable recommendations to ensure compliance. This might involve modifying certain aspects of the data initiative, implementing additional safeguards, or seeking further legal counsel. Consider including a checklist or step-by-step guide to help the organization ensure all compliance boxes are ticked off.

Step 3: Engage Experts   When dealing with complex legal and regulatory environments, it's beneficial to engage with experts in the field. As I've suggested in previous chapters, always seek input from legal counsel, compliance officers, or industry experts when writing this part of the plan to ensure that all bases are covered.

Step 4: Integrate Ethical Considerations   What might be legal isn't always ethical. Beyond legal and regulatory compliance, address any ethical considerations that are related to the data initiative. Highlight any potential ethical concerns and propose solutions that align with your organization's values and ethics.

Warning

Companies often prioritize quick success and overlook areas such as bias, privacy, and transparency. They may release their product to the market without accounting for, let's say for example, bias in the answers of a fine-tuned foundation model. Their excuse is "We'll fix that later," which is the sort of mindset you need to avoid.

Step 5: Educate and Train Stakeholders   Your recommendations should extend to the broader organization. Propose training sessions, workshops, or informational campaigns to ensure that everyone involved in the data initiative knows and understands these frameworks. You can revisit the case studies we went through in Chapter 13 to support your work here.

Step 6: Summarize and Highlight Key Actions   At the end of the section, provide a summary of key action items. This will serve as a quick reference guide for those implementing the data initiative and help them prioritize legal and ethical compliance. Consider all applicable legal, regulatory, and ethical frameworks to strengthen the integrity of your data strategy. This will ensure it adheres to the highest standards of compliance and ethical practice.

> **Warning**
>
> Always consult an attorney to get a sign-off on a legal recommendation before executing. There's a lot that can go wrong, and you are introducing massive risk if you fail to contact a licensed attorney about legal issues.

> **Bonus resource**
>
> Download an example recommendation for GDRP compliance for free at www.data-mania.com/book.

Resource Allocation and Budget

A meticulously detailed resource allocation and budget is behind every successful data initiative. This section is responsible for providing financial and logistical support for the strategy. This is where you'll allocate money, resources, and people for each phase of the strategy.

A clearly defined resource allocation and budget empowers organizations to navigate their data-driven objectives while mitigating the risk of unforeseen financial or resource-based constraints.

What to Include in a Resource Allocation and Budget

Table 17.1 details the components you should include in the Resource Allocation and Budget section of the plan.

Resource Allocation and Budget Best Practices

The following best practices will help you prepare a Resource Allocation and Budget section that is comprehensive yet simplistic.

Start with Historical Financial Records   If similar projects or initiatives have been undertaken by your company in the past, use them as a starting point. Analyze previous budgets, actual expenses, and outcomes. Using real-world figures and evidence gathered from past experience helps you prepare budget estimates that are realistic for your company.

Table 17.1   Resource Allocation and Budget Components

Component	Description
Financial estimates	Detail expected costs for each phase, such as technology purchases, software licenses, consultancy fees, and training.
Human resources	List personnel requirements, including both existing employees and potential hires. Specify roles, responsibilities, and estimated compensation.
Infrastructure and technology	Outline specifications and costs for required infrastructure upgrades and new technology platforms.
Contingency funds	Set aside a budget for unexpected expenses. Doing this reduces the risk of setbacks that are caused by unexpected costs and ensures that the project's progress remains uninterrupted.
Return on Investment (ROI) projections	Present an analysis of the initiative's expected financial returns. This will help leadership prioritize strategy elements and understand how expenses compare.

Engage Relevant Stakeholders Don't make assumptions about costs and resource needs. Involve the departments or teams that have a direct role in the project, including those from IT, data science, HR, and operations. Seek their input on accurate cost figures, potential challenges, and resource requirements to support the formation of a realistic budget.

Tip

When you're speaking to stakeholders about the costs and resources required, be sure to detail both long-term and immediate costs. A data strategy often necessitates making an upgrade to complex infrastructure or buying a third-party license. Make sure you've secured the necessary budget in advance.

Prioritize the Budget Not all expenses will be upfront. Break down your budget by project phases or milestones. Prioritizing like this ensures that critical components are funded first. Breaking down expenses makes it easier to gain approval by demonstrating progress at each phase.

Include a Top-Level ROI Analysis You do not need a hyper-detailed ROI analysis. Instead, focus on the overall comparison between the expected investment costs and the potential benefits they can yield within a certain timeframe. It's always challenging to predict ROIs to precision. A high-level ROI analysis like this high-lights the potential value of the data initiative while guiding stakeholders in assessing its feasibility and benefits. This approach simplifies the complex dynamics of ROI projections and enables a concise and effective representation of anticipated results.

Separate Capital Costs From O&M Costs   Budgeting and financial planning for a data strategy initiative requires you to differentiate between capital costs (CapEx) and operating & maintenance costs (O&M). This helps you delineate the financial structure of the project, leading to better resource allocation, more accurate forecasting, and more effective long-term strategic planning.

This distinction is important because breaking these out helps with:

- **Improved financial forecasting**—By categorizing expenses into CapEx and O&M, organizations can more accurately forecast both short-term and long-term financial needs.
- **Tax implications**—There are often different tax implications for CapEx versus O&M. While capital costs might be amortized over several years, operating costs are typically deducted in the year they occur.
- **Performance metrics**—The differentiation allows organizations to establish separate performance metrics based on capital efficiency and operational efficiency.

Bonus resource

Visit www.data-mania.com/book for detailed instructions on how to break CapEx apart from O&M.

Stakeholder and Departmental Alignment

The Stakeholder and Departmental Alignment section helps ensure that all relevant parties are on the same page and are collaborating to achieve a shared goal. At this point, you will have already gathered a lot of valuable information from stakeholder interviews and compiled best practices to address potential challenges. Now, you need to create a plan that all departments and stakeholders can agree upon for the data initiative moving forward.

Table 17.2 Stakeholder and Department Alignment Components

Component	Description
Stakeholder mapping	Detail the primary and secondary stakeholders. This clarifies who will be directly impacted by the data initiative and who might have indirect interests.
Feedback mechanisms	Highlight relevant insights from stakeholder interviews. By referencing actual feedback, you're underscoring the value of the collaborative process. You're also showing that you've considered (and integrated) their feedback into the process.
Communication plan	Outline how you plan to communicate with different stakeholders and departments. Include updates, changes, and important milestones for the data initiative.
Alignment activities	Recommend workshops, training sessions, or meetings to promote deeper alignment with stakeholders.
Potential challenges and solutions	Identify potential departmental conflicts or challenges based on your stakeholder interviews and analysis. Develop proactive strategies to anticipate and address them early on.
Metrics for alignment success	Establish metrics to track the continued alignment of stakeholders and departments throughout the data initiative's lifecycle. These metrics provide a quantifiable way to monitor progress.

Table 17.2 details what you should include in the Stakeholder and Departmental Alignment section of the plan.

Although technologies and data are important, the success of any initiative often depends on how effectively people with varying perspectives and motivations work together toward a shared goal. This section emphasizes the importance of human and organizational factors in implementing a data strategy.

Bonus resource

Download an example recommendation and challenge activity for stakeholder and departmental alignment at www.data-mania.com/book.

Training and Hiring Recommendations

The Training and Hiring Recommendations section should act as a guide for maximizing the potential of your existing workforce and hiring budget. You have already conducted a data literacy and skill gap analysis in Chapters 11 and 12. In Chapter 15, you formulated detailed recommendations for training and hiring required to support the data initiative. Now, it's time to summarize your training and hiring recommendations within a written plan.

> ### Tip
>
> Both the gap analysis and the training and hiring recommendations should be included in the appendix of your data strategy.

To keep this section brief, provide only a general overview of your recommendations and direct your readers back to the appendix for a deeper explanation that supports those recommendations. Making concise recommendations ensures that they're actionable and credible. This helps you build a strong case that ultimately helps you get the stakeholder support you need.

> ### Bonus resource
>
> Download an example and challenge activity for training recommendations at www.data-mania.com/book.

Risk Management and Contingencies

Data initiatives face unexpected challenges and threats as a matter of course. The Risk Management and Contingencies section acknowledges, evaluates, and prepares for these uncertainties. This type of planning decreases risk while supporting a seamless and timely execution. Table 17.3 details what you should include in the Risk Management and Contingencies section of the plan.

By detailing here both the broad organizational risks as well as the nitty-gritty ones, your organization can undertake the data initiative with maximum levels of preparedness and assurance.

Table 17.3 Risk Management and Contingencies Components

Component	Description
Technical risk identification	List potential technological risks that could arise, such as system failures, software bugs, and cybersecurity threats.
Operational risks	Acknowledge risks associated with project delays, misalignment between departments, or resource unavailability.

Component	Description
Risk assessment	For each of the risks you've laid down, use a risk matrix to assess the likelihood and potential impact. Once you know the severity of the risks, you can make efforts to reduce their impact (and in the best-case scenario, eliminate them).
Mitigation strategies	Describe what steps you'd take to reduce the likelihood or impact of each risk.
Contingency plans	What happens if the risk actually does materialize? Make sure to clearly define the steps you'd take, such as immediate technical responses, communication channels, and long-term technical adjustments.
Review and update mechanisms	Even though you have strong systems in place to mitigate risks, it's recommended that you have regular review cycles for the risk management strategy. For this, you'll need to consider future risks associated with technological advancements, new vulnerabilities, or lessons learned.

Monitoring and Management Mechanisms

Throughout the lifecycle of a data initiative, it's important to ensure that it remains aligned with its objectives, meets performance benchmarks, and can adapt to any emerging challenges or changing circumstances. The Continuous Improvement Section lays out the structure and processes through which the project will be routinely supervised and steered.

Within this section, you should clearly define the metrics and KPIs that will gauge the success and effectiveness of the data initiative in real terms. KPIs offer tangible, quantitative benchmarks for success. They help stakeholders measure progress and results against set goals. Metrics and KPIs also provide real-time insights into the effectiveness of the project's execution and highlight areas for improvement.

Table 17.4 details what makes for an effective KPI.

Table 17.4   Components of an Effective KPI

Component	Description
Technical KPIs	Identify KPIs to measure the technical success of the initiative. This may cover aspects like data quality, system uptime, and query response times.
Monitoring tools	Specify the tools and software that will be employed to continually assess these KPIs.
Audit intervals	Determine how often you'll measure the initiative against these KPIs. Regular audits can help identify and address issues promptly.
Adjustment protocols	Outline the procedures for making adjustments or refinements based on insights gleaned from these KPIs. This will allow flexibility and adaptability to changing conditions or requirements.

Advanced Project Management for Data Strategies

Earlier in the chapter, I encouraged you to delegate the project management requirements associated with the execution of your data strategy. While it's true that a data strategist fulfills an executive leadership role, they must be aware of the various options available for management requirements as well. This knowledge supports the executive in overseeing the execution, in which project and product management are included.

When you delegate management, you need to oversee that management to ensure that each step is planned and managed well. This requires that you take a project management approach specific to your data initiative, as opposed to the traditional type of project management approach utilized for projects that have well-defined scopes and very predictable outcomes. The best examples for this would be data migration activities, basic integration tasks, and reporting and analytics.

Table 17.5 provides a quick overview of how project management methods vary greatly between well-defined processes (with low risk) versus those for data initiatives that you've chosen.

Traditional project management approaches heavily rely on timelines, budget constraints, and resource availability. In contrast, with data and AI projects, your project or product manager should also account for additional factors like data quality, data accessibility, and insights garnered from each step.

In traditional project management approaches, you have clear, well-defined stages with minor volatilities. The most familiar example of this approach (as shown in Table 17.5) is the good old waterfall model. Another relevant approach here is the Projects In Controlled Environments (PRINCE2) method, which is linear in nature and emphasizes two core factors: "Organization" and "Control."

Notice that traditional approaches will almost always rely on well-defined, static project scopes and are not designed for accommodating many revisions in between. You may not return to the stages you've already completed because development happens in a linear manner with these types of projects. Each stage here is predictable.

In contrast, the project management approaches you'll use for your data initiatives should always be highly flexible and have built-in access to repeating cycles of exploration, development, testing, and evaluation. This is helpful in adapting plans based on the uncertainties that are inherent to the data initiatives you've chosen. These uncertainties can arise from a plethora of scenarios, from new data sources, to new data insights that are derived in late stages of the project, from

Table 17.5 Management Approaches for Data Intensive Projects

Attribute	Traditional PM	Agile PM
Framework, Methodologies, and Principles	Waterfall Model, PRINCE2	Agile Methodologies (Scrum, Kanban), Machine Learning Operations (MLOps) Principles
Relies on	Timelines, budget constraints, and resource availability	Timelines, budget constraints, and resource availability as well as data quality, data accessibility, and insights garnered from each development stage.
Project stages	Clear, well-defined project management stages that are linear in nature. Each stage is predictable, and there are few disruptions in terms of technology, business requirements, and user feedback. Typical stages include: Initiation > planning > execution > monitoring > closure	The stages are more dynamic and iterative in nature. The requirements related to each stage may change due to the project's evolving nature, such as stakeholder feedback, regulatory changes, or unexpected technological changes. Typical stages include Concept and ideation > inception and planning > iterative development and testing > review and feedback incorporation > deployment and evaluation > continuous improvement
Risk	The assumption is that most risks can be anticipated and mitigated well in advance.	Risk here is more multifaceted – due to complex interdependencies between technology, data, regulations, and changing user needs. Consequently, it's much more difficult to anticipate such risks compared to that of traditional projects.
Response Type	Reactive	Proactive

changing model performances to regulatory compliance issues, even plain-ol user feedback. In the face of such uncertainty, your project management approach must be flexible and agile (pardon the pun!)

Tip

Your project management approach should also be dynamic and iterative, due to the volatile nature of the space, as well as the requirements for multiple iterations of the same activity such as data collection, transformation, and analytics. Additionally, you need to be prepared to quickly adapt to changing data laws and guidelines, which may force you to restart from earlier checkpoints in time, in the worst case, undoing a lot of effort.

The following are some project management tips to help prepare you and your project manager for overseeing the execution of your data strategy.

Use Agile Methodologies

Be prepared and responsive toward the changing requirements of the data initiative. Take a proactive stance, not a reactive one. This ensures that you're ready to work with your team to address any challenges—be they related to technology, business, or compliance. Instead of waiting for something to happen and then fixing it, plan for the worst and expect the best.

Be Mindful of Data Risks

Be prepared to face risks related to data quality, breaches, and compliance, just to name a few. This is really part of the data risk management we discussed back in Chapter 13. If you've been following the guidance provided in this book, then you already have a strong monitoring system in place for addressing data-related technical issues as they occur. You are already in sync with the compliance team for addressing legal and compliance issues, if any. In this case, you're already prepared and have little to worry about. If you're delegating project management, however, it's your responsibility to make sure that your project manager is prepared for these risks as well.

Maintain Strong Communication

Make sure to maintain a clear line of communication with all parties, whether those be technical teams, high-interest, high-influence stakeholders, ethics and compliance teams, or others. Remember, there's no such thing as overcommunication. Clearly document all conversations, ideas, and feedback for future reference. When you're presenting updates, use visual aids and easy-to-understand dashboards so that stakeholders can quickly understand and make decisions.

Use the Tools at Your Disposal

Technology is your friend. Use the tools at your disposal to automate as many repetitive tasks as possible—for example, status updates, reminder emails, and task assignments—so the team has plenty of time to actually execute the strategy.

Use project management tools to track timelines, budget, and resources. Use real-time collaboration and communication tools to coordinate with team members.

Wrapping Up Your Strategic Plan

In this segment, we look at what you need to build well-supported conclusions and appendix sections for your data strategy plan. Although we cover this in one segment, there should be two distinct sections of your plan.

The Conclusion Section

The Conclusion section is where you'll bring together all of the plan's key points. This should define the organization's future trajectory and make it clear for your audience to understand the direction the organization should take. It should:

- Summarize the technical direction identified in the strategy.
- Articulate the path forward, including the next steps or phases.

The following are the earmarks of a strong conclusion:

- **Clarity**—Avoid introducing new ideas or complexities.
- **Conciseness**—Keep it brief but impactful. This is your last chance to persuade and motivate.
- **Consistency**—The conclusion should be in line with what is proposed and discussed throughout the strategy.
- **Sequential**—Clearly articulate the next steps, making it easy to move from planning to action.

Table 17.6 details what you should include in the Conclusion section of the strategy.

The Appendix and Supporting Documentation Section The Appendices and Supporting Documents section serves as a repository for all the data, reports, diagrams, and other information that supports your data strategy plan. It acts like the foundational layer for your plan. While not every reader will go through this section in detail, those who wish to delve deeper should be able to find everything they need here.

Table 17.6   Conclusion Section Components

Component	Description
Recap of core tenets	Review the plan's core objectives and strategies, which set the groundwork for your organization's future direction.
Expected impact	Be sure to discuss the expected outcomes on both technical and business fronts. Remember, the executives or stakeholders to whom you're presenting are interested in the value this brings to the organization.
Call to action	You want to end your conclusion with a call to action. What should be done immediately after the plan is approved?
Refer to appendices	If there are any further details or data that support your conclusion, direct your readers to the relevant appendices.

A Complete, Organized, Relevant, and Up-to-date Appendix   The primary objective of the appendices and supporting documents is to:

- Store technical data in detail that supports the body of the plan.
- Serve as a go-to resource for stakeholders seeking additional information or clarification.

The following attributes are characteristics of a strong appendix:

- **Complete**—Include all the documents that are referred to in the plan.
- **Organized**—Clearly label each appendix and create an index for easy navigation.
- **Relevant**—Only include documents that directly support or elucidate points made in the main plan.
- **Up-to-date**—Ensure that all information, especially contracts or quotations, is current.

The Core Components of an Appendices and Supporting Documentation Section   The following are the core components of a data strategy plan appendix.

Detailed Technical Specifications   Include specifics that couldn't be accommodated in the main document due to their technical nature or level of detail. For example, you may include the details of the data models, ETL processes, or algorithms that will be used.

Architecture Diagrams   Diagrams that visually represent the data infrastructure, workflow, or system architecture can be extremely helpful for technical stakeholders. As part of this, you can include an architecture diagram clearly showing how different data sources are integrated.

Vendor Contracts   If you plan on using third-party services, tools, or platforms, you can include contracts, quotations, or terms of service here. For instance, you may add a copy of the contract with the cloud service provider or the software licensing agreements for a tool.

Other Supplemental Information   You can include any other information that adds value or context to your plan. This could range from cost estimates to project timelines. Here, you can include a Gantt chart showing the project timelines and milestones. You can also include the technical specifications and requirements of the data project in this section.

The Appendices and Supporting Documents section provides specific context for all your undertakings. Some stakeholders may be interested in going through this before they give full buy-in. By drafting this section carefully, you ensure that your plan is resistant to scrutiny, anticipatory of potential questions, and provides clear explanations of complex points while keeping the main document as concise as possible.

Tools, Technologies, and Resources for Streamlined Implementation

Based on my years of experience in the field, I have some recommendations for tools and technologies for each of the phases we looked at in this chapter. Make sure you do your own research and properly evaluate each before opting for any one of them.

Tools for Legal, Regulatory, and Ethics

For data initiatives that involve compliance with GDPR and CCPA regulations, and others such as Lei Geral de Proteção de Dados (LGPD), you can opt for OneTrust. It provides customized solutions for different industries and jurisdictions—while also being up-to-date with the latest laws and guidelines around privacy, ethics, and compliance. It also has provisions for addressing the data subject access request

(DSAR)—which is a user inquiry made to a company to know how it's handling and processing their data—by streamlining data intake, automated data redaction for sensitive information, and centralized reporting.

An alternative is AI-powered Clarip, which helps companies comply with data privacy requirements across multiple channels such as web, mobile, and cloud platforms. It offers similar features and functionalities along with provisions for breach response, i.e., implementing custom rules for data breaches based on needs. It also offers a dispute resolution platform that allows customers/end-users to log privacy violations and concerns.

If your data project revolves around the use of a foundation model, then you can consider using Responsible AI Toolbox kits provided by different organizations such as:

- Microsoft Responsible AI toolkit by Microsoft
- Responsible Generative AI Toolkit by Google
- Responsible AI tools and resources by Amazon

These can help you continuously monitor the output of your AI models from inception up to post-deployment for equitability, reliability, privacy, and transparency.

Note

You can also refer to Figure 13.1 in Chapter 13 to explore explainability for LLMs if your data project/initiative has to do with output from LLMs.

Resource Allocation and Budget Tools

For resource allocation and budget purposes, you can try using Smartsheet. It's an advanced project management and collaboration tool you can fully customize for resource allocation and budget tracking. You can also create different budget management templates and intuitive dashboards to track your real-time expenditures against budget allocations—which is really important for your data project.

You can also explore Planview, which is a project portfolio management software. It offers plenty of features such as top-down planning for quick prioritization, resource management, time reporting, effort analysis, and what-if analysis. These features will help you quickly allocate and deallocate resources to changing needs, compare expenditure vs. budget, and make important decisions with respect to the objectives you've set.

Stakeholder and Departmental Alignment Tools

Your best bet for communications tools is to use Slack, Trello, or Airtable to enable clear and up-to-date communication with all your stakeholders. You can create separate channels to clearly segregate your messages, documents, and other essentials meant for different groups or departments. These tools also provide integration with other project management tools.

Training and Hiring Recommendations Resources

After you've identified the skills gaps, you can use courses from Coursera, Udemy, Pluralsight, and LinkedIn Learning to help the team learn new tools and technologies related to the data initiative they'll be working on. Based on your budget, you may also consider an instructor-led course that is much more interactive and helpful for the team.

There are several job boards and platforms such as Indeed, Workable, and ZipRecruiter that can help you hire the right talent for your data initiative. You can also try Upwork if you're looking for contract hires. Make sure to clearly note your requirements and when evaluating candidates for your initiative, focus on their work experience and the projects they've worked on. Another way to find great candidates is through networking events and workshops—personally, I've seen a lot of talent at these venues.

Risk Management Solutions

Consider using LogicManager for risk management purposes. It's a robust risk management software that provides you with tools for identifying, assessing, and monitoring risks. This platform is really valuable for developing contingency plans and ensuring that risk management practices are integrated throughout your data initiative life cycle. You can also use its dashboard to display and monitor all your risk management processes.

Other tools that I recommend for different aspects of risk management are:

- **Splunk**—For technical risk identification
- **RiskWatch**—For risk and compliance assessment
- **PagerDuty**—For incident response management

Monitoring and Management Tools

To monitor the performance of your data initiative, you can use simple visualization tools like Tableau or PowerBI. You can consider using Datadog for cloud applications. Through Datadog, you can monitor, troubleshoot, and optimize applications that run on any infrastructure—focusing on quick resolution of errors and latency.

You also need to have clear metrics before you begin your evaluation. For example, if your data initiative centers around the use of LLMs, then you need to evaluate the responses that are being returned to users. Typically, here, you'd be looking at the fluency and coherency of responses, the factual accuracy, and other subjective factors you decide based on your data initiative.

For complex projects, there is usually no fixed metric you can use. Your team will usually need to define custom metrics based on what you see as the "success" of your data initiative. Then, they'll need to write custom scripts (say, in Python) to evaluate parameters that'll tell them how close they are to your key performance metric. Again, the metrics are usually subjective and will require multiple discussions with stakeholders to finalize the set.

This Is Just the Beginning

If you're reading this, then I know two things about you. First, you're a powerful and dedicated reader. And second, you're a self-determined go-getter who has the perseverance, and now the strategic skills, needed to start designing data and AI strategies that drive exponential business growth.

Moving forward from the pages of this book, please know that strategic mastery is not an overnight matter. You're now equipped to begin building and leading powerful data and AI strategies, but this is just the beginning. As the old adage says, "Rome was not built in a day."

Be gentle with yourself as you progress from strategic novice to expert. Each new strategy, each new project, each new client will bring their own subtle nuances from which you will learn. Celebrate the fact that you're part of the upper-most echelon of technical workers who know how to leverage their technical expertise in building a low-risk, high-reward data strategy from the ground up.

The website that comes with this book (www.data-mania.com/book) is fully stocked with all the strategy-building resources you could need. Those assets are like cheat codes to building high-performance strategies, so make sure you've got them in your arsenal. If you'd like to continue the growth strategy journey with me, then I invite you to join my newsletter community, The Convergence: https://data-mania.com/newsletter

And last, but not least, if you need proven and accomplished growth marketing leadership support, I'd love to have a conversation about working together to drive more efficient bottom-line revenue for your company. Even if it's help with technical execution that's on your mind, I have world-class partners to help you by supporting any data and AI project and product implementation requirement. Feel free to reach out to me directly on LinkedIn at: https://www.linkedin.com/in/lillianpierson/

Index